For 10 years, author Ralph Buntyn spent many hours with renowned United Nations correspondent and United Israel World Union founder David Horowitz. They engaged in lengthy discussions about his foundational views drawn from his experience and unique vantage point in the two world bodies. *The Book of David* is based on his personal notes, extensive archival records and reflections from these conversations.

In Horowitz's autobiography *Thirty-three Candles* published in 1956, he wrote: "*Thirty-three Candles* undoubtedly calls for a sequel because much has occurred on the world scene since 1944, most of it confirming its major thesis. I feel I shall have to bow to this demand." *The Book of David* is dedicated to fulfilling Horowitz's request for an historical accounting of the period that followed.

The Book of David

DAVID HOROWITZ:
Dean of United Nations Press Corps and
Founder: United Israel World Union

By Ralph E. Buntyn

innerQuest Books • ASHEVILLE, NORTH CAROLINA

www.innerQuestBooks.com
www.ChironPublications.com

innerQuest is a book imprint of Chiron Publications
Interior and cover design by Danijela Mijailovic
Printed primarily in the United States of America.

ISBN 978-1-63051-583-6 paperback
ISBN 978-1-63051-584-3 hardcover
ISBN 978-1-63051-585-0 electronic
ISBN 978-1-63051-586-7 limited edition paperback

Library of Congress Cataloging-in-Publication Data

Names: Buntyn, Ralph E., author.
Title: The book of David : David Horowitz, Dean of United Nations Press Corps and founder, United Israel World Union / by Ralph E Buntyn.
Description: Asheville : Chiron Publications, [2018] | Includes bibliographical references and index.
Identifiers: LCCN 2018041709| ISBN 9781630515836 (pbk. : alk. paper) | ISBN 9781630515843 (hardcover : alk. paper)
Subjects: LCSH: Horowitz, David, 1903-2002. | Journalists--United States--Biography. | Zionists--United States--Biography. | Reporters and reporting--United States--Biography. | United Israel World Union--History--20th century. | United Nations Correspondents Association--History--20th century.
Classification: LCC PN4874.H647 B86 2018 | DDC 070.92 [B] --dc23
LC record available at https://lccn.loc.gov/2018041709

"It hath been told thee, O man, what is good,
And what the LORD doth require of thee:
Only to do justly, and to love mercy, and to walk humbly with thy God."

The Book of Micah 6:8

"And they shall beat their swords into plowshares,
And their spears into pruning hooks;
Nation shall not lift up sword against nation,
Neither shall they learn war anymore."

The Book of Isaiah 2:4

In Dedication

To the memory of David Horowitz whose voice was not of one crying out in the wilderness-but of one echoing in the halls and chambers of the House of Nations—tirelessly supporting and defending the land of Israel, the people of Israel, and the causes of justice and peace as prescribed by the prophets of old.

Acknowledgements

To special friends, Dr. James D. Tabor and Ross Nichols whose motivation and encouragement provided continued inspiration to finish this work.

To the many members of United Israel World Union seeking an ancient path in search of a better tomorrow.

To my editor-in-chief, Dr. Leonard Cruz, whose literary skills improved my work and whose wise counsel improved my life.

To Chiron Publications Manager Jennifer Fitzgerald, whose patience and guidance helped me to successfully navigate the publication process.

Finally, to my dear wife Rebecca whose love and support have made all the good things real.

CONTENTS

Foreword

This wonderful book by my friend and associate Ralph Buntyn brings together for the first time the remarkable story of the last 57 years of the extraordinary life of David Horowitz who I had the privilege of knowing and working with for the last 12 years of his life. In this foreword, I wanted to relate a bit of background and connections with David Horowitz from my own perspective and experience as an academic and university professor.

I first encountered the name David Horowitz in 1989 when I was teaching at the College of William and Mary. I am a professor of ancient Judaism and early Christianity, now at the University of North Carolina at Charlotte, but at that time I was doing some research on contemporary Jewish ideas about the legendary "Lost Tribes of Israel." In looking through the massive *Encyclopedia of American Religions* I came across the entry for a Jewish organization called United Israel World Union, founded in 1944, of which I had never heard. I was, of course, familiar with the various branches of contemporary Judaism such as Reform, Conservative, modern Orthodox, Hasidic, and Reconstructionist, but UIWU was new to me, as was its founder David Horowitz, a Swedish born immigrant, whom I learned, was the first accredited correspondent at the United Nations. I decided to write Mr. Horowitz a letter of inquiry, since I had read that his organization represented a Jewish outreach to non-Jews, many of whom he was convinced might be part of the "Lost Tribes" of Israel.

David responded within a week or so, a lovely personal two-page letter, typed on United Israel World Union letterhead, but with a note requesting a reply to Room 373, Press Section, at the United Nations in New York. David himself, not a secretary, had clearly typed the letter personally and it appeared to be from an older non-electric typewriter. I was more than intrigued. That was in March 1989 and David was weeks away from his 86th birthday. Thus, began a close bond and working relationship that lasted until his death in 2002 at age 99.

David and I began to exchange letters over the next few months and I became more and more intrigued with this remarkable man and his fascinating biography. David was born in 1903 in Sweden, the son of a well-known cantor, Aaron Horowitz. The family immigrated to the United States in 1914 and David received an Orthodox Jewish upbringing in Worcester, MA and Wilkes-Barre, PA where his father served the local Orthodox congregations. I learned that he had traveled to the Holy Land in what was then British Mandate Palestine in 1924 at age 21. He had spent three years there, becoming fluent in Hebrew and studying the Bible with various rabbis and teachers. He returned for more studies in 1932-34 and worked for the next decade translating and publishing a massive work of biblical interpretation titled *The Bible in the Hands of its Creators*, authored by Moshe Guibbory, his primary biblical teacher in Jerusalem. David wrote an extensive account of these early years in his riveting 500-page autobiography, *Thirty-three Candles*, published in 1949. David sent me a signed copy of the latter work and I will never forget staying up all night Passover of 1990 reading it through until early dawn. I simply could not put the book down and all I could think of was "what happened next"? That is the reaction of almost everyone I have talked to who has read that book. Now at last, Ralph Buntyn has provided us with what might be called "Volume 2" of Horowitz's amazing story.

The following year, July 1990, on my way to Israel to do some archaeological investigations related to the Dead Sea Scrolls, I arranged to meet David Horowitz face-to-face at his United Nations office. We spent an enjoyable day together exchanging ideas and learning more of one another's interests and work—and our conversation continued late into the evening. Over the next twelve years I saw David many times in New York or his cottage in New Jersey, and even traveled with him on his last trip to Israel in 1993. We became close friends and associates in many common ventures and I began to write regularly for his *United Israel Bulletin* and attend the annual meetings of UIWU.

David's illustrious 57-year career as a veteran UN correspondent is well documented and covered in detail for the first time in this present volume, *The Book of David*, by historian and UIWU archivist Ralph Buntyn. Not only was David present at the 1945 founding meeting of the United Nations, but he was the first accredited correspondent and founder of the United Nations Correspondents Association, serving as president several terms and receiving countless awards and accolades. What is less known are such things as his pioneering efforts at brokering peace between Israel and the Arabs through his personal correspondence with King Abdullah I, grandfather of King Hussein of Jordan, his behind-the-scenes influence at the UN, and with President Truman, leading to the establishment of the State of Israel in 1948, his tireless efforts to bring Romanian archbishop Valerian Trifa to justice for Nazi war crimes, and his work on behalf of freeing Soviet Jewry—including direct confrontations with Premier Nikita Khrushchev at the United Nations. David was a friend of every UN Secretary General, including Swedish born Dag Hammarskjöld, every president and premier of Israel, from Ben Gurion to Netanyahu, and countless world leaders, presidents, and ambassadors over his 55 years of active service. The stories are endless, and Ralph Buntyn has captured them all for us, written in an engaging style but with full documentation from thousands of documents, including private letters and even hand-written notes. *The Book of David* tells it all for the first time.

David Horowitz wore two hats. Besides his notable work at the United Nations he continued his interest in biblical studies through the founding of United Israel World Union in 1944. UIWU is acknowledged as the first American Jewish organization whose primary purpose is to educate non-Jews regarding the foundational faith of the Hebrew Bible and the values and prophetic ideals of the teaching of Moses and the biblical Prophets. UIWU is a non-sectarian educational outreach now in its 75th year and still thriving with an active and impressive board of directors and a worldwide membership. Its goal is neither to "convert" non-Jews to Judaism nor to begin a new religion, but to represent to the broader world the prophetic vision of a universal "House of prayer for all peoples," founded on the ideals of the Torah and Prophets.

I first met Ralph Buntyn through personal correspondence in the 1990s, but happily face-to-face in 1993 in New York at the grand celebration of David Horowitz's 90th birthday and the 50th anniversary of United Israel World Union. What a gala affair that was, bringing together David's friends and associates from throughout the world in tribute to both his work at the United Nations and his educational work through UIWU. Ralph and I have spent hundreds of hours together since, including times with David, trips to Israel together, and various executive and personal meetings here in the United States over the years. There is no one who has dug deeper and exhibited more passion for the task of this book—relating the remarkable 60-year career of David Horowitz as Dean of the United Nations Press Corp and founder of United Israel World Union. I heartily and with the greatest pleasure commend to your reading *The Book of David*.

Dr. James D. Tabor
Professor, University of North Carolina at Charlotte
President, United Israel World Union

Introduction

As World War II drew to a close there were three things not yet in existence: United Israel World Union, the United Nations, and the State of Israel. By the end of 1948, one person would be involved in establishing all three. His name is David Horowitz, and, for the next fifty-four years, he would devote his life to all three causes.

He was the founder and president of United Israel World Union (UIWU), a global movement dedicated to propagating the ideals of the Torah faith on a universal scale. He was the Dean of United Nations Correspondents serving a vital role in the world organization since its inception and until his death. He was a Zionist, a true Lion of Judah, who worked tirelessly for the establishment and well-being of the State of Israel.

Yet, like a force greater than the sum of its parts, Horowitz left us a legacy much greater than the significant contributions he would make to each of the three causes. Capturing this legacy was the task I decided to undertake in the fall of 2014.

Horowitz published an autobiography in 1949 covering the thirty years from 1914 until 1944. Entitled *Thirty-Three Candles*, the book chronicled events in his life as an early Zionist pioneer in British Mandate Palestine and his strange encounter with a prophetic figure, and it continued through the compilation of a massive Jerusalem research project that ended in post-World War II New York in 1944. It was at this point that forty-one year old Horowitz's life would be profoundly redirected.

Attempting to write an unfolding fifty-four-year story of the life and times of an individual whose journalistic offerings alone in this period would fill volumes is an unrealistic and futile expectation. Horowitz had written over 2,500 syndicated columns alone. The UIWU archives, consisting of United Israel Bulletins, copies of letters and correspondence, photos, and daily press releases from the UN to multiple sources globally, easily account for over 50,000 documents. Yet, there was this treasure trove of information just sitting there that had never really been adequately mined.

I decided on a course of action. All documents would be arranged in chronological order. I would begin at the beginning in 1943-44, a time when Horowitz founded UIWU and began his journalistic career at the United Nations and conclude in 2004. It centers on key events that took place in the life of David Horowitz, his UN career, UIWU, and the events of the Middle East, with particular attention focused on the new State of Israel. Key world events appear in the narrative adding historical context.

From the fast-paced newsbyte coverage to the penetrating stories behind the stories, we are presented with a history in review of the days of destiny that make up the latter half of the twentieth century.

Ralph Buntyn
Asheville, North Carolina
2018

Part One

Chapter 1

He Walked with Kings and Rulers

Born in Malmo, Sweden in 1903, David Horowitz and his family immigrated to the United States in 1914 during World War I, settling in Worcester, Massachusetts. He was one of eight children of Cantor Aaron and Bertha Horowitz.

As a toddler at the synagogue where David's family worshipped in his hometown of Malmo, the rabbi once placed his hand on David's head and proclaimed, "David, you will go before kings and rulers." This would literally and metaphorically prove to be the case.

David made his first visit to what was then British-occupied Palestine as a young Zionist pioneer in 1924 and remained through the end of 1927. This was to be the first of many trips to pre-independent Israel where he would work in Jerusalem while mastering Hebrew and developing an extensive knowledge of Judaism.

In late 1927, Horowitz had a remarkable encounter with a prophetic figure, one Moses Guibbory, who at the time was living in the northwest area of Jerusalem in the Sanhedria tomb area. This association changed and shaped his entire life. Horowitz details this meeting in his 1949 autobiography, *Thirty-Three Candles*.

Following an intensive year working with Guibbory, Horowitz became editor and publisher of the mammoth 2,000-page compendium of biblical research based on the work of Moses Guibbory.

Following a sharp break with Guibbory in 1943, Horowitz' life was profoundly redirected. Out of the pangs of the past grew a movement, a world structure, founded upon the principles of Israel's ancient laws. It came at a time when, as Horowitz expressed, "it appeared to me that I had been forsaken by God and man, this development vindicated my faith in the One in whom I had always placed my trust." The movement was named United Israel World Union. It was incorporated on April 17, 1944, under the laws of the State of New York, as an educational, Mosaic Institution to function in all countries.

In 1945, Horowitz obtained press credentials at the newly-formed United Nations under the auspices of World Union Press, an arm of United Israel World Union. He was present at the opening sessions in San Francisco and at Lake Success, NY. Horowitz's decades of chronicling the official affairs of the General Assembly, the Security Council, and the Secretary General's office, helped to make him an unparalleled authority on the world organization. "He was the institutional memory of the United Nations," stated CNS news U.N. Bureau Chief, Serge Beaulieu.

It is this period—post-1945—and the rich history of the founding of two world organizations that will be the subject of the Horowitz saga. His role in both could only be described as providential.

Journalist Vanni Cappelli, son of Horowitz's longtime friend and press associate, John Cappelli, wrote a moving tribute to Horowitz entitled, "He Walked with Kings and Rulers" which was published on March 6, 2003 in *The Jewish Press*. Cappelli wrote:

What everyone will always remember about him with loving joy is his smile. That smile that captured the hearts of Metropolitan Opera greats like Enrico Caruso and Geraldine Farrar when he was an office boy at the Old Met in 1918. He appeared in a group photograph taken on the occasion of the legendary tenor's last visit to the opera house shortly before Caruso sailed back to Italy and passed away in the summer of 1921.

It is the same smile, which shines forth in numerous pictures taken over the course of almost six decades at the United Nations that hung above his cluttered desk. They show Horowitz greeting and engaging with the great and the obscure, the saints and the sinners, the statesmen and the journalist. The images include Elie Wiesel and Nikita Khrushchev, Menachem Begin and Andrey Vyshinsky, Dag

Hammarskjöld and Benjamin Netanyahu, Eleanor Roosevelt and U Thant.

The UN is supposed to be about dialogue and David was always ready to answer the invective with its opposite—a calm reasoned response based on passion. That is why he was so beloved, and everyone was willing to talk to him. When you talked long enough with David Horowitz, the invective became dialogue—you just couldn't help it.

There was a simple, compelling reason for this, and it went far beyond his venerable age or his standing as the dean of UN correspondents. It was that Horowitz represented, as no one else I have ever met, the ancient ideal upon which the world organization was supposed to be founded, and which it has so often fallen short of in its troubled history— the Brotherhood of All Mankind. His own adherence to this truth was a constant reproach to the hypocrisy of the world body. Yet, incredibly, this passionate defender of the State of Israel was never anti-UN.

"In all my 40 years and more of knowing him," John Cappelli once said, "not once did he ever raise his voice in anger. That was the reason that all of the other correspondents, even those from the Arab world who would refuse to attend a press conference given by an Israeli diplomat, would come to see, and talk with, David." In later years, many more would come to pay homage, Jews and Gentiles, faithful and unbelievers, advocates of freedom and supporters of tyranny.

Chapter 2

Dialogue with an Arab King

January 17, 1945. David Horowitz was motivated to write a letter to the Emir of Trans-Jordan, Abdullah bin al-Hussein. Copies of United Israel World Union Bulletins were sent along with references made to select articles. Also included was a copy of the United Israel Constitution which stated in part, its all-embracing aims and purposes: "Peace in wisdom and understanding in the love of our Creator whom all true souls should serve."

The history of the geopolitical entity created in Palestine under the British administration was known as the "British Mandate of Palestine" and was first carved out of Ottoman Southern Syria after World War I. British civil administration in Palestine operated from 1920 until 1948. The "controversy over Zion" was fast becoming the burdensome stone.

In his letter, Horowitz suggested to the Emir that the "Palestine Question" be approached on the basis of the decrees of a higher power. Horowitz stated: "Could it not be solved between brethren if we begin with the premise that *Abraham* was our common father and that his God was the one true God for all of us?"

The next procedure should then be to take "the words and the works of the prophets of the Bible, including the wisdom of the Koran which upholds the Bible, and base all solutions on what these works promised."

Abdullah bin al-Hussein (1882-1951), along with his brothers Ali, Feisal and Zeid, had led the Arab forces of the Great Arab Revolt against Ottoman rule. Between 1916-1918, he worked with the British guerrilla leader, T.E. Lawrence (of Lawrence of Arabia fame) playing a key role as architect and planner, while leading guerrilla raids on garrisons of the Ottoman occupation forces.

Trans-Jordan was formed on April 21, 1921 when the British created a protectorate with Abdullah bin Al-Hussein as Emir. Independence was gained on May 25, 1946, as the Hashemite Kingdom of Transjordan (renamed simply as Jordan in 1949), with Abdullah as its king.

To Horowitz's surprise, within two months after sending the letter, he received a lengthy reply from Emir Abdullah, dated March 2, 1945. The original letter was written in Arabic with an English translation. The Arabic letter was signed by the Emir in red ink.

Of course, the Emir was sure to look on any Jewish person as being in favor of a Jewish State in Palestine and questioned Horowitz's motives. He also implied that he did not want Jews settling in Palestine and differed on Horowitz's proposal that the Arabs and Jews use the Bible and the Koran as the basis for adjudicating the Palestine question. Thus began a nearly two-year long correspondence and dialogue between the two.

April 1945 was active with historical developments: after months of declining health, President Franklin D. Roosevelt died on April 12th; Vice-President Harry S. Truman succeeded him, becoming the 33rd President of the United States; the second annual assembly of United Israel World Union was held in Washington, DC on April 28th; at the same time, delegates were gathering in San Francisco to hold meetings that would lead to the founding of the United Nations; and on April 30th, Adolf Hitler committed suicide along with Eva Braun, his long-term companion, in his bunker in Berlin. On May 8th, V-E Day marked the fall of Nazi Germany and the end of World War II in Europe.

On May 29th, Horowitz answered Emir Abdullah. He began by citing detailed passages from the Koran which confirmed the validity of the Tanach (Torah) and which upheld the laws of Moses. He also pointed out that it was Moses who had first set the historic boundaries of Israel as constituting an eternal heritage of the children of Israel.

He countered the Emir's belief that the Koran superseded the Tanach in total. He said: "the Koran, as I have noticed, does not add nor does it diminish from the laws of Moses and the prophets. On the contrary, it champions the same." He then proceeded to offer definitive statements in the Koran confirming the Hebrew scriptures. Therefore, it follows that the injunctions in the Bible are as binding upon the Arabs as they are upon the Jews and the Christians.

In closing, Horowitz would express: "Would not the All-Wise and Just, the One God of all, be mocked unless the definitive statements and plans which He gave in the Bible were given careful study and consideration in the light of all available facts."

After two months without a response, Horowitz sent another letter to Amman dated July 30, 1945. Included was a copy of the newly published July-August 1945 edition of the United Israel Bulletin that contained his story on "The Palestine Problem," which appears to have been written with Emir Abdullah in mind.

Two points in the article are worth mentioning. Horowitz began by attacking the British for being two-faced and creating disillusionment among both Jews and Arabs in Palestine. The other point was to state that the "twelve tribes" constituting the whole house of Israel, must likewise fully realize that the children of Islam are their full cousins through Abraham and by virtue of their faiths which uphold Moses and the prophets, all must accept Sinai as the mountain of all mountains of truth. All stem from one source. All worship the God of Israel.

September 2, 1945. The Empire of Japan officially surrenders aboard the battleship *USS Missouri*, bringing the hostilities of World War II to a close.

Later that month a reply from the Emir arrived. Horowitz described the letter as being friendlier in tone. The Emir seemed to be agreeing that the British were playing a double game in their Palestine policy, stating that: "the politics of the matter has its tricks and snares." After expressing more of his views, Abdullah closed by quoting *al-Fātiḥah Sura 1* from the Koran "Dispute ye not the People of the Book except in a friendly manner, so you are to have good action from us and more." Horowitz would respond with another lengthy reply on October 9, 1945, continuing the dialogue.

There would be no exchange between the two for almost a year. The Emir was up for "a big promotion." He became King of the independent nation of Jordan on May 25, 1946, becoming one of the first Arab leaders to adopt a system of constitutional monarchy during the newly emerging era of the contemporary Arab World. October 1946 brought the final exchange between the two.

In his letter of October 5, King Abdullah remarked: "Personally, I know you and your faith" and expressed his understanding that David Horowitz was a man "to do according to his faith and national prestige." He closed with the words: "Please accept my friendship." This was to be the last message from the King.

Horowitz sent King Abdullah a short note on October 22, saying: "that God would one day re-establish His Kingdom on earth" and "when the Prophet comes he will right all things for all mankind." He then expressed the wish "that peace may come and that we may dwell as brethren again according to the Book."

In 1949, Abdullah entered secret peace talks with Israel, including at least five with Moshe Dayan. News of the negotiations provoked a strong reaction from other Arab states.

On July 20, 1951, King Abdullah traveled to Jerusalem for his regular Friday prayers along with his young grandson, Prince Hussein. A lone gunman on the steps of the Al-Aqsa Mosque assassinated the King. The conspiracy-backed execution was motivated by fears that the old king would make a separate peace with Israel. Miraculously, a bullet also meant for Hussein, deflected off a medal he was wearing given to him by his grandfather, thus sparing his life. The young Prince Hussein would later become King Hussein I of Jordan and enter into a peace agreement with his Israeli neighbors. And Horowitz would live to file the story.

"I'm very happy," said Horowitz. "You know when Abdullah was assassinated by an Arab fanatic, Hussein was a fifteen-year old boy and saw it happen. He has his memories."

Chapter 3

A Biblical Answer to the
UN Controversy over Zion

For nearly two years, Horowitz exchanged correspondence with the King of the Hashemite Kingdom of Jordan, Abdullah bin Al-Hussein. Central to their dialogue was the Palestine question and the notion of whether the ancient texts of the Bible and Koran could play a role in the resolution of key issues.

In February 1947, the British, succumbing to the problems and pressures from Palestine and at home, announced they were referring the Palestine Mandate question to the United Nations. This spurred a beehive of activity at the UN. Horowitz, sensing that the timing was right, was about to take his case directly to the big house.

As a prelude, David spent considerable time discussing and interviewing several Arab and Muslim delegates including Dr. Charles Malik of Lebanon, Dr. Fadhil Jamali of Iraq and M. Asif Ali, a Muslim delegate from India. He posed the same question to all delegates: "Do you think the Bible and the Koran could be used as the basis in solving the Palestine Problem?" Responses were mixed, however, several contended that the impasse included a deeper religious element that the ultimate solution might have to face.

Following these encouraging responses, United Israel World Union sent a letter to the Chairman of the UN's Political and Security Committee, Lester B. Pearson, suggesting the World Organization consider using the Bible and Koran to help settle the Arab-Israeli dispute over Palestine.

On April 28, 1947, fifty-five nations of the world, representing the greater part of mankind, took seats in the New York City Building at Flushing Meadows, Long Island. They had been summoned in special session to begin deliberations over the vexing and seemingly unsolvable issue of Palestine. In the May-June 1947 edition of *United Israel Bulletin*, Horowitz authored an article entitled: "Controversy over Zion comes to United Nations." In a letter to Pearson, Horowitz stated both the purpose and reason for the appeal:

> As an international Anglo-Hebrew Organization, chartered under the laws of the State of New York, we have a deep interest in the fate of Palestine. We wish, therefore, to submit the following for the consideration of the Fact-Finding Commission, which it is the duty of your committee to elect for the study of the seemingly unsolvable Palestine Question.

Horowitz then proceeded to recommend that the Commission give serious and careful consideration to the two historic documents that constitute the life-pattern of the Jewish and Arabic peoples, namely, the *Bible* and the *Koran*. After a gentle reminder to the Commission that all other previous approaches to the solution to the problem of Palestine have failed, he stated: "We recommend that your Committee include these world-recognized documents as evidence to be considered in the study." It seemed incumbent then upon the cousins, the Arabs and the Jews, to recognize fully what is actually inherent in the Palestine question.

The proposal included three main points: 1) that these documents are honored by both peoples and are also recognized by world courts; 2) they establish these peoples' statehood status, and 3) they indicate the extent of their historic domain in the Middle East.

On June 2, 1947, UIWU received a reply from the Commission. It expressed thanks for the submission promising "that the Committee would give the fullest consideration to every relevant opinion" and then asking the United Israel organization to submit its views regarding Palestine on or before June 26.

Throughout the deliberations, the eleven-nation Special UN Committee had before it a memorandum which was submitted by UIWU and which was duly acknowledged both by the Chairman of the Special Committee and by Secretary-General Trygve Lie himself. The memorandum gave the members of the Committee the full opportunity to know what the Bible had to say on this issue.

The four-page memorandum pointed out that legislative bodies and courts recognize the Bible to the extent of having all oaths of fealty and honor sworn by it, giving indisputable logic that this ancient document be given foremost consideration by members of the Special Committee. The memorandum also stated that its recorded history be examined in the light of genealogy and that the rights, claims, and deeds it has attributed to the peoples linked to the Holy Land should be properly evaluated.

Carefully laid out and emphasized in the memorandum were the facts that the Koran, religiously observed by all true Muslims, never invalidated the Bible and upheld the Bible as the highest authority portraying Hebrew leaders such as Noah, Abraham, Isaac, Moses, David and a host of others, as holy prophets whose utterances were accepted as inspired word. Each year all true Muslims honor Moses by commemorating the festival *Nebi Musa*. And it was this same Moses who originally set the biblical borders of the Holy Land for all the tribes of Israel as an everlasting statute. Definitive statements from the Koran were then set forth that confirmed the Hebrew Scriptures, thus making the biblical injunctions equally as binding upon all true believers to obey. Scriptural references were given that pertained to the issues of the biblical boundaries of Palestine, land deeds, and inheritances, as well as the covenant blessings given to Ishmael with the Arabian territory defined.

Evidence was submitted that served to prove that the original mandate looked upon Transjordan as an integral part of Palestine proper. Article 7 of the "Convention between the United States and Britain" regarding "Rights in Palestine" was signed in London on December 3, 1924 and was ratified by the President of the United States on March 2, 1925. The case had been duly presented, the evidence carefully laid out for consideration, and it was time for the closing statement.

Reading like an oracle penned from an ancient prophet, Horowitz made his impassioned closing argument to the committee representatives of the nations:

> All of the above facts are self-explanatory and need no further comment. The picture is clear, and brave men, truthful men, God-fearing men, should know what to do in the sight of an all-seeing God who is known to all mankind from the Bible as The God of Abraham, the God of Isaac, and the God of Jacob, the Holy One of Israel. He it is who swore to give Palestine to Israel. For nearly two thousand years the wandering Jew has never once ceased hearing the eternal threat: Go back to Jerusalem from whence you came. The Jew has now come to the end of the road and Jerusalem too, has become forbidden ground. The cry of the ancient prophet still rings: *Let My People Go!*

Following an intensive investigation of the many-sided Palestine problem, the Special UN Committee succeeded in completing its arduous tasks. A decision had been made. On September 1, 1947, Secretary-General Trygve Lie had the Committee's recommendations on his desk. It was indeed recommended that Palestine be partitioned into a Jewish state and an Arab state. But not according to the ancient blueprint. The efforts of United Israel World Union had failed to influence the Pearson Committee.

On November 29, 1947, the vote on Israel's future was held at the UN. The UN vote, thirty-three to thirteen (with ten abstentions), favoring the establishment of a Hebrew State in Palestine came between 5:30 and 5:45 PM on Sabbath evening, the 16th day of Kislev, 5708. The Zionists accepted the partition plan with some reluctance, and the Arab countries, along with the Arabs of Palestine, flatly rejected the plan, but that story will have to wait, and it is a saga that continues.

At United Israel's 5th meeting held on April 18, 1948, Horowitz reported on the results of the UN Assembly Special Committee's decision. He stated: "As long as the UN fails to follow God's blueprint for Palestine, it will fail to solve the problem. It will always remain in our official records that we brought to the attention of the United Nations the plan of the Bible for Palestine."

Though Horowitz and United Israel did not achieve the success they were hoping for, he was not deterred. He would soon embark on another campaign that would prove to be highly successful-one that would influence a sitting President and a vote for Israel's statehood.

Chapter 4

When Prophecy Echoed
in the White House

When, on November 29, 1947, the UN General Assembly voted
to recommend the partition of Palestine into a Jewish and an Arab state,
France, the Soviet Union, and the United States were the major powers
that supported the resolution. Horowitz had also worked intensely
behind the scenes to help influence crucial Latin American votes
needed to pass the partition plan. The UN appointed a commission
composed of representatives from Denmark, Czechoslovakia, Panama,
Bolivia, and the Philippines to implement their resolution. The British
gave notice that they would evacuate Palestine by August 1, 1948,
although they later decided to terminate the mandate earlier, on
May 15.

Violence in the Holy Land broke out almost immediately after the
UN announcement. The Arabs declared a protest strike and began to
instigate riots. By the end of the second week ninety-three Arabs,
eighty-four Jews, and seven Englishmen had been killed and scores
were injured. The chairman of the Arab Higher Committee said that
the Arabs would "fight for every inch of their country." Two days later,
the jurists of Al-Azhar University in Cairo called on the Muslim world
to proclaim a *jihad* (holy war) against the Jews.

As the rioting intensified, the U.S. State Department convinced
President Truman to propose that the partition plan be suspended in
favor of a UN trusteeship over Palestine, warning that the longer the
violence continued, the angrier at the United States the Arab world

would become. This policy shift, however, caused great consternation to world Jewry.

In the spring of 1948, Truman's public approval rating stood at thirty-six percent, and the President was nearly universally regarded as incapable of winning the upcoming general election. All the polls showed his Republican opponent, former New York governor, Thomas E. Dewey, far ahead in the race. Truman's chances for re-election were considered very slim. It was during this time that Horowitz met up with an old friend and a luncheon conversation that led to an engaging new development.

Horowitz's activities took him to Washington often where he met Martin F. Smith, an official of the Department of Justice, for lunch. Smith who was formerly associated with Congress was an old friend of President Truman and, like Truman, was a deep student of the Bible and prophecy. During their meetings, Horowitz and Smith would almost always discuss prophecy in the light of present-day events as relating to Israel and America.

President Truman had long taken an interest in the ancient history of the Middle East and the events related in the Bible. During their meeting, the discussion turned to Smith's friend, Mr. Truman, and the Presidential campaign. Both agreed that Truman's chance for re-election was very poor. As they spoke about the Bible and prophecy as relating to the Jews returning to Palestine, Horowitz told Smith that America's new policy was contrary to God's will. He added that, because of this, Truman, as head of the nation, had found disfavor in the sight of God and man. Then, in a sort of wishful way, Horowitz said: "Possibly if Truman would heed my counsel, he might still at this late hour stand a chance of re-election." Smith, looking serious and taking the statement in earnest, said: "Tell me, and I will tell the President."

Somewhat taken aback by this sudden challenge and realizing that Smith was serious, Horowitz told him: "Truman should know, first of all, that no man or electorate had put him into the White House. He got in through an act of God when Franklin D. Roosevelt died on April 12, 1945 a week or so after it was revealed that Mr. Roosevelt had made certain commitments to Ibn Saud and the Arabs. Hence, it is clear, that God does not want Truman to listen to every dissenting voice, as he has up until now in matters of State and Foreign Policy. God wants him to do what he thinks is right himself."

"Moreover," Horowitz continued, "the problem of Palestine is not exclusively a Jewish one. American Christian voters, nurtured on Hebrew tradition as based on the Bible, have always connected the Jew with the Holy Land. When they read in their daily papers that Truman was wavering on this matter, permitting the State Department to play politics that's not in the interest of the people of the Book, they lost their faith in him. They saw a weak man who changes his mind with every wind. Therefore, unless your friend, Mr. Truman, realizes these facts and rectifies the wrong done the Jews, he will fail history and lose. He will have to convince the American people by doing something spectacular in the matter of the Jews and Palestine so as to electrify the world." Mr. Smith listened intently, and as they parted, he promised he would go to the President and press the matter with him.

A week later, in a *New York Times* dispatch reporting Mr. Truman's weekly press conference, the President was quoted among other things, as having said: "I don't care what happens to my own political career personally. I am going to do what *I think* is right." During this press conference reporters seemed to be witnessing a new Truman. He became more "unpredictable." He began to act more on his own and his ratings in the public eye began to rise.

Fighting in the undeclared war in Palestine gradually escalated. From November 30, 1947 through February 1, 1948, 427 Arabs, 381 Jews, and 46 British were killed, and many more were wounded. In March alone, 271 Jews and 257 Arabs died in clashes. The UN continued to debate Trusteeship over Palestine, but there seemed to be insufficient support in the UN General Assembly to adopt this change of policy. The UN partition resolution was never suspended or rescinded and on May 14, 1948, the Zionists declared the independent state of Israel, as the British finally left the country.

Against vigorous opposition from his Secretary of State, George Marshall, President Truman did the unpredictable. He extended immediate recognition to the new state *eleven minutes* after it declared itself a nation. Marshall believed the paramount threat to the U.S. was the Soviet Union and feared that Arab oil would be lost to the U.S. in the event of war. He warned Truman that: "the U.S. was playing with fire with nothing to put it out." There was other opposition in the State Department as well.

Truman had indeed electrified the world by recognizing the State of Israel to the dejection of Israel's enemies. The General Assembly of the UN went into a tantrum. Not even the American delegation under Warren Austin had known what Truman would do.

It seemed that President Truman had taken seriously the message conveyed to him by Smith, perhaps becoming a modern Cyrus (Cyrus the Great, King of Persia, issued the decree of liberation ending the Babylonian captivity of the Jews). Horowitz was in the press gallery in Flushing Meadows that late Friday afternoon when news of Truman's recognition of Israel was announced in the General Assembly. During their next meeting, Smith told Horowitz that soon after their previous discussion, he contacted President Truman and related every word he had heard from Horowitz. He said that Truman listened intently and became strangely quiet. "I have seen Mr. Truman many times and in many moods," Smith said, "but never did I see him so dead earnest and serious as at the close of our meeting this time."

The 1948 Presidential Election will always be remembered for Harry Truman's stunning come from behind victory. The defining image of the campaign came after Election Day, when an ecstatic Truman held aloft the erroneous front page of *The Chicago Tribune* with a huge headline proclaiming, "Dewey Defeats Truman."

Chapter 5

A Decade of Change:
The Greatest Generation

Israel, the Jewish State in Palestine, was born on May 14, 1948. The day after Israel declared its independence, five Arab armies; Egypt, Syria, Trans-Jordan, Lebanon, and Iraq invaded Palestine in an effort to prevent Israel from coming into being. The Arab war to destroy Israel failed. The cost to Israel was enormous, both in human loss and economic cost. Because of their aggression, the Arabs wound up with less territory than they would have had if they had accepted partition, and the United Nations would be faced with a huge Palestinian refugee issue. Israel expected its neighbors to accept its independence as a fact and negotiate peace. This was not to be. With the exception of Iraq, the other four Arab countries signed armistice agreements with Israel in 1949. It would take another thirty years before an Arab state would agree to make peace with Israel.

Nineteen-forty-eight was winding down. On September 14, 1948, the symbolic ground-breaking ceremony of the United Nations permanent headquarters located in the Turtle-Bay area on the East Side of Manhattan took place. The event marked the beginning of the actual work of excavation for the thirty-nine story first building. Horowitz once remarked that he "watched the UN compound go up brick by brick." October 24 was declared United Nations Day to commemorate the coming into force of the United Nations Charter, one of the greatest international undertakings in history. October 24th was observed each year thereafter throughout the world as United Nations Day.

During the same period, Dwight David Eisenhower was installed as the thirteenth president of Columbia University. Some interesting sidelights on the appointment: the number thirteen happens to be both America's and Israel's peculiar symbol. Nearly all the emblems on the Great Seal of the United States run in groups or clusters of thirteen. America started with thirteen colonies, Israel with thirteen tribes. Also, thirteen is the numerical value of the Hebrew word "echad" (meaning one). Eisenhower was taking over the reins of the only university in the world whose official seal carries the Hebrew name YHVH as its most imposing symbol.

Once again America stood at the head among the nations of the world in espousing the cause of Israel. The January-February 1949 issue of the United Israel Bulletin covered the story of the December 2, 1948 session of the Security Council in which U.S. Spokesman, Dr. Philip C. Jessup, delivered a stirring appeal urging Israel's immediate admission as the fifty-ninth member of the United Nations. Dr. Jessup's declaration indicated clearly where President Truman stood on Israel.

On March 4, 1949, the Security Council recommended Israel for admission to the United Nations. The vote, coming at about 5:40 pm (almost midnight in Israel) was nine in favor, one against (Egypt), and one abstention (England). Horowitz was present on May 11th, the twelfth day of Iyar, 5709, at approximately 7:30 pm, when the United Nations congregated in its General Assembly Building at Flushing Meadows and admitted Israel as its 59th member nation. He summed up the prevailing emotions as the event unfolded:

> It was a dramatic occasion. As the vote was taken there prevailed an air of tense alertness, vigil, and almost breathlessness. Even some of the most seasoned newsmen showed emotions that revealed their innermost feelings. Most of them, having followed the Israeli case from the very outset of the struggle, had hoped for just this sort of development. The vote, 37 in favor, 12 against with 9 abstentions, came as a climax to a drama upon which the eyes of the world had been focused for a long time. For the Jews, the event seemed Messianic in scope.

A story about Herbert Hoover's plan for Palestine appeared in the November 1949 edition of the United Israel Bulletin. Hoover, a former U.S. President (1929-33) and a Quaker, was known as "the great humanitarian" for his many relief initiatives that fed war-torn Europe during and after World War I and similar efforts post World War II. He had proposed a plan for the many displaced Palestinian refugees following Israel's War of Independence.

Although much has been written regarding the refugee issue, for the sake of brevity only an overview is provided. The Palestinians left their homes in 1947-48 for many reasons. Thousands of wealthy Arabs left in anticipation of a war, fleeing to neighboring Arab countries to await its end. Thousands more responded to Arab leaders' calls to flee out of the way of the advancing armies and in a few cases the Israeli forces did expel Arab residents from villages.

The best estimates from census records show that no more than 650,000 Palestinian Arabs could have become refugees. Reports by the UN mediator on Palestine arrived at an even lower figure of 472,000. There were no welcome mats in neighboring Arab countries for the displaced refugees and the UN would become essentially a welfare agency for the Palestinians.

Hoover's proposal was that Iraq be made the scene of resettlement of the Arabs from Palestine. Quoting directly from Hoover's plan:

In ancient times the irrigation of the Tigris and Euphrates valleys supported probably 10 million people. The deterioration and destruction of their irrigation works by the Mongol invasion centuries ago and their neglect for ages are responsible for the shrinkage of the population. My own suggestion is that Iraq be financed to complete this great land development on the condition that it is made the place of resettlement of the Arabs from Palestine. This would clear Palestine completely for a large Jewish emigration and colonization.

A suggestion to transfer the Arab people of Palestine was made by the British Labor Party in December 1944, however, no adequate plan was proposed as to where or how they would go. There is room for many more Arabs in Iraq than the total of Arabs in Palestine. The soil is more fertile. They would be among their own race, Arab-speaking and Mohammedan.

The Hoover Plan was submitted to the Anglo-American Committee of Inquiry on Palestine in December 1945. Speaking in Kansas City on December 27, 1948, President Truman made reference to the Hoover Plan as a possible settlement of the Arab refugee problem brought about by the war in Palestine. He viewed it as a way to relieve the plight of the refugees while also benefiting Iraq since Palestinians excel at both agriculture and construction.

Israel was now a member nation of the UN and was ready to take its place at the big table. The alphabetical seating arrangement of the United Nations delegates at all committee meetings placed Israel in a rather uncomfortable position. Directly at Israel's left sits Iraq, then Iran and India. At her right is Lebanon. These states, which voted against Israel's admission into the World Body, seemed none too pleased with their immediate seating partner.

The UN experience would lead to Israeli delegate Abba Eban making his famous observation while commenting about the UN General Assembly: "If Algeria introduced a resolution declaring that the earth was flat, and that Israel had flattened it, it would pass by a vote of 164 to 13 with 26 abstentions."

The decade of the 1940s was one of immense change. Horowitz's life became profoundly redirected. As previously stated, UIWU was founded as a world organization and Horowitz began a long and successful career as a United Nations Correspondent.

An impressive endorsement of the UIWU came from famous French author and playwright, Edmund Fleg. Interviewed at his Paris home, Fleg stated, "The advent of United Israel World Union in the new world is without a doubt a sign of a new beginning in American Anglo-Jewish life. It is my sincere hope that United Israel will spread to all parts of the world. The idea has a message for tomorrow."

It was a year of many accomplishments, but David Horowitz was about to close 1949 with an event that would change his life.

Chapter 6

What a Difference a Year Makes!

Times Square: December 31, 1949. The countdown was underway. Happy New Year…Happy New Decade!

David Horowitz was invited to a New Year's Party in Greenwich Village to celebrate the new beginning. During the party the subject of Israel and the Middle East was raised, and Horowitz was asked for an insider opinion. Some, not wanting to mix merriment with politics, objected rather loudly. Hearing the commotion, a Ms. Nan Reilly, seated just inside an adjacent room, spoke out loudly, "It's regarding Israel. Let him speak!" And so, with Ms. Reilly's vociferous endorsement, Horowitz addressed the revelers on why he felt it was the British, more than the Arabs, who were responsible for the hostility and conflagration against Israel.

Following his address, Horowitz introduced himself to his young outspoken supporter. They spent much of the remaining evening in conversation and ringing in 1950 together. As Horowitz would discover later, Ms. Reilly had a similar history of supporting Israel's struggle for independence. Born in 1910 to an Irish father and English mother in Longford, Ireland, Nan's childhood and early adolescence were spent like any other Irish child of that period, living on a rural farm with lots of chores and a warm family and community life. Unfortunately, that idyllic existence came to an end when Nan was only a teenager. First, she lost both of her parents; then, her aunt and uncle, who had brought her to America, also died.

Bereft of relatives while still in her teens, Nan studied nursing and obtained her certification. It was during this period of loss that she began to make close friends in the Jewish community, both among her patients and other acquaintances. This new circle became her adopted family. Nan developed a fierce loyalty to the Jewish people and became an outspoken supporter of an independent State of Israel and an opponent of all forms of anti-Semitism.

Nan also became an ardent supporter and worker for the pro-Irgun "American Committee for a Free Israel," which was led by the noted Samuel Merlin and Peter Bergson and supported by other such notables as Ben Hecht and Billy Rose. Igrun was a Zionist paramilitary organization. In connection with this work, she met and befriended the young Irgun leader, Menachem Begin, thus meeting the great Israeli leader before David Horowitz did.

As the New Year unfolded, Middle Eastern issues continued to occupy the UN agenda. The General Assembly led by a coalition of Arab, Muslim, Catholic and Soviet bloc states voted for the internationalization of Jerusalem. In reaction, the Israeli government proclaimed Jerusalem to be its capital and the Knesset was transferred there. Most countries, however, refused to move their embassies to Jerusalem.

The General Assembly also established the UN Refugee Works Administration (UNRWA) beginning with a $54 million budget, to assist in employing refugees on relocation projects in Arab lands. Arab governments refused to cooperate with any plan designed for economic integration and the UNRWA remained a relief agency.

New developments were also underway at United Israel World Union. David Horowitz announced plans to visit Israel after a long absence. He was returning as a correspondent for the UI publication and as head of United Israel World Union. His purpose was to make a comprehensive survey of conditions prevailing in Israel after statehood and explore possibilities for assisting in program development of a more unified educational system.

After meeting Horowitz at the New Year's party, Nan Reilly began to take a greater interest in the activities of United Israel World Union, becoming a member of its editorial staff and assisting at United Israel's Fifth Avenue office in her spare time.

Speaking at a meeting of the New York unit of United Israel on the eve of the biblical New Year, 1 Nisan 5710 (March 18, 1950), Horowitz emphasized that "the battle of the sword" for the redemption of Israel must be accompanied and followed by "the battle of education" towards the unity of all Israel in common with all nations. "The Mosaic Code," stated Horowitz, "is not mere religion in the ordinary sense of the word. It is a *philosophy of life* applicable to all peoples and all times." He announced that United Israel was expanding to include a more extensive program in the educational field and that a new United Israel Welfare Fund would be established to assist in the newly expanded program.

In an interesting development, the Jordan radio station in Amman announced plans to launch a series of Hebrew broadcasts. The programs were seen as the first move toward Jordan's recognition of the Jewish state. The Amman station would be the only Middle Eastern station that referred to the new Jewish state of "Israel." During April 1950, the council of the Arab League adopted a resolution forbidding its members to agree to peace with Israel. They also refused to recognize the annexation by Jordan of the West Bank and east Jerusalem, calling it illegal.

On June 11, the Jewish National Fund announced the establishment of the Harry S. Truman Village in Israel. Vice-President Alben Barkley expressed the hope that the agricultural colony bearing the name of the President will "serve not only as a testimonial to President Truman's efforts on behalf of the Jewish State, but also as a firm link which will bind together the oldest democracy in the New World with the youngest born after the World War in a firm union against all aggression."

April brought the 7th Annual Meeting of United Israel, several favorable reviews for Horowitz's autobiography *33 Candles,* and an extensive interview by New York radio station WLIB commentator Estelle Sternberger, during which Horowitz explained how United Israel began and discussed the purpose and goals of the organization.

Events were heating up on other fronts: Egypt closed the Suez Canal to Israeli ships and Israeli commerce; in June, North Korea invaded South Korea; the UN Security Council, acting in absence of the Soviet Union, voted military sanctions and called on its members to repel the invasion; President Truman authorized the use of American forces.

On the 19th day of Tishre, 5711 (September 30, 1950), the Sabbath of the Feast of Tabernacles, members of United Israel World Union from various parts of the country converged on West Olive, Michigan, at the estate of Lewis Goodin, Vice President of the Union, to dedicate a New Hebrew altar. Scores of visitors from surrounding cities came to witness the historic dedication, including the Mayor of Grand Haven and the leading Rabbi of Muskegon. The New York Times, the Jewish Telegraphic Agency and all the local newspapers had representatives covering the biblical ceremony.

With United Nations Day only three days away, David Horowitz finished the final draft of an article entitled, "America's Destiny, The United Nations and the World." He completed it in the United Nations Press area at Lake Success on October 21, 1950, and the first copy was dispatched that same day to President Harry S. Truman.

David arrived at Flushing Meadows on the morning of October 24th, UN Day.

Everything was in readiness for President Truman's arrival, where he was scheduled to be the final speaker. Along with a number of newsman and security personal in the hallway, David witnessed Truman's entry. Truman's address on the role and vision of the United Nations was moving and passionate, citing the promise in Isaiah that "swords shall be beaten into plowshares and that nations shall not learn war anymore."

Following the adjournment of the Assembly, a special UN reception was held for President Truman. Horowitz was standing nearby the President with a couple of White House correspondents. As the President was turning to leave, he looked over at Horowitz, smiled, and chuckled, "well, well!"

It had been a year filled with change and progress. United Israel World Union was experiencing incredible exposure and growth, and David was becoming much more involved in UN activities. As 1951 came into being, David Horowitz and Nan Reilly were married. Truly, what a difference a year can make.

Chapter 7

Twin Flames of Freedom: An Eternal Bond

Building off the previous year's success and momentum, United Israel World Union continued to expand. Newlywed UIWU President David Horowitz sent a letter to Israeli Prime Minister David ben Gurion regarding the establishment of colonies in Israel. United Israel also announced the formation in Greater New York City of a Young Men's and Young Women's Anti-Discrimination Auxiliary under the name "B'nai Sinai." It was a program designed to unify and strengthen the ranks of an Israeli youth of a new age, one born out of the Hitlerian holocaust. It offered renewed hope and faith in the eternal ideals of their heritage born at Sinai. Response and growth was widespread among the young men and women of the Empire City and the organization soon had its own officers and committee heads.

On April 22, 1951, United Israel held its 8th Annual Meeting and announced plans for the building of the organization's second Hebrew altar to serve a growing congregation in West Virginia. The dedication was scheduled to take place in the town of Wilbur during the Feast of Tabernacles in October.

The Korean War intensified. China intervened by sending two hundred thousand troops to support North Korea. On April 11, U.S. President Harry Truman relieved General Douglas MacArthur of his Far Eastern command.

May 1951 marked a new chapter in American Zionism, and David Horowitz witnessed firsthand many of the new developments. The Zionist Organization of America's "Salute to Israel" rally was held at New York's Madison Square Garden on the evening of May 13th, commemorating the third anniversary of the State of Israel. The pageant entitled "Twin Flames of Freedom" was presented at the rally that drew over 20,000 spectators.

The marvelous pageant, conceived by Israeli Ben Aronim and produced by Isaac Van Grove, linked the destinies of the oldest and youngest world democracies. It drew a sharp parallel in the struggle of the United States and Israel to achieve independence. The very nature of this unique pageant symbolized the link that would bind the two democracies into a bond of eternal friendship involving ongoing cooperation and coordination of action and activities.

The celebration continued as two warships of the Israeli navy arrived in New York harbor on a goodwill tour of American ports. It marked the first visit of any unit of Israel's armed forces. Representing the world's youngest navy, the warships (frigates) named "Misgav" (Secure Haven) and "Haganah" (Defense) were veterans of Israel's War of Independence. Members of the crew were from over thirty different countries. Many bore the brand of Auschwitz and other Nazi death camps and had personal, dramatic stories to share of survival and migration to Israel. Mrs. Nan Reilly, new United Israel associate editor and David's new wife, interviewed Israeli sailors during the warship's New York visit for United Israel World Union.

David Horowitz personally met and interviewed several members of Hollywood's leading personalities appearing in New York for the festivities. Peter Hanson, Joan Taylor and Nancy Hale were among Paramount's Golden Circle who spent time with David at a luncheon held at the Waldorf Astoria Hotel on May 15th. For Israel and the United States, it was a golden celebration.

An Israeli bond drive of one half billion dollars opened in the U.S. Following an extensive tour of leading American cities on behalf of the bond issue drive, Prime Minister David ben Gurion left New York on the afternoon of May 31st aboard the Queen Mary. At Paris, he boarded an El Al Israeli national plane for the return trip to Israel. On the eve of his departure, ben Gurion made the following statement at a meeting with the representatives of the press: "I am returning to Israel profoundly moved by the warmth and cordiality of the reception which Mrs. ben Gurion and I have experienced on all sides during our stay in this country. In Washington, twice I had the opportunity of meeting with President Truman and of learning firsthand of his deep personal interest in the welfare and development of Israel."

In late August 1951, Horowitz returned to Israel. He was fortunate to have arranged a meeting with Israeli Prime Minister David ben Gurion. The occasion of the visit marked the presentation of United Israel's first symbolic flag to the State of Israel at the behest of the West Olive unit in Michigan. The Premier accepted the flag enthusiastically and later expressed his appreciation in a letter to the Michigan congregation. Dated August 29, 1951, the Prime Minister wrote:

> Your kind letter of August 20th was conveyed to me by Mr. David Horowitz. I was deeply moved by its contents and by your fine gesture in sending us your symbolic flag. I have told my colleagues in the Government of Israel of your letter and of your gift. The flag I will hand over to the State of Israel and, in accordance with your wishes, it will be kept in Jerusalem, the Holy City, the capital of our State.

On October 14, 1951, the second United Israel altar was dedicated at Wilbur, West Virginia. The Clarksburg Telegram of October 15 carried a full report of the dedication in a front-page story. By early 1952, however, United Israel began experiencing financial difficulties and announced that they were no longer able to have the United Israel Bulletin published. It was replaced by a number of "Personal Letters" consisting of several legal sized pages with a bulletin-like format. The last magazine style bulletin appeared in March 1952. It was not until April 1957 that the bulletin reappeared, this time in a tabloid form.

In Personal Letter #5 of July 1952, Horowitz reported that he had a new column titled *"Behind the Scenes at the United Nations"* which the Western Jewish News of Winnipeg, Canada, had assigned to him to write for the publication. A leading magazine in Bombay, India and the "Jewish Herald" in Johannesburg, South Africa soon picked up the column as a regular feature. In the first few columns, Horowitz referred to Mrs. Eleanor Roosevelt's participation at the United Nations in connection with her deep understanding of Israel. When she read the columns, Mrs. Roosevelt wrote Horowitz a nice note of appreciation.

During July 1952, King Farouk of Egypt was dethroned by a bloodless coup led by Gamal Abdel Nasser, Anwar al-Sadat, and others. Israeli Prime Minister Ben-Gurion, in a Knesset speech, extended the "hand of friendship" to the new Egyptian regime and privately offered economic and political assistance, which Egypt responded to favorably. Private conversations would continue until December 1954.

Returning from a trip to Spokane, Washington in October, Horowitz stopped over in Kansas City, Missouri and had a long visit with one of President Truman's closest friends, Eddie Jacobson. Jacobson and Truman had once been business partners and buddies during World War I. It was believed that Jacobson had also influenced Truman on the matter of the recognition of the State of Israel. Horowitz later received a letter from Jacobson telling him that he had finished reading *33 Candles* and that he planned to visit him at the UN in November.

On November 9, 1952, the first president of Israel, Chaim Weizmann, died while in office. In a little-known fact, Prime Minister David ben Gurion offered Albert Einstein the position of president. While the office of the President of Israel is a largely ceremonial position with the real executive power lying in the hands of the Prime Minister, Einstein declined the honor, saying he was "deeply moved by the offer, but didn't consider himself suited for the position." Yitzhak Ben-Zvi succeeded Chaim Weizmann as president.

In the November 1952 Presidential election, former five-star general and Columbia University President, Dwight David Eisenhower defeated Adlai Stevenson and became the 34th President of the United States. Under the new U.S. administration, Israel soon learned just how much they missed President Harry Truman.

Chapter 8

When Israel Was a Child...

Nineteen-fifty-three began with a new United States Presidential administration. With the transition from Truman to Eisenhower, the U.S. began to distance itself from Israel. A new Middle East policy began to take shape that influenced American decision-makers for the remainder of the century. The greatest danger, in the view of the new administration, was the Soviet Union. U.S. policy throughout the 1950s was primarily shaped by the effort to contain the spread and influence of Communism.

Israelis were disappointed by the Arabs refusal to recognize its existence after the 1948 War of Independence. They were discouraged further by the policies of the new Eisenhower administration, which ranged from apathetic to seemingly hostile. Eisenhower thought that the previous administration had been excessively partial to Israel and he resolved to follow a more even-handed policy on the Arab-Israeli conflict.

The foreign aid program for Israel that Truman had initiated after the 1948 war was quickly reduced. Aid was used as a lever to extract concessions. The Israelis were encouraged to make territorial concessions in exchange for peace with the Arabs. The new president also refused to sell arms to Israel and showed little tolerance for Israeli policies.

In fairness, it is important to understand the forces at work in the shift of U.S. policy. In addition to the growing cold war with the Soviets, Eisenhower faced a potent challenge in Arab nationalism. There were two issues at play. First, there were the lingering vestiges of British and French imperialism in the Arab world. The fact that the U.S. was formally allied with Britain and France aroused considerable popular resentment in the Arab world. A second issue was Zionism. The fact that the U.S. had played a key role in the creation of Israel aroused even deeper Arab resentment.

The basic dilemma became another all too familiar political juggling act. The U.S. had to keep the Arab states favorably disposed toward the West and, thus, keep the region's oil reserves and strategic positions accessible, while at the same time, remaining committed to Israel's survival and security, a position that caused deep resentment in the Arab world.

The new nation of Israel was a mere child, yet five years old, learning to live a new life of self-determination, while surrounded by a world of hostile forces committed to its destruction. Would it survive? Could it? What were the odds? If we could pause and tear a page from history that shows us a picture of the new five-year-old, what would the child look like? How was it behaving?

Fortunately, we have such a record today. As the U.S. shifted its Middle Eastern policy, we are allowed a look back at the old family photo. David Horowitz, serving as a Special Correspondent for "The Voice," a Los Angeles publication with the largest Jewish circulation in the West, had returned from an extended stay in Israel and offered a full report of his findings in the June 12, 1953 issue of the publication. The following is Horowitz's assessment of the new nation in his own words.

JERUSALEM: My three-month visit to Israel, having afforded me the opportunity to traverse the country and study carefully almost every phase of life here, has left me with the following impressions:

1) Israel as a whole is the most dynamic and promising little country in the world. The sturdy, energetic Israelis are creating a commonwealth along this Mediterranean crescent which, judging by the present intensive activities,

has all the signs of becoming a second little "America." Settlements dotting the nation are expanding and thriving at a pace unequalled in history. Possibilities here are as great as they were in the early days of colonization in America. The wise and the foresighted are putting a stake in this land and now is the time of opportunity. Four or five years hence might be too late in order to get in on the ground floor.

2) Opportunities for foreign investors in nearly every field of endeavor are greater now than ever. The Mapai-General Zionist Coalition, opening a new trend, has enhanced the situation. Former restrictions placed on private enterprise have been relaxed. The political trend is moving more and more towards the center, away from Mapai-Mapam influences (note: Mapai was the largest left-wing political party, General Zionists, the centrists' political party, and Mapam, a left-wing labor party with Marxist ideology). My survey has shown that more than 30 percent of the population is independent of Party affiliation. Also, many within the Mapai-Mapam Parties find themselves favorably disposed to the new trend. Here lies a great power for the future, a power that may well prove decisive during the next elections.

3) Despite the present economic difficulties, and they are many, no nation in history has doubled its population in so short a time. With population growth from 650,000 to 1,450,000, the state is moving ahead uninterrupted with numerous national projects. These include roadways, waterway improvements and port developments. Most important, Israel's military strength has more than tripled since the War of Independence. The leading cities of Jerusalem, Tel Aviv, Haifa, Tiberius, Beersheba, Ashkenlon, Rishon, Petah Tikvah, Ramleh, Afuleh and Acre, have all embarked upon large-scale municipal programs which will make these vital centers equal major tourist attractions.

4) Israel is the most music and art-loving country in the world, even surpassing Italy. The strains of the great masters are heard daily from almost every house with the new songs of Zion as happy interludes. There is singing in the streets and dancing during festivals and holidays. The Sabbath in Israel is truly Sabbath. Shops and factories close early Friday afternoon and some two hours before sundown the streets become deserted. Thus, universal acceptance of the Sabbath by all Israelis is remarkable. The seventh day rest transcends affiliations. It is a holy day of peace and relaxation for all. While it's true that only a minority go to the synagogue, the majority rejoice in the delights of the Sabbath under the canopy of the clear skies, enjoying the seas, lakes and rivers and the many glories this land has to offer. Saturday is indeed Sabbath.

5) As for the Arabs remaining in Israel, their lot has never been better. A buyer of tobacco took me to several Arab villages recently. With us, went an official of the company buying the rich tobacco leaves. He carried a briefcase containing 10,000 Israeli pounds. After the tobacco bales were weighed, the Arab growers were paid on the spot. The inspector revealed to me that during the Mandate days, the Arabs often had to wait up to a year until payment was made, and they themselves had to go into the city from their villages begging payment, thus losing valuable time that could be spent working their plantations.

6) In one of these villages I was invited into the home of an Arab member of the Knesset. A flagpole over this home flew the blue and white flag of Israel. For the Arabs living in this village, this emblem meant something new and good. For they are their own witnesses to the fact that since this flag has flown over their village, their conditions have improved a hundredfold. This was evident by the joyful and happy expressions of their children who did not appear any different from the Israeli children of their neighbors.

Meanwhile, on the world scene, Soviet dictator Joseph Stalin died. The United Nations and North Korea signed a truce agreement ending the North Korean invasion of South Korea. King Hussein bin Talal, the grandson of King Abdullah who was assassinated in 1951, assumed the throne in Jordan. King Hussein's rule extended throughout the cold war and four decades of Arab-Israeli conflict.

At the United Nations, Dag Hammarskjold, Swedish diplomat and economist, was elected the new Secretary-General of the UN after Trygve Lie's resignation. David Horowitz and Dag Hammarskjold were both Swedes. They became good friends and the fact that they shared the same birthplace gave them great chemistry. Their friendship and respectful working relationship continued until Hammarskjold's tragic death in 1961.

An exhausted Prime Minister David Ben-Gurion announced his intention to withdraw from government and was replaced by Moshe Sharett, who was elected the second Prime Minister of Israel in January 1954. (Ben-Gurion later returned to government in 1955 and was re-elected as Prime Minister.)

In an article written by Adam Garfinkle entitled "The Triangle connecting the U.S., Israel, and American Jewry may be coming apart," and published in Tablet Magazine on November 5, 2013, Garfinkle reported:

> For President Harry Truman, the Jews of America stood for the Jewish people in history as mediated through the prism of Anglo-American Protestantism. Truman actually cried when Chief Ashkenazic Rabbi Yitzhak Herzog told him during his White House visit on May 11, 1949, what he as President had done, in broad meta-historical terms, for the Jewish people. In a private meeting after Truman left the White House, he replied to the thanks offered by the head of the Jewish Theological Seminary by answering his host, "What do you mean helped create Israel, I am Cyrus; I am Cyrus!

For the young child Israel, a new era was underway...and a long, long exile had ended.

Chapter 9
The Gathering Storm

The year 1954 began with an all-too-familiar sameness. A January issue of *The New York Times* reported that King bin Saud of Saudi Arabia had urged the sacrifice of ten million Arabs to "uproot the cancer" of Israel, while infiltration attacks inside Israel by Arab guerrillas continued on a frequent basis.

David Horowitz became involved in controversy when the editor of a small mid-western newspaper, James M. Watkins, accused him of advocating the conversion of Christians to Judaism. In the February 23, 1954 edition of *"The Restitution Herald"* of Oregon, Illinois, Mr. Watkins criticized Horowitz for being a Jewish missionary, along with the frivolous charge that he somehow had near complete control of Israeli news. Watkins charged that "Since Horowitz controls most of the press dispatches that go to the nation of Israel, as well as that which is sent out in this country, we can assume that he expressed the official viewpoint of the nation (Israel)."

Reacting to Watkins' editorial, Karl Baehr, Executive Director of the American Christian Palestine Committee (a pro-Israel Christian group), in a letter that was printed in the March 30 edition of *The Restitution Herald,* tried to dissuade any anti-Semitic or anti-Jewish feelings among Watkins' readers.

Responding to both Watkins and Baehr, on April 13, 1954, Horowitz sent a reply to *The Restitution Herald* in which he defended his views and his press dispatches. In reference to a specific passage, he remarked that the statement was not his, but that of "a Catholic, Malcolm Hay, author of the book, *The Foot of Pride* (Beacon Press, Boston 1950). "A book," Horowitz suggested, "that Watkins and every true Christian ought to read." Hay's book carefully chronicles the roots of Christian anti-Semitism.

U. S. Middle East policy continued to focus on containing the Soviet Union. The Arab States often played the superpowers off against each other in an effort to win concessions from one or the other. One Arab ruler, however, stood in the middle of everything: the inter-Arab rivalries, opposition to Western imperialism, Eisenhower's bid to create a regional alliance, and the perpetuation of the war with Israel. That man was Gamal Abdel Nasser. Over the next two decades, Nasser was to be an extremely forceful and charismatic advocate of radical Arab nationalism and of resistance to Western domination.

This was an especially active time at the United Nations, and Horowitz's role as a journalist took on an intensive tempo. In addition to his many hours interviewing delegates and ambassadors from various nations, he had considerable contact with Israeli Ambassador Abba Eban and new UN Secretary-General Dag Hammarskjöld. He also interviewed Pierre Mendès-France, then President of France's Council of Ministers, during his visit to the world organization.

Horowitz, persistent as always, continued his campaign to get the Israel-Arab dispute settled by the utilization of the Bible and the Koran. During August 1954, he attempted to persuade Egypt's chief UN delegate Major-General Abdel Hamid Ghaleb to accept his plan and received a most interesting and candid response. Ghaleb emphatically stated to Horowitz that he and all religious Egyptians believe in the Torah as much as in the Koran and they venerate Moses as one of the holiest men to have appeared on earth. He said further that "if the people in the Middle East turned to the Torah and the Koran for guidance instead of accepting their own narrow views, peace could come to the region. Allah is the same God worshipped by Israel, and this one God certainly does not want them to quarrel and fight over questions which, in the final analysis, are disposed of by Him anyway."

Ghaleb revealed that Egyptian President General Mohammed Naguib (who appointed Ghaleb), during his premiership, often visited synagogues and was sincere in his desire to come to some under-standing with Israel. Having restrained his innermost feelings, he succeeded in escaping the fate that befell the late King Abdullah of

Jordan whose mind was open for negotiations with Israel. But, as recent developments showed, he was overruled. On September 28, 1954, Egypt seized the Israeli merchant vessel "Bat Galim" in the Suez Canal. The issue was brought before the UN Security Council with the fiasco continuing into 1955 before a resolution was reached. In February 1955, Israeli Defense Minister Pinhas Lavon resigned following the uncovering of an Israeli intelligence network in Egypt. David Ben Gurion returned to government as Defense Minister.

David Horowitz's first visit to Israel had taken place in 1925 when Israeli pioneering was at its height. Subsequent trips were taken in 1932, 1951 and 1953. In March 1955, he made his fifth trip to Israel. This time, countless hours were spent in interviews with officials at Jerusalem's UN headquarters. Horowitz also took the time to conduct a little United Israel business.

Horowitz met with former Irgun leader Menachem Begin, then a member of the Israeli Knesset on behalf of the second largest party, Herut. Mr. Begin expressed his concern that the greatest threat facing Israel at the time was guerrilla warfare. He also gained an audience with Israeli President Yitzhak Ben-Zvi, who had served in the Jewish Legion together with Ben-Gurion and was among the signers of the Declaration of Independence on May 14, 1948. The Israeli President showed a deep interest in United Israel World Union and said he would extend an official welcome to any UIWU group. Horowitz would later remark, "President Ben-Zvi is a great scholar who has shown a profound interest in the fate that has befallen Israel's tribes scattered all over the world."

Before leaving Israel, Horowitz visited some old friends, the Tritto family, now residing in Safed in the Galilee region. Esther, her husband Eliezer and family were among scores of other Italians, all former Catholics who had embraced the Hebrew faith and who came to Israel from the south Italian town of San Nicandro in 1949. He happily reported that they had established firm roots in Safed and were helping to build Israel.

As April 1955 came to a close, France was hit with Arab threats and protests for shipping arms to Israel. Jordan also threatened to boycott French goods and the Foreign Ministers of both Syria and Lebanon protested the French action. Egypt requested that the Negev be detached from Israel. Just another busy day at the office of Middle Eastern affairs.

In June, Horowitz became a charter member of "Judaism Universal," a new international society for the propagation of the Hebrew faith as a world religion funded in New York City. Blessed and endorsed by Rabbi Menachem Mendel Schneerson, "Judaism Universal" adopted the following three-point program: to reclaim the Jewish youth; to Judaize the Jews; and to draw within the sphere of Jewish life neglected Jewish communities in isolated parts of the world and non-Jewish populations who hunger after universal truth and righteousness.

During a national election in Israel, David Ben-Gurion was again elected Prime Minister as well as Defense Minister. Moshe Sharett became Foreign Minister.

U.S. officials continued to reach out to Gamal Nasser. Egypt was offered promises of arms and help in building the Aswan Dam. Nasser instead began to import arms from the Soviet Bloc to build his arsenal for a confrontation with Israel. He announced, however, a new tactic on August 31, 1955: "Egypt has decided to dispatch her heroes, the disciples of Pharaoh and the sons of Islam, and they will cleanse the land of Palestine."

These "heroes" were Arab terrorists, or *fedayeen*, trained and equipped by Egyptian Intelligence to engage in hostile action on the border and infiltrate Israel to commit acts of sabotage and murder. Such terrorism violated the armistice agreement provision that prohibited the initiation of hostilities by paramilitary forces. Nevertheless, it was Israel that was condemned by the UN Security Council for its counterattacks.

The escalation continued with the Egyptian blockade of the Straits of Tiran, Israel's only supply route with Asia. Less than two weeks later, on October 25, Egypt signed a tripartite agreement with Syria and Jordan, which placed Nasser in command of all three armies. As 1955 drew to a close, Nasser made clear his intent. In an interview with New York Post reporter Paul Sann, he explained, carefully and quite clearly, "that Egypt would *never*, under any circumstances, consider peace with the Jewish State."

Even as war clouds gathered over the Middle East, history reminded us once again: One should never say never.

Chapter 10

Back to the Desert: War over Suez

The Suez crisis was a crucial turning point in world history. It marked Britain's demise as the pre-eminent Western power in the Middle East and the assumption of that role by the United States, a role the U.S. continues to play to this day.

It rankled the Eisenhower administration that Egypt began to buy arms from the Soviets, unleashed the *fedayeen* on Israel, and blockaded the Straits of Tiran. Further deterioration of U.S.-Egyptian relations occurred when Nasser threatened to turn to the Soviet Union for funding of the Aswan Dam project and to extend diplomatic recognition to Communist China.

In January 1956, David Horowitz learned that UN Secretary-General Hammarskjöld planned to visit both Cairo and Tel Aviv in efforts to ease tensions in the region. He was scheduled to meet with both Nasser and Ben-Gurion. Horowitz made a personal written appeal to the Secretary-General, stating, in part: "Since your flight to Cairo and Tel Aviv has been announced as a good will visit, you are in an excellent position to drive home the points you wish to raise with both President Nasser and Prime Minister Ben-Gurion. They must meet if peace is to come in the Palestine Zone."

Horowitz continued:

When you see Nasser, you might mention that Egypt played a vital role in Old Testament history as evidenced so wonderfully in the fascinating story of Joseph and his brethren who found refuge in Egypt under a kind and benevolent Pharaoh. For a period of 400 years the Hebrews lived and thrived with their cousins the Egyptians, until Providence ordained them to leave and become an independent nation under the leadership of Moses, whom Islam venerates as *Nebi Musa*.

When you see David Ben-Gurion, you might open the Bible and show him Isaiah chapter 19, verses 24-25, when prophecy of the future speaks of an Israel and an Egypt at peace and as constituting a blessing in the midst of the earth.

Just before his departure to the Middle East, Hammarskjöld expressed his thanks to Horowitz, remarking that he considered the counsel to be of great value and hoping that his own personal intervention might bring a measure of success.

Other attitudes were shifting politically. The new Socialist government of France, headed by Guy Mollet, had grown increasingly close to the new Israeli government, politically, diplomatically, and militarily. The alliance with France proved to be crucial for Israel in the years to come. The French became Israel's primary source of arms for roughly a decade and provided the key elements that ultimately allowed Israel to develop a nuclear capability.

At the end of January, former President Harry Truman, Eleanor Roosevelt, and labor leader Walter Reuther issued a joint statement urging the U.S. provision of defensive arms to Israel to help protect itself from the introduction of Communist arms to Arab countries in the Middle East.

France immediately informed the U.S. that Mystere jet fighters would be sent to Israel. The U.S. made it known it would not object to the sale of arms to Israel by France or Britain but continued to defer action on Israel's request for U.S. arms.

On February 26, 1956, Cantor Aaron Horowitz, David Horowitz's father, was hailed as the dean of American Cantors in an impressive tribute to his 60 years of service to Orthodox Judaism. The testimonial dinner event, sponsored by B'nai Jacob Synagogue, brought forth messages of tribute to Cantor Horowitz and his wife from regional, state and national personages. Among the many tributes in messages were those of President Eisenhower, Governor George M. Leader and

Herman Wouk, iconic Pulitzer Prize-winning author whose works include *The Caine Mutiny, Winds of War,* and *Marjorie Morningstar.* Mr. Wouk described the testimonial to Cantor Horowitz as a rare and splendid event. The author cited a traditional Hebrew concept that in each generation there are thirty-six unknowns whose spiritual ministrations enable the rest of the world to survive. Wouk concluded that Cantor Horowitz's career might well place him in that category. It was a most high tribute for Cantor Horowitz and a special time for a proud son.

In June 1956, Britain withdrew from Egypt, ending seventy-four years of military occupation and Foreign Minister Moshe Sharett was replaced by Golda Meir in the Ben-Gurion government. Following Britain's withdrawal, Nasser responded by announcing that he was nationalizing the British-owned Suez Canal Company and would use toll revenues to finance the Aswan Dam Project. Britain regarded Nasser's action as intolerable and began advocating a military intervention to reverse it. The U.S. strongly opposed military action and pressed for a diplomatic solution to the crisis.

From Israel's perspective, the continued blockade of the Suez Canal and Gulf of Aqaba, combined with the increased *fedayeen* attacks and buildup of Arab arms, were untenable. David Ben-Gurion decided to launch a pre-emptive strike with the backing of the British and French governments. The three nations subsequently agreed on a plan whereby Israel would land paratroopers near the Canal and send its armor across the Sinai Desert. The British and French would then call for both sides to withdraw from the Canal Zone, fully expecting the Egyptians to refuse. At that point, British and French troops would be deployed to "protect" the Canal.

On October 29, 1956, Israel attacked Egypt. "Operation Kadesh" began with a paratrooper drop near the Mitla Pass, about 30 miles from the Suez Canal. The U.S. government received no prior notice of the British-French-Israeli plan. Eisenhower was infuriated and immediately sent a message to David Ben-Gurion urging the withdrawal of forces. Ben-Gurion ignored the request. The U.S. sought a UN Security Council resolution calling for an Israeli withdrawal.

Britain and France vetoed the U.S. resolution and addressed a joint ultimatum to Egypt and Israel to withdraw from the Suez Canal area.

On October 31st, French and British warplanes destroyed most of the Egyptian air force in raids on air bases near the Suez Canal. The Soviets informed President Nasser that they would not go to war over the Suez. Jordan and Syria rejected his appeal for military support. He ordered a withdrawal from Sinai to concentrate forces to repel the impending British and French invasion.

Given the pretext to continue fighting, the Israeli forces routed the Egyptians. The IDF armored corps swept across the desert, capturing virtually the entire Sinai by November 5th. That day, British and French paratroopers landed near Port Said and amphibious ships dropped commandos onshore. British troops captured Port Said and advanced to within twenty-five miles of Suez City before the British government agreed to a cease-fire.

Meanwhile back home, the Republican incumbent, Dwight D. Eisenhower, defeated challenger, Adlai E. Stevenson, for another term as U.S. President in a rematch of their contest four years earlier.

Israel's failure to inform the U.S. of its intentions, combined with ignoring American entreaties not to go to war, sparked tensions between the countries. Pressuring Israel to withdraw included a threat to discontinue all U.S. aid, impose UN sanctions, and expel Israel from the United Nations. Additional pressure from the Soviets, the U.S. and the UN forced Britain, France, and Israel to end their attack on Egypt. Nasser's regime was saved.

By the end of the fighting, Israel held the Gaza Strip and had advanced as far as Sharm al-Sheikh along the Red Sea. A total of 231 Israeli soldiers died in the fighting. U.S. pressure resulted in an Israeli withdrawal from the areas it conquered without obtaining any concessions from the Egyptians. This sowed the seeds for a later war with Egypt in 1967. The only thing Israel gained for giving up all the territories it had won was the U.S. assurance that its shipping lanes would be kept open.

On December 23, the last British and French troops left the Suez Canal region. Gamal Abdel Nasser's prestige at home and among Arabs was undamaged. In fact, his greatest influence and popularity was just beginning.

Chapter 11

The Ides of April—Twin Anniversary Celebrations

Dateline: January 1957. Following the 1956 Suez Campaign, President Eisenhower launched an initiative that became known as the "Eisenhower Doctrine" to secure the Middle East against Soviet aggression by aiding any nation against overt armed aggression from any other nation controlled by international Communism. Congress adopted the doctrine in March.

Saudi Arabia's King ibn Saud visited Washington at the invitation of Eisenhower, the first official visit of an Arab head of state. During Eisenhower's eight years in the U.S. presidency, no Israeli was so honored.

In March, the Suez Canal reopened after clearance by the UN salvage crews of ship hulks that had been sunk to block the entrance during the Suez crisis.

United Israel World Union began republishing the *United Israel Bulletin* in a new format in April. This edition, released during the Passover redemptive season, was the first published since the last printed magazine appeared in March 1952. During the interim, a number of United Israel newsletters had been published periodically. In the April bulletin, it was reported that movie stars Marilyn Monroe, Carol Baker and Elizabeth Taylor had all, at various times, embraced the Decalogue Faith of Moses following long periods of contemplation and study of the Hebrew Scriptures.

In July, David Horowitz was instrumental in creating the "United Nations Correspondents Fellowship," to foster closer understanding and fellowship among the correspondents at the UN. The move was unanimously embraced by the association and lauded in written letters of endorsement by Ambassadors Abba Eban of Israel, Dr. Djalal Abdoh of Iran, Alberto F. Canas of Costa Rica and UN Secretary-General Dag Hammarskjöld himself.

In early August, Evangelist Dr. Billy Graham told David Horowitz in an exclusive interview, that God's word with respect to Israel's future boundaries as promised in the Bible-from the Euphrates to the Nile-cannot fail eventual fulfillment. Dr. Graham agreed that the return of the Jews to the Holy Land marks one of the great turning points in the history of the world.

As 1957 drew to a close, it became apparent that the "Eisenhower Doctrine" was not a great success. Middle Eastern governments were generally eager to accept U.S. aid under the new program, but Arab public opinion was hostile to the doctrine, seeing it as an effort to impose Cold War thinking on the Arabs by pressuring them to join an anti-Soviet alliance. Consequently, few Arab governments publicly endorsed the program.

It was announced in early 1958 that David Horowitz had been elected to the Executive Committee of the Foreign Press Association—a fitting recognition for the many contributions Horowitz had been making to the association.

The American Committee for Israel's 10th Anniversary announced that the inauguration of the celebration would take place on April 24th at Independence Hall in Philadelphia. The city was the cradle of America's independence and the home of the famous Liberty Bell containing the Old Testament inscription, "Proclaim ye liberty throughout the land to all the inhabitants thereof." Former U.S. President, Harry S. Truman, the first head of government to recognize the newly-born state ten years earlier, and Israeli Ambassador Abba Eban were scheduled to be the featured speakers during the unique ceremony.

During a television interview, leading CBS newsman, Edward R. Murrow, asked former President Truman: "You moved immediately to recognize Israel after it was created. Do you have any regrets about that?" Without hesitation, Truman replied: "Not the slightest...I know the history of that section of the world fairly well. There was the Balfour Declaration on the creation of the State of Israel. They hesitated and prolonged the situation. When it became my time to make the decision and there was a chance to create the State of Israel, as had been promised, I just carried out the agreements that had already been made. I've never been sorry for it, because I think it's necessary that there be a State of Israel. It's going to stay there no matter what they (the Arabs) think or what they do. Because the Israelites will take care of themselves as they always did in historic times."

Israel's 10th birthday was not the only significant event being celebrated in the month of April 1958. United Israel World Union was also observing the 15th anniversary of its existence. Remarking that the great Hebrew prophets prophesied the rise of the Third Hebrew Commonwealth in a period of stress and trial among nations, David Horowitz drew a providential connection between the two events, saying that: "despite the confusion among nations, two great rays of hope and fulfillment beam on the world horizon: Reborn Israel in two dispensations—United Israel World Union and the rising Hebrew Commonwealth on the ancient site."

"Notables Hail United Israel World Union on Its Fifteenth Anniversary," announced the front-page headline of the April edition of the United Israel Bulletin. Leaders from all walks of life, among them professionals, rabbis, and laymen alike, joined hundreds of others in hailing the successful endeavors of United Israel on the occasion of its 15th anniversary. Among the many rabbis who praised the constructive, Torah-reviving activities of United Israel were: Dr. W. Gunther Plaut of St. Paul's Mt. Temple; Rabbi Arthur Meyerowitz, Scarsdale, N.Y., a member of the N.Y. Board of Rabbis; and Rabbi Samuel S. Lerer of Temple Sholem, Hollywood, California. In addition, the world-renowned Lubavitch Rebbe, Menachem M. Schneerson, sent a special Passover message along with his best wishes and blessings.

Especially meaningful to Horowitz, was a message from London from former Catholic Priest, Abraham Isaac Carmel, congratulating United Israel on its fifteenth birthday. Dr. Carmel, the first and only fully ordained Catholic priest to have adopted the Hebrew faith, hailed United Israel as a "heaven-sent" movement that has "created a new era in Jewish history." In an open letter Dr. Carmel wrote: "As a proselyte to Orthodox Judaism, and the first Christian Priest to enter the Hebrew family, I write to offer my warmest congratulations on your 15th birthday. I personally owe a great debt to David Horowitz and his wonderful work. It was a heaven-sent revelation to me to learn of the amazing activity of David Horowitz and United Israel World Union."

In still another open letter to United Israel, which was titled "Time for rededication and to open the gates of Sinai," Dr. Hirsch Loeb Gordon, world-renowned leader in the field of neuropsychiatry and research, offered the following remarks: "On the occasion of the 10th anniversary of the Republic of Israel and the 15th of United Israel World Union, we should all rededicate ourselves to the rebuilding of our ancient Fatherland and to the propagation of our ancient faith universally." Dr. Gordon, a giant in his field, held six doctorates and four masters in several different fields, and had served in the Neuropsychiatric Consultants Division, Office of the Surgeon General and was the past National Commander of the American Palestine Jewish Legion of World War I. In his stirring endorsement of the work of United Israel World Union, Dr. Gordon said: "Your movement to send the Chariot of YHVH across the firmament of the pagan world to finish the mission begun at Sinai and crush the false idols is most inspiring."

Perhaps Rabbi Samuel Lerer of Temple Beth Sholem expressed it best when he said: "I wish to convey my deep gratitude for your dedicated work in bringing the Judaic faith unto the nations of the earth. Your missionary work that brings pure monotheism and Torah-faith to mankind, which is now merely a trickling spring of clear water, will eventually develop into a great fountain that will break forth into many springs from which humanity will drink."

Two fitting anniversary tributes; one to Israel reborn in their ancient prophetic homeland; the other to the emergence of an organization calling for a return to the Decalogue Faith of Moses for all mankind.

Chapter 12

Out of Africa

In April 1958, the celebrations and tributes marking the 10th Anniversary of the Republic of Israel and the 15th of United Israel World Union were in full swing.

On the world scene, General Charles de Gaulle became Prime Minister of France as a result of the Algerian crisis and was given special powers by the French Parliament. In a reply to Israel's Prime Minister David Ben-Gurion's message of congratulations, the new premier stated: "I salute the courageous nation of Israel, with which France maintains solid ties of friendship and shares the same spiritual ideal."

It is worth mentioning that in the midst of hostilities toward the young nation of Israel, the Druze people who represented a religious minority reflected a most welcome and refreshing attitude of acceptance. Rooted in Ismailism, a branch of Shia Islam but whose social customs differ markedly from those of Muslims or Christians, the Druze are Arabic speaking citizens of Israel who serve in both the Israeli Defense Forces and in politics.

In a new publication issued for the Druze community in Israel by the Ministry of Religious Affairs, a number of leading Druze hail the State of Israel and emphasize their loyalty to it. Sheikh Salih Adu Rukun, in discussing the duties of which a man owes his country and government writes: "We are duty bound to love our country, for there are strong ties between us. We were born and bred among a people which God gathered from all the corners of the earth into its promised land, and which is turning this holy land into a Garden of Eden in fulfillment of the words of Isaiah. We are a branch of the Israeli nation, and its ways have become ours."

On May 11th (21 Iyar, 5718), Mrs. Bertha Chazan Horowitz, eighty-four, wife of Cantor Aaron Horowitz, spiritual leader of Congregation B'nai Jacob, and mother of President David Horowitz passed away. She was taken into the bosom of the Eternal's grace, fittingly, on Mother's Day.

In a meeting with Ambassador Daniel A. Chapman, Permanent Representative of Ghana to the UN, David Horowitz congratulated him on their first anniversary of its independence. In March of 1957, Ghana became one of the first African nations to declare its independence from European colonization.

A number of years before Ghana became independent, hundreds of Gold Coast Bible students became interested in United Israel World Union and in 1955 some of them, under the guidance of several schoolteachers, organized a unit of United Israel in the province. In subsequent years, Headmaster Immanuel Johnson Kumi of Presby Village School in Kwaboanta, himself a convert to the Hebrew faith, corresponded regularly with David Horowitz. Photos and reports about unit activities in Ghana have appeared in past United Israel Bulletins.

Ghana maintains a close association with the State of Israel and there's a story behind it. Had it not been for an American black woman, Marguerite Cartwright, a roving correspondent for the *Pittsburgh Courier*, Israel today would never enjoy the close and friendly relations with the new, important West African state of Ghana. Both Marguerite and her husband, Leonard Carl Cartwright, played a vital role in the events that led to the Ghana-Israel relationship.

It all happened in the year of the Bandung Conference. The Conference was the first large-scale meeting of Asian and African states, most of which were newly independent, which took place on April 18-24, 1955 in Bandung, Indonesia. From a sobering perspective, the twenty-five countries that participated at the conference represented nearly one-quarter of the earth's land surface and a total population of 1.5 billion people. En route to Bandung, Marguerite Cartwright, a type of modern Queen of Sheba, visited what was then the Gold Coast and interviewed the leaders of the country, including Prime Minister

Kwame Nkrumah. Through many discussions, Cartwright convinced Nkrumah and his colleagues that, upon Ghana's attainment of independence, Israel would be the most logical country to call upon for technical, cultural, maritime, civil and administrative assistance. She cited Israel's enormous success in these areas during its short period of independence.

At first, Nkrumah appeared skeptical, being fully aware of the strained Arab-Israel relations, and seemed to dismiss the thought. The persistent Marguerite Cartwright, however, kept pressing the positive results that would accrue from relations with the Jewish State. Finally, Nkrumah agreed to be open to the idea.

Fortified with this mandate, Marguerite attended the Bandung Conference and, on her way back, stopped in Israel. There she conferred with Golda Meir, Moshe Sharett and others. Realizing the great importance and significance of Cartwright's mission, the Israeli leaders lost no time in putting the Foreign Office machinery into motion. The results were hugely successful. Trade agreements were signed, and an Israel-Ghana shipping line was established, opening doors of trade and industry between the two countries. Both nations benefited greatly from the mutual exchange of goods. Ghana became the first African country to establish diplomatic relations with the nation of Israel. Marguerite Cartwright became the darling of the Israeli Foreign Office and one of the best friends that Kwame Nkrumah could have. She became friends with David Horowitz. For more than three decades, her newspaper columns appeared regularly in *The Pittsburgh Courier* and *The New York Amsterdam News*. She died in 1986 at the age of 76.

High summer had arrived, and the Middle East was busy being the Middle East. In July, Iraq's pro-Western monarchy was overthrown. King Faisal II and Premier Nuri es-Said were murdered. Fearing that his own regime would be next, Lebanon's President Camille Chamoun appealed to the U.S., Britain, and France for military aid. Following the invocation of the Eisenhower Doctrine the next day, the U.S. sent 14,000 Marines to land on the coast of Lebanon to protect it from a United Arab Republic or Communist invasion.

King Hussein of Jordan then sought military aid from Britain to withstand United Arab Republic and Communist threats after the revolt in Iraq. British paratroopers landed in Jordan and remained there until October 29.

During Israel's 10th anniversary celebration, Prime Minister David Ben Gurion, who had a great interest in biblical research, opened his Jerusalem home to monthly bible study groups in which he himself was an active participant. The Prime Minister made it clear that this present generation of Jews was the last generation of bondage and servitude and the first in redemption, thereby bringing the Messianic ideal of deliverance from a long and wearisome journey. This vision of Jewish and universal redemption fostered a sense of spiritual closeness and bond to the sacred books of the Hebrew faith.

By now, the Eisenhower administration was convinced that challenging Egypt's Nasser was counterproductive. In late 1958, it quietly abandoned the Eisenhower Doctrine and decided to seek an accommodation with Nasser. This decision was facilitated by an unexpected deterioration in relations between Nasser and the Soviet Union. The result was a modest U.S.-Egyptian rapprochement lasting for the rest of Eisenhower's term and into that of his successor.

Ghana and Israel maintained mutual ties, but later severed their relations in the wake of the Yom Kippur War. For the next four decades they maintained only basic ties through Nigeria. They later restored full diplomatic relations, mutual economic growth and an abiding friendship.

Today in Sefwi Wiawso, located in southwest Ghana, there remains a Jewish community who call themselves "The House of Israel" and claim to have roots in the Ten Lost Tribes of ancient Israel. They built themselves a synagogue in 1998, a simple, rectangular concrete building and painted it a brilliant blue and white to match the Israeli flags that hang above the doorways.

Chapter 13

An Iconic Symbol

On New Year's Day 1959, Cuban President Fulgencio Batista resigned and fled to the Dominican Republic, thereby clearing the way for the Communist revolutionary, Fidel Castro, to seize power in February. Cuba became the first Communist state in the West. In another first, Soviet Premier Nikita Khrushchev toured parts of the United States and met with President Dwight Eisenhower at Camp David.

It was announced in Jerusalem that the Government Statistical Office reported that the population of Israel had reached 2,022,500. Of this number, 1,801,806 were Jews.

The purpose and message of United Israel World Union continued to gain popularity and widespread approval both here and abroad, attracting leading professionals in various fields. A number of noted surgeons, authors and other distinguished leaders attended a January 18 meeting of United Israel held at the Dr. M. J. McDonald Reception Studio adjacent to the Union's headquarters at 507 Fifth Avenue. Among those present were the famous physicians Dr. Harry Cohen and Dr. Sholom Shakin, both active in numerous humanitarian endeavors and brotherhood activities. Present also, was author Shlomo Dov London, executive director of Keren Or, a center in Jerusalem for blind and disabled children. All joined in lauding the universal brotherhood program of United Israel and called for greater support to the movement's worldwide activities.

The meeting opened with an invocation by Falasha Rabbi Hailu Moshe Paris, the spiritual head of the Congregation Beth B'nai Israel located at 204 Lenox Avenue, New York. Rabbi Paris had spent a year studying in a Jerusalem Yeshiva, arriving in the Holy Land aboard the same Israeli ship as United Israel's officer Avraham Fuhrman in the summer of 1957. Born in Ethiopia, Rabbi Paris himself is a remarkable story. He became a lifelong, close friend of David Horowitz, supporting the mission and work of United Israel World Union for many years. He also served as a member of United Israel's Board of Directors.

On April 19, a treaty of friendship between Israel and Liberia was signed in Monrovia, the capital of Liberia. Joining other African states such as Ghana and Nigeria, they sought the opportunity to acquire the advanced technologies that the State of Israel had to offer. They viewed the Jewish State as their solution to the problem of securing modern techniques in agriculture, science, industry and medicine without pawning their future to the departing colonial powers. The Arab states in Africa—Libya, Morocco, Tunisia and the UAR, whose influence kept Israel out of the Bandung Conference—moved to block the new friendship, but they failed to do so.

During the 16th Annual Meeting of United Israel on April 26, the national board unanimously approved a new United Israel World Union emblem. The new insignia holds special significance because of its unique design and the little-known story behind it. Five years earlier, noted artist and sculptor, Dr. Rene Shapshak and his wife Eugenie, moved from Johannesburg, South Africa into the famous Chelsea Hotel on 7th Avenue located in downtown Manhattan. Born and educated in Paris, Shapshak was an alumnus of the prestigious Ecole des Beaux-Arts in Paris that produced such giants as Claude Monet and Pierre Renoir.

Dr. Shapshak had become a world-renowned artist and sculptor, bringing his artistic and cultural contributions to many countries. His art is represented in Buckingham Palace, in the Rothschild, Schiff and Schonegevel Collections in England and Athens, Greece and in the Smithsonian Institute in Washington, D.C. He did sculptures of Mahatma Ghandi and John Cecil Rhodes of Great Britain. His Rhodes sculpture resides in the Rhodes Museum at Bishop's Stortford, England. Among his sculptures in New York City are those of Cardinal Francis Spellman, Dr. Leo B. Mayer and Playwright Arthur Miller. In 1956, Dr. Shapshak had the privilege of sculpting a bronze bust of former

President Harry S. Truman. The sculpture was placed in the Hall of Fame at the Ben Yehuda National Museum in Jerusalem, Israel. It was unveiled in Israel on Truman's 73rd birthday.

Now, about that new United Israel emblem: Dr. Rene Shapshak was a close friend of David Horowitz and an active member of the United Israel organization. It was Dr. Shapshak who personally designed the new insignia. Brilliantly conceived, the Seal itself represents a dynamic activating Wheel with a spinning Star of David in which the Earth revolves and on which is the Levitical escutcheon with the Ten Commandments. It honors YHVH as the true Savior as indicated in the ancient Hebrew script *YHVH Hu Go'alenu*. On the periphery of the spinning wheel are the remaining symbols of the twelve tribes of Israel. The special seal remains today our official logo appearing on all organizational documents and stationary.

In the summer of 1959, David Horowitz began a multi-part series entitled *An Answer to Thomas Paine's Age of Reason*. Paine (1739-1809), author of *Common Sense, The Rights of Man, The Crisis,* and *The Age of Reason*, was an English and American political activist, philosopher and revolutionary. His *Common Sense* became the clarion call that led to the independence of the thirteen American colonies and freed the States from the tyranny of monarchial rule. The insightful series of expositions written by Horowitz received high praise from noted scholars, rabbis and scientists, including Professor Robert H. Pfeiffer of Harvard and Luxembourg's Chief Rabbi Dr. Charles Lehrman.

From Tel Aviv came a strong endorsement and a call to action. Reuven Ben Arje-Lev, author of *Halicha Ladror*, a history of the great liberation movements and the Jewish spirit that inspired them, appealed to United Israel World Union for the creation of a Torah Center in Israel. Calling United Israel "the right association for such a center," Ben Arje-Lev declared "United Israel has proven its faithfulness in this very task for many years. Its message is already being heard in many parts of the world, and those whom it brings to the Torah have become members of the Hebraic community." Referring to such a center as the building of the *Gate to Zion*, he stated "Israel awaits United Israel in action!"

On October 7 in Baghdad, a group of Baath Party gunman tried to assassinate, but only wounded, Iraq's ruler, General Abed al-Karim Qasim. One of the gunmen, twenty-two-year-old Saddam Hussein, was forced into hiding.

October brought another surprising international story. The heir to the ancient Irish Throne, H. R. H. Raymond Moulton Nathan Seaghan Donogh VI, of the House of O'Brien of Thomond, officially identified himself with Israel and Jewry on the strength of his family genealogy that traces his line to ancient Israel. Both Donogh VI, his wife Sarah Loreta Santos, as also their two children, Prince Turlogh and Princess Grania, considered themselves Israelites in the full sense of the term. They announced they would be seeking affiliation with an established Hebraic Temple of worship.

Having been informed of United Israel World Union, Donogh VI, himself a 33rd degree Mason, immediately contacted them and submitted official documents (duly notarized by the Lord Mayor of Dublin and Magistrate Benjamin Shaw, P. C., a past President of the United Hebrew Congregation of Dublin), testifying to the true genealogy of the Royal and Imperial House of O'Brien of Thomond. The principality of Thomond, (which includes Shannon) at the time had a population of over 90,000, most of which were Roman Catholic. David Horowitz described the revelation as "living proof of Ireland's Hebraic ancestry."

In December, United Israel also played a major role in hosting an important and influential foreign guest. Outstanding leaders within the three branches of the American Jewish Rabbinical world joined hands with United Israel World Union in organizing a reception committee to greet the arrival of the noted Japanese convert to Judaism, Professor Abram Setsuzau Kotsuji, a descendant of Shinto priests. Professor Kotsuji, 60 years of age and acknowledged as Japan's top Hebraist and author of a Hebrew grammar, was the former tutor of Emperor Hirohito's brother, Prince Mikasa.

A special reception was held for Professor Kotsuji at the Plaza Hotel. Among those who honored the newcomer to Israel's ranks were officials of United Israel, the Jewish Information Society, officials of the Histadruth Ivrit and some of New York's outstanding Rabbis and business leaders. In his address, Professor Kotsuji related the story of his early life as a boy in Japan and how he had turned to the Jewish peoples and Judaism. He told of later being interrogated by Nazi-inspired Japanese army officers for befriending the Jews, and in the face of death, his miraculous escape to safety through an incident he felt was the providential hand of God in his life.

Prior to his arrival in America, Professor Kotsuji was in Israel where he delivered several lectures and was officially brought into the Abrahamic covenant in Jerusalem in the presence of Rabbis and Israeli officials. Fittingly, Dr. Rene Shapshak also designed the new emblem for the Institute of Hebrew Culture that Professor Kotsuji had established in Japan. Dr. Shapshak presented the new design to Mr. Kotsuji on behalf of United Israel before his return home.

In 1959, the United States added their last two states. The territories of Alaska and Hawaii were ratified as the 49th and 50th states respectively. The decade of the 50s had drawn to a close. By its end, the world had largely recovered from World War II, but a new cold war between the rival super-powers of the Soviet Union and the United States had grown hot. Like special chapters in a grand story, a new decade was about to be written.

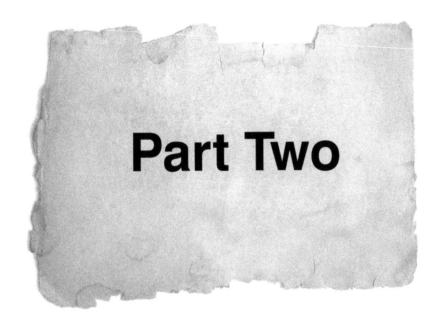

Part Two

Chapter 14
Bringing the Torah to Harlem

The decade of the 1960s had arrived and the United Nations had a new occupant. A huge bronze sculpture with the inscription "Let Us Beat Our Swords into Plowshares," created by Soviet artist Evgeny Vuchetich, had been presented to the United Nations on December 4, 1959, by the Government of the USSR. The sculpture, depicting the figure of a man holding a hammer aloft in one hand and a sword in the other, which he is making into a plowshare, is meant to symbolize the human wish to end all wars by converting the weapons of death and destruction into peaceful tools that are more beneficial to mankind. The phrase originates from the Biblical book of Isaiah (2:3-4), and its theme is repeated in the books of Joel (3:10) and Micah (4:3). The impressive statue is located in the North Garden of the United Nations Headquarters and remains today as much an inspirational ideal as it is an elusive reality.

Sammy Davis Jr., the famous entertainer legend, finally told the whole story of why he had chosen to convert to Judaism and share the fate of the people of Abraham. The lengthy feature story appeared in the February issue of *Ebony Magazine*. From his modest beginnings in the Harlem neighborhood of New York City and an itinerant lifestyle to his incredible success as an actor, comedian, singer and dancer, Davis's story is riveting and extraordinary. Contending with the prevailing racism of that period, Davis refused to appear in any clubs that practiced racial segregation. The action led to the integration of several venues in Miami Beach and Las Vegas. In 1954, he lost his left eye in an automobile accident. One day on a golf course with Jack Benny, following his conversion to Judaism, Davis was asked what his handicap was. "Handicap?" he replied. "Listen, talk about handicap: I'm a one-eyed Negro Jew!" This became a signature comment, recounted in his autobiography, and in countless articles.

Davis became a regular reader of the United Israel World Union Bulletin and, included in the United Israel archives today, are copies of letters exchanged between Davis and David Horowitz.

The United Nations Correspondents Circle, an experiment in seeking better understanding and fellowship among reporters from politically antagonistic regions in all parts of the globe, marked the occasion of its third anniversary. The fellowship of UN correspondents had managed to bring together some ninety highly opinionated, and sometimes rather emotional correspondents, who represented news-papers, wire services, magazines, radio, and television media of nearly thirty nations. The background story of the group's beginning is worth sharing.

Horowitz conceived the idea for an informal fellowship of UN news representatives in 1957. At the time, David served as a special correspondent in the U.S. for the American Association of English-Jewish Newspapers and the Israeli papers *Heruth* and *Ha'Olam Ha'Zeh* of Tel Aviv. His column, "Behind the Scenes at the United Nations," regularly appeared in 35 newspapers in the U.S., Canada, Italy, South Africa and Israel. Horowitz felt the need to stress the common interests of correspondents, rather than frictions, and the need for a mutual effort to learn more about the attitudes of various UN delegations and regional blocs. The organization was also needed to dispel the atmosphere of isolation and unfriendliness in which many correspondents felt they were working.

Thinking in international terms came easily for Horowitz. After all, of Jewish descent, he was born in Sweden, naturalized in America, married an Irish girl and maintained close professional connections with Israel. Clearly, tolerance and goodwill were the basic aims of his effort.

Appearing as the guest at the celebration luncheon of the UN Correspondents Association, former President Harry Truman was asked by correspondent David Horowitz about his historic decision to recognize Israel at the moment of its birth and how he felt about it as the young State celebrates its 12th birthday. Never hesitating, Truman replied that he would do it all over again today. He added that the prophets and judges of ancient Israel had laid the foundation for the American form of government and that the heirs of those great people are not doing so badly themselves today. It was vintage Harry Truman.

On May 11, 1960, German war criminal Otto Adolf Eichmann was captured in Buenos Aires, Argentina. Eichmann had been a Nazi SS lieutenant colonel and one of the major organizers of the Holocaust. In 1959, David Ben Gurion learned that the notorious Nazi war criminal was likely living in hiding in Argentina and ordered the Israel foreign intelligence service, the Mossad, to capture the international fugitive alive for trial in Israel. The covert operation succeeded, and Eichmann was smuggled out of Argentina aboard the same El Al Bristol Britannia aircraft that had a few days earlier carried Israel's delegation to the official 150th anniversary celebration of Argentina's independence from Spain.

As we shall discuss, later, in greater detail, David Horowitz, who also suffered personal family loss in the holocaust, played an important role in exposing and bringing to justice Nazi war criminals residing in the United States.

The 17th Annual Meeting of United Israel World Union took place on Sunday, April 17th with a majority of the international board members present. Special greetings were conveyed from those as far away as Israel, Germany and Ghana. A highlight of the affair was the presentation of a Torah Scroll to the Wilber, West Virginia Mid-Western headquarters of United Israel, followed by an inspiring ceremony. The scroll was a gift from Dr. and Mrs. Howard L. Werner of Glencoe, Illinois. Dr. Werner, a noted psychiatrist and philanthropist, was an officer of the Chicago Information Society for the Propagation of Judaism.

The young black Rabbi who first learned of United Israel World Union when he met United Israel officer Avraham Fuhrman while traveling to Israel in the summer of 1957, had begun attending various organizational functions and held similar views to those of David Horowitz. He had become the spiritual leader of Congregation Beth B'nai Israel in Harlem. Befriended and encouraged by Horowitz, it soon became evident that this youthful Rabbi was born an academic. Even the simplest question elicited a detailed, fact-heavy answer. The destiny of this gifted teacher had an unusual and most remarkable beginning.

Hailu Moshe Paris was born an orphan in Addis Ababa, Ethiopia on October 17, 1933 and adopted by Eudora Paris from the orphanage when she migrated to Ethiopia in 1935. Following Italy's invasion of Ethiopia as a prelude to World War II, they were forced to flee the violence of Mussolini and the fascist invaders. On board a ship bound for America, Eudora Paris carried with her a carefully wrapped bundle and an adopted Ethiopian two-year-old named Hailu. When the ship pulled into the port of Bremen, Germany late in 1935, Nazis boarded looking for Jews. The bundle was wrapped in a blanket, which also covered her young son's shoulders. "They rounded up everyone sitting nearby" she would later say. They looked at Eudora and her child, but because of the color of their skin, the Nazis never suspected they were Jewish. "They ignored us because they never thought black people could be Jews" said Eudora. It was later expressed "that it was the one time racial prejudice about what a 'real Jew' looked like worked in their favor." The carefully wrapped bundle that Eudora Paris was carrying to America was a Torah Scroll destined for a synagogue in Harlem.

In his twenties, Hailu Paris attended Yeshiva University in New York, earning a degree in Hebrew literature and a master's degree in education. He later taught Talmudic courses at the Israelite Rabbinical Academy in Queens and was an assistant and, later, head rabbi at the black Temple of Mt. Horeb in the Bronx.

Rabbi Paris became a vocal advocate for African Jewry. He became a bridge between the African-American community and Ethiopian community. Teaching that the descendants of the biblical Israelites had spread across the continent of Africa was a history which at that time was considered radical and controversial. This gifted teacher would spend decades campaigning on behalf of Ethiopian Jews. He made trips to Ethiopia where he worked with the Beta Israel and the Falash Mura, a related group of Ethiopians with Jewish family connections. He also served on the board of the American Association of Ethiopian Jews and was an early activist on behalf of their immigration to Israel.

In 1977, the State of Israel recognized the Beta Israel community of Ethiopia as Jewish. More recent cultural and genetic studies suggest that the Lemba of South Africa and the Igbo of Nigeria may also have Jewish roots. Alongside his central role in the black Jewish world, Rabbi Hailu Moshe Paris also made crucial connections to mainstream Jewry, working to foster interaction between black and white Jewish communities. He remained a lifelong friend of David Horowitz and strong advocate of United Israel World Union where he also served as a member of its board of directors.

As the dog days of summer 1960 wound down, there remained an air of uneasiness and uncertainty in America regarding possible Vietnam entanglement. There was also the question of who our next leader would be as the U.S. presidential election drew near; plenty of time left for a few surprises, as we shall see.

Chapter 15

U.S. and UN: Under New Management

A new decade was well underway. The year 1960 had frightened us all with the release of the shocking psychological-thriller-horror film, *Psycho*, directed by Alfred Hitchcock; alarmed us by placing over 900 "military advisors" in South Vietnam; and had given us a new President after eight years of the Eisenhower administration. To paraphrase Bob Dylan, "The times, they were a-changin'."

The 1960 Presidential election was the closest since 1916. Democrat John Fitzgerald Kennedy narrowly defeated Republican Vice President Richard M. Nixon to become the 35th President. In doing so, Kennedy became the first Catholic and, at age forty-three, the youngest person ever elected to the office. Kennedy won by a mere 113,000 votes; almost 69 million people voted.

When Kennedy came to power, he became the next man up in the juggling act of Middle Eastern politics. He made a remarkably serious effort to reach an accommodation with the forces of indigenous Arab nationalism. He believed that the best way to deal with Arab nationalists was to treat them with respect, allow them to make their own foreign policy decisions, and offer them generous assistance in developing their countries internally. He also downplayed Cold War themes, stressing local concerns instead. Kennedy also tried to strike a balance between ensuring Israel's security and pressuring them to make concessions to its Arab neighbors. Whereas Eisenhower had kept the new nation at arm's length, Kennedy established much friendlier relations with Israel.

Prior to becoming President, John Kennedy had made two visits to Israel. He had these observations regarding his trips.

In 1939 I first saw Palestine, then a barren and unhappy land under alien rule. In 1951, I traveled again to the land of the River Jordan, to see first-hand, the new State of Israel. The transformation that had taken place was hard to believe. For in these twelve years a land had been born, a desert had been reclaimed, and the most tragic victims of World War II had found a home.

In the words of British author Israel Zangwill: "The land without a people waited for the people without a land."

Following the 18th Annual Meeting of United Israel World Union on April 2, 1961, it was announced that Harry Leventhal, prominent philanthropist and co-publisher of the United Israel Bulletin had been named a vice-chairman for the committee supporting the "Salute to General Omar N. Bradley Dinner." The dinner affair, sponsored by the Eleanor Roosevelt Cancer Foundation, would be held at the Waldorf Astoria Hotel on the evening of May 30. President John F. Kennedy was to attend as the main speaker and Bob Hope would serve as Master of Ceremonies.

In early July, Dr. Rene Shapshak, sculptor and United Israel Bulletin Art Editor, was back in the news. It was announced that Shapshak had been commissioned by the Eliezer Ben Yehudah Museum authorities to execute a large-scale monument dedicated to the renaissance of the Hebrew language as inspired by the late Ben Yehudah. The monument was scheduled to be erected in the museum in Jerusalem.

On September 18, 1961 tragedy struck. A Douglas DC-6 airliner crashed near Ndola, Northern Rhodesia (now Zambia). Secretary-General of the United Nations, Dag Hammarskjold and fifteen others perished in the crash. Hammarskjold was en route to Ndola to negotiate a cease-fire between "non-combatant" UN forces and troops of President Moise Tshombe of Katanga. The circumstances of the incident were never clear. A British-run commission of inquiry blamed the crash on pilot error and a later UN investigation largely rubber-stamped its findings. Later evidence suggested otherwise.

Dag Hammarskjöld was a true statesman and diplomat in every respect and became personally and actively engaged in the world problems facing the United Nations. In a 1955 visit to China, Hammarskjold negotiated the release of 11 captured U.S. pilots who had served in the Korean War. He was involved in struggles on three of the world's continents and approached them through what he liked to call "preventive diplomacy."

As previously mentioned, David Horowitz and Hammarskjöld became good friends. Shortly after Hammarskjöld became Secretary-General, Horowitz presented him with a gift of an Aztec stone head that Horowitz himself had brought back from Mexico some years previously. It became a colorful and unique paperweight for the Secretary-General's new desk.

Horowitz often communicated with Hammarskjöld before he left on diplomatic missions. One such case was the intervention in the 1956 Suez Crisis when Horowitz made a personal written appeal to the Secretary-General before he left to meet with Egyptian President Nasser in Cairo and Israeli Prime Minister Ben-Gurion in Tel Aviv. Of Hammarskjöld, Horowitz remarked, "[he] was able to understand people psychologically; he could almost read their minds. He was very, very clever, and had an intuitive quality that is rare in individuals."

In 1960 when Hammarskjöld was working to defuse the Congo Crisis, he came under intense pressure from elements within the United Nations, led by the Soviet Union. They demanded his resignation and the replacement of the office of Secretary-General by a three-man directorate with a built-in veto, known as the "troika." Horowitz, knowing Hammarskjöld's sensitivities well, sent the Secretary-General a letter to his apartment in New York, to comfort him. In the letter, he cited a quotation from the Bible. He recalls that Hammarskjöld responded immediately to the letter, with "a beautiful note."

The circumstances of the tragic death of Dag Hammarskjöld were, and remain, shrouded in mystery. For more than half a century, three separate inquiries have been unable to come to a definitive conclusion about what happened on that fateful night. As recently as March 16, 2015, UN Secretary-General Ban Ki-moon appointed members to an Independent Panel of Experts to examine new information relating to the tragic event. The panel's ninety-nine-page report, released on July 6, 2015, assigned "moderate" value to nine new eyewitness accounts and transcripts of radio transmissions. Those accounts suggested that Hammarskjöld's plane was already on fire as it went down and that other jet aircraft and intelligence agents were nearby. Additional new evidence may exist which, for national security reasons, was and remains classified by several governments more than fifty years after the fact.

Four years after the crash, David Horowitz visited Sweden, returning home to see his own birthplace, and to see Uppsala, where Hammarskjöld had grown up. He decided to visit Backakra, the farm Hammarskjold had bought with the hope that it would one day be his retirement home. When Horowitz entered the farmhouse, he saw books, paintings, and sculptures, either collected by Hammarskjöld, or gifts he had received. One thing caught his attention. On the desk in the library, which was a replica of Mr. Hammarskjöld's Park Avenue study, there was a family crest he used as his seal. Mounted above it was an Aztec stone head—the one given to the Secretary-General by Horowitz shortly after they met in 1953. David Horowitz remarked that he left Backakra that day "with a heavy heart and a mood of sadness".

Hammarskjöld was awarded the Nobel Peace Prize posthumously in 1961, having been nominated before his death. In 2011, *The Financial Times* wrote that Hammarskjold "has remained the benchmark against which later UN Secretaries-General have been judged." Historian Paul Kennedy hailed Hammarskjold as "perhaps the greatest UN Secretary-General we've ever had".

U.S. President John F. Kennedy regretted that he opposed the UN policy in the Congo and speaking of Hammarskjöld, said: "I realize now that in comparison to him, I am a small man. He was the greatest statesman of our century".

As the turbulent year of 1961 moved to a close, an Israeli war crimes tribunal sentenced Adolf Eichmann to die after he was found guilty on all counts of crimes against humanity during the holocaust.

U Thant, a Burmese diplomat, was appointed to succeed Hammarskjöld as the new Secretary-General of the United Nations.

Chapter 16
Remember Amalak: Justice in Ramla

In January 1962, the Foreign Press Association, consisting of some 200 foreign correspondents from all regions in the world, unanimously elected David Horowitz as General Secretary succeeding Zivko Milic of Belgrade, Yugoslavia. Horowitz, at the time, represented a number of foreign papers in Canada, Italy, South Africa and Israel and had been an active member and officer of the association for eight years.

In January, Horowitz also delivered two lectures; one before a Manhattan branch of the American Jewish Congress and another at Congregation Beth Sholom in Teaneck, New Jersey, on the universality of the Hebraic faith.

Professor Abraham S. Kotsuji, head of the Institute of Hebrew Culture in Japan arrived in the United States during the month of April and attended the 19th Annual Meeting of United Israel as an honored guest. He spoke to the group briefly about his work in Japan. Also attending were well-known Israeli educator, Dr. Israel Ben Zeev and internationally renowned artist and sculptor, Dr. Rene Shapshak.

A few minutes past midnight on June 1, 1962, Otto Adolf Eichmann was executed by hanging at a prison in Ramla, Israel. The German Nazi SS lieutenant colonel was one of the major organizers of the Holocaust. He personally facilitated and managed the logistics of mass deportation of Jews to ghettos and extermination camps in German- occupied Eastern Europe during World War II. In his last hours, Eichmann remained defiant and unrepentant. Refusing a last meal (asking instead for a glass of red wine) and the traditional black hood, he was hanged.

The historical irony in this demonstration of poetic justice was not lost. The engineer and supervisor of Hitler's "final solution" resulting in the systematic murder of six million Jews had met his fate at the hands of a Jewish tribunal. He stood before Jewish judges in a nation established by Jews. Within four hours of his execution, Eichmann's body had been cremated at a secret location, and his ashes scattered in the Mediterranean Sea, outside of Israeli territorial waters, by an Israeli Navy patrol boat.

July provided another first in the changing U.S. policy with Israel. President Kennedy agreed to the sale of HAWK anti-aircraft missiles, the first major weapons system to be supplied by the United States. The main source of Israel's weapons was France, whose support was critical in enabling Israel to meet its defense needs. The HAWK sale was significant not only because it was the first major direct arms transfer from the United States to Israel, but also because that system required that Israeli soldiers be given extensive training in the United States and that spare parts be supplied to Israel.

On October 22, President Kennedy delivered a nationwide televised address on all of the major networks announcing the discovery of Soviet medium range ballistic missiles in Cuba and the administration's plan to implement a strict quarantine on all offensive military equipment under shipment to Cuba. The tense, thirteen-day (October 16-28) political and military stand-off between the United States and the Soviet Union played out on television worldwide and was the closest the cold war ever came to escalating into a full-scale nuclear war. The situation eased on October 28 when it was announced that Kennedy and Khrushchev had reached an agreement. Results of the agreement were the complete withdrawal of Soviet missiles from Cuba, withdrawal of American nuclear missiles from Turkey (a secret part of the agreement at the time) and an agreement that the U.S. would never invade Cuba without direct provocation. The naval blockade of Cuba was lifted on November 20th. The Cuban Missile Crisis confrontation that had brought the world to the brink of nuclear disaster ended.

In November, the first Annual Dinner of the Tarbuth Foundation, created by Dr. Emanuel Neumann with the view to advance Hebrew culture, was held at the Pierre Hotel in Manhattan. Some 300 of America's outstanding Jewish leaders and educators attended the unique event. The keynote speakers were former French Ambassador to Israel, Monsieur Pierre E. Gilbert, and former Israeli Ambassador to the UN, Abba Eban, who at the time was serving as Israel's Minister of Education.

Former Ambassador Gilbert, who did more perhaps than any other person to cement Israel-French friendship during one of the most critical moments in the history of the Jewish State, the 1956 Suez crisis, was a Catholic who had been educated in a Jesuit school. In his address, the Ambassador declared that the Hebrew language alone "can bring out the true meaning of the Bible" and that the Jewish peoples "had been chosen by God to bring Monotheism to the whole world." Gilbert further revealed that "a new world gradually opened up before my eyes" through the study of Hebrew. "At first, as a linguist and a philologist" he told the distinguished audience, "I discovered the beauty of the Bible. In addition to its religious, historical and philosophical interest, it is a colossal literary monument. Now that I have read it in the Hebrew text, which is the only one able to bring out all its values, I find it to be the most captivating book I've ever read."

The surprise of the evening came when Gilbert began to speak in fluent Hebrew to the amazement of even the scholars in the audience, including Harry Orlinsky, the editor-in-chief of the New Jewish Publication Society (NJPS) translation of the Torah.

On March 6, 1963, David Horowitz departed for his sixth visit to the Holy Land. Following a three-week visit in Israel, Horowitz traveled to Turkey for a special occasion.

The Turkish Government had invited the United Nations correspondent to be its guest for a week. The Turkish Press Association, representing reporters of all the leading Turkish dailies and agencies, paid special tribute to Horowitz at a reception given in his honor at the press club in Izmir, Turkey. The Association officers presented him with a certificate making him an honorary member of the Association. Following the reception, a press conference was held at which Horowitz answered questions relating to the basic issues facing the United Nations. Among these were Vietnam, Cyprus, and the Middle East.

In Ankara, the capital of Turkey, Horowitz was feted at a special dinner given by the heads of the Ministry of Information and Press. Mr. Ben Yitzchak Yaakov, the Israeli Charge d'Affairs, was among the invited guests. During his stay, David met with other officials, including the Governor of Istanbul State, Niyazi Aki and its Mayor, Necdet Ugur. He also visited the Jewish community leaders who spoke very highly of the Turkish Government, which had close and friendly relations with the State of Israel.

After four weeks of intense activity, that included some well-deserved recognition, both in Israel and Turkey, a tired, yet inspired Horowitz was finally back home. During this commemoration year of United Israel's 20th anniversary, Horowitz received a personal, hand-written letter in English, and the envelope was also hand-written with the back flap containing only two letters: B.G. It was from David Ben Gurion. The former Prime Minister concluded his letter by quoting a passage from Isaiah 62, writing it in Biblical Hebrew. The hand-written letter dated July 27, 1963, remains on display today in the David Horowitz Memorial Library archives located at United Israel World Union's headquarters.

Horowitz had experienced a remarkable year. There was yet another award as The Deadline Club, New York City Chapter of Sigma Delta Chi, and America's most outstanding professional journalism fraternity, selected him for "distinguished journalistic achievement" for United Nations reporting.

Chapter 17
The Change in Spain

Dateline: November 22, 1963, Dallas, TX. John Fitzgerald Kennedy, the 35th President of the United States, was on the final leg of a fund-raising and political fence-mending campaign through Texas to help ensure his reelection in 1964. What had been a successful and enjoyable trip for Kennedy and his wife, Jackie, was brought to an abrupt and horrific end as the President's motorcade passed through Dallas's Dealey Plaza at approximately 12:30 p.m. CST. Lee Harvey Oswald, an expert marksman, fired three shots from a mail order rifle and, within seconds, had inflicted a mortal wound on Kennedy and seriously injured Texas Governor John Connally. The Governor, along with his wife, Nellie, were accompanying the Kennedys on their way to the Dallas Trade Mart for a luncheon event in an uncovered 1961 Lincoln Continental convertible limousine. This fact was taken full advantage of by the assassin who was perched in a sixth floor window of the Texas School Book Depository building with a clear view of Dealey Plaza and the open convertible carrying Kennedy below.

Vice President Lyndon Baines Johnson was sworn in as our 36th President on Air Force One in Dallas just two hours and eight minutes after the assassination took place. He took the oath of office administered by U.S. District Judge Sarah T. Hughes, with a distraught Jacqueline Kennedy standing at his side.

The new President quickly inherited pressing problems, including the war in Vietnam and the Middle East juggling act. Kennedy's effort to balance conflicting interests in the Middle East, already faltering by late 1963, collapsed altogether under President Johnson, who gave up on even attempting a balanced approach. Instead he assumed a frankly partisan stance. He sided openly with the Shah of Iran against his internal opposition, with the conservative Arab regimes against Nasser's Egypt, and with Israel against the Arab states as a whole.

With the dawn of 1964, United Israel World Union entered its twenty-first year of global activities. Links on behalf of a universal Torah faith had been established on five continents and a sure foundation had been laid in re-born Israel. United Israel held its 21st Annual Meeting on Sunday, April 26. Highlight of the meeting was the announcement by Rabbi Irving J. Block, spiritual leader of The Brotherhood Synagogue in Greenwich Village, New York, of the gift of an antique Indian (Calcutta) Torah scroll to the West Olive, Michigan unit of United Israel.

In early 1965, a most unusual and little-known story began to unfold. An article written by Shlomo Nakdimon entitled, "Sequence of events favoring Jewry marks change in Spain," appeared in the February 1965 issue of the United Israel Bulletin. In the article Nakdimon indicated that reports from Spain during the past six months all indicated that the nation of the infamous Inquisition was moving quickly ahead to rectify the great wrongs inflicted upon the Jews. These wrongs had led to restrictions against their descendants up to our modern times. Nakdimon called it "an unusual and intriguing development which may well have led to a reawakening and a stirring of Generalissimo Francisco Franco's 'Jewish spirit' and to the realization of a true universal faith applicable to all mankind."

The renowned Yiddish writer and radio commentator, Shelomo ben-Israel earlier in the month (February 1, 1965) published an article in *The Jewish Daily Forward* in which he recounted how a Spanish correspondent at the United Nations one day last summer discussed Franco with his colleague, David Horowitz. The Spanish correspondent stressed the fact that the Generalissimo was probably a descendant of the Marranos, and thus a Jew by origin. Moreover, he reiterated the fact, already widely known, that Franco aided hundreds of Jews fleeing from Hitler's pursuit during World War II.

A thought immediately flashed through Horowitz's mind: Why not try to stir the dormant little "Jewish spark" residing deep in Franco's bosom by sending him a copy of his autobiography, *Thirty-Three*

Candles. David autographed the volume and dispatched it in May of 1964 to Madrid. The autograph, in effect, read: "Your Excellency, Generalissimo Francisco Franco, in appreciation of what I have learned from a Spanish colleague here at the UN, namely, of the great aid you gave many fleeing Jewish refugees entering Spain from Nazi persecution during World War II, and in the knowledge that we may share a common heritage, I am happy to send you this, my book, which I trust will bring you many hours of pleasant and contemplative reading."

Some six weeks after the book was mailed, Mr. ben-Israel points out, Mr. Horowitz received a telephone call from the office of the Spanish delegation to the UN informing him that an official letter had arrived for him from Madrid and asking if he would please come and pick it up. Believing possibly that some secretary or official may have formally acknowledged the book, Mr. Horowitz went to pick up the letter. When he opened it, he noted to his amazement that Franco himself had signed the letter. The Generalissimo expressed his gratitude for the volume and especially for the sympathetic autograph. When the Spanish correspondent at the UN was shown the letter he, too, thought it incredible that Franco himself should have found it important enough personally to acknowledge receipt of *Thirty-Three Candles.*

"Franco's letter was dated July 4, 1964," ben-Israel notes. "And two months later, in September, the Spanish Cortes (Parliament) suddenly took up a bill which called for the elimination of a law which had restricted the religious rights of both Jews and Protestants in Spain." This news, continued ben-Israel, "created a sensation. But, as it happened, the influence of the Catholic Church in Spain being so deeply rooted, that, despite all efforts of some liberals, the proposed bill was relegated to the sidelines."

However, on the eve of the New Year, when Franco delivered his "State of the Union" message, "the Generalissimo dropped a small bombshell," as *The New York Times* commented on the event editorially. "He came out in favor of the exercise of freedom of conscience. But in clearer language, this could only mean that he favors passage of the bill, which has been stalled in the Cortes since September. Since the Spanish Cortes is like a rubber stamp for General Franco, it must be presumed that a statute on religious rights will be enacted this year." *(The bicameral legislature of the Kingdom of Spain)*

But this did not mark the end of the new turn of events in Spain under the new Franco. "Last month," ben-Israel observed, "something happened in Spain that has not occurred since the Inquisition: namely, no Spanish head of state had received Spanish Jewish representatives in 473 years." In January 1965, Franco broke the precedent. He received in a friendly audience the heads of the Jewish communities of Madrid and Barcelona—Max Mazin and Alberto Levi—discussing with them the status of the Jews. The only previous meeting recorded in history took place between King Ferdinand and the great Jewish sage Isaac de Abravanel, who served as the King's aide. Abravanel had tried in vain to have the King and Queen Isabella rescind the decree expelling Jews from Spain.

Concluding his article, Shelomo ben-Israel asks: "Does Franco in truth feel proud of his Marrano descent? Did a mystic book bearing the title *Thirty-Three Candles* really influence him? Did the foregoing acts and reforms and new bills come about as a result of this influence? Possibly. One day, perhaps, a historian will come forth and give us the answers..."

Generalissimo Francisco Franco died just after midnight on November 20, 1975 at the age of eighty-two, just two weeks before his eighty-third birthday. In Spain and abroad, the legacy of Franco remains controversial. The length of his rule, the suppression of opposition, and the effective propaganda sustained through the years has made a detached evaluation almost impossible. The reasons behind Franco's late actions that moved to rectify wrongs of the Inquisition remain somewhat mystifying and unknown. We are indeed left to speculate. However, one of the forgotten pieces of the story might well have been the effort of United Israel President David Horowitz.

Chapter 18
Among Jethro's People

In January 1965, Horowitz was elected First Vice President of the Foreign Press Association, a forty-eight-year-old organization of over 300 correspondents representing every region of the world. Mr. Horowitz also moderated the UN Correspondents Round Table bi-weekly radio program heard over station WEVD in New York. Prior to his election to this new post, he served as General Secretary of the association for three years.

In early March, Horowitz left New York bound for Sweden and Israel. It became an extended trip lasting over six weeks. Landing in Stockholm, this was an exciting and much anticipated time for Horowitz. It was his native country and having been born in Malmo, this was his first return since his family left Malmo at the outbreak of World War I in October 1914. During his stay, *Arbetet,* the leading daily newspaper in Malmo, ran a long article in its March 19th issue with a headline calling Horowitz a "Malmo-born World-Citizen." The article by well-known Swedish writer Nils Anderson featured a three-column photo showing Horowitz standing by the house at Parkgatan number twenty-one, where he had lived as a young boy. *Dagens Nyheter,* Stockholm's leading daily, which is circulated throughout Sweden and whose U.S. and UN correspondent was Sven Ahman, also carried two stories on Horowitz's visit. While in South Sweden, Horowitz also visited Backakra, the farmstead of his old friend, the late Secretary-General of the UN, Dag Hammarskjöld.

Following two weeks in Sweden, Horowitz returned to Israel where he spent another four weeks, from March 21 to April 20. This was his seventh visit to the land of Israel. It was a busy and agenda-driven schedule with his days filled with interviews, meetings, talks and visits in various parts of the State. One of the scheduled events, however, stood out as special and something Horowitz had waited a long time to experience.

For many years, Horowitz had looked forward to finding some way of coming into closer contact with the heroic Druze communities of Israel who had played such a vital role in aiding the outnumbered Palestinian Jews to win their life and death struggle during the 1948 War of Independence. Druze soldiers also fought side by side with Israeli troops during the Sinai campaign against Egypt.

The Druze are an Arabic-speaking religious minority rooted in Ismailism, a branch of Shia Islam. Jethro of Midian is considered an ancestor of all Druze and revered as their spiritual founder as well as chief prophet. In the book of Exodus, Jethro is called a priest of Midian and became father-in-law of Moses after he gave his daughter, Zipporah, in marriage to Moses, thus making the Druze related to the Jews through marriage. This view has been used to represent an element of the special relationship between Israeli Jews and Druze.

The opportunity for Horowitz finally arose thanks to a colleague in the Foreign Press Association of New York, Salman Falah, the son of a Druze Sheikh. Falah agreed to write several letters of introduction for David, among which was one to his father, Sheikh Hammoud Falah of Kfar Samia in Galilee, and another to Sheikh Lavib Abu Rukum of Isfiyah, a former member of the Knesset.

Salman Falah was a correspondent in the U.S. and the UN for the Israeli Arabic daily *"Al Yam"* while at the same time, a student at Princeton University majoring in Oriental studies. He was the first in Israeli-Druze history to go abroad to complete his studies. Salman received his M.A. at Hebrew University. In addition to the letters of introduction, Salman had also written to his family and friends regarding Horowitz's visit. One of the letters was sent to his brother Faris, a well-known Druze attorney with offices in the historic city of Acre.

Horowitz spent two eventful days with the chieftains of the remarkable Druze communities and left us with the following first-hand account of his meetings in his own words:

Salman had thus opened the door for me to visit those people in Israel's midst whom I had so long yearned to meet and commune with. The very people whose noble modes of life and mighty exploits I had previously only read and heard about. The people whose prophet of veneration, Jethro, the father-in-law of Moses, was a true partner of the "great legislator" in both deed and word. He had given both succor and haven to the youthful son of Amram and Yocheved (Moses) during his most trying years as a refugee from Egypt and who later, after the exodus in the wilderness, also acted as the wise counselor to the over-burdened Hebraic leader.

These were the people of Jethro, whose faithfulness to Moses' people to this very day had remained steadfast and unshaken, as was evidenced by the pro-Jewish stand they had taken when the children of Esau and Ishmael sought once again to destroy Jacob's seed. And now, at last, I was to find myself the honored guest of an entire Druze village, Kfar Samia, situated on the heights of the Western Galilean Mountains.

Horowitz continued,

Upon my arrival, I was met by Faris in Acre and driven to the village where all the village fathers, headed by Sheikh Falah were congregated at the Falah homestead waiting to greet me. The royal welcome took me by complete surprise. No head of state could have received a warmer reception. The dramatic scene was reminiscent of Bible days. In spirit, in demeanor, even in attire, these Druze had not changed, and this is what fascinated me. Despite this, they all possessed a keen perception of modern life.

Sheikh Falah, the epitome of nobility and kindness, escorted me into the spacious living room as the village fathers followed, taking seats around the room. After having conveyed the greetings of the village's favorite son, that of my friend Salman, and after reporting on his fine progress in America, Sheikh Falah, in a prayerful mood, said: "when I beheld you as you arrived at the threshold of our home, it was like seeing my own son coming back, praised be Allah.

There was continuous serving of the famous Druze coffee, possibly the best in the world, during the ensuing hour preceding the feast, which had been prepared in my honor. As I sat here in the presence of these people, all highly intelligent, fiercely righteous appearing, with sharply penetrating glances, proud, yet imbued with a spirit of humility and exuding warmth of love and affection, I had the absolute feeling of kindred affinity.

I expressed my heartfelt gratitude: "I am greatly honored to find myself in your midst as one of you, and I thank the Almighty for having blessed me with this visit and for your acceptance of me as a brother in the family. I am familiar with your great history, your veneration of Jethro, and the valiant part you played in aiding the descendants of Moses in their most critical moment in modern times. I bless Allah-YHVH for this privilege."

One of the schoolteachers translated. There were happy nods of approval all around and expressions of thanks to God.

Following this "communion," Sheikh Falah escorted me into the dining room where a huge table was fabulously set up to a king's delight. Before seating ourselves, mother Falah came out to greet me heartily along with other members of the family.

The sumptuous meal was followed by a tour through the village. There were signs of prosperous activity all around. A new school was being erected and the road to the village was being widened and paved. All signs pointed to the fact that the emergence of the State of Israel was to the Druze as happy an occasion as it had been to their Jewish brethren, both of whom had suffered a similar bitter fate under the British and the Arabs.

My next meeting with the Druze took place about a week later in the autonomous Druze Religious Court in Haifa where Faris Falah had set a date for me with the three chiefs

(Judges), Sheikhs Salman Tarif, Labib Abu Rukun, and Hussian Elayan. Here too, I was received royally. A later visit to the Isfiyah village on the Carmel left me once again, feeling perfectly at home.

Horowitz summarized his thoughts about his experience by saying:
My meeting with the Druze was indeed a highlight of this my seventh visit to the Holy Land. I took leave of these, Jethro's beloved people with the feeling of profound peace and contentment, a feeling of having been reunited with brothers and sisters long separated from the family. Surely, Moses and Jethro must be smiling in their places of holy repose in the face of the 20th century reunion of their offspring.

The number of Druze people today exceeds over one million worldwide. They reside primarily in Syria, Lebanon, Israel and Jordan. Other communities, however, live outside the Middle East, in Australia, Canada, Europe, Latin America and the United States. In Israel today, the Druze form a religious minority of about 140,000. They are Arabic-speaking citizens of Israel and serve in the Israel Defense Forces just as most citizens do. Members of the community also serve in leadership roles in the military, law enforcement and medicine.

In November 2015, a Druze delegation toured the United States to promote Israel, speaking at schools, organizations, and with various media outlets to spread understanding and awareness of their community's place in Israel's multicultural society.

Chapter 19
The Strange Saga of "Eddie" Abrahams

When the West Olive, Michigan congregation of United Israel World Union dedicated their new Community Center on the 7th day of Sukkoth, October 17, 1965, the group received a most treasured gift. A rare Indian Torah Scroll encased in a beautifully ornamented silver container was consecrated. The Torah was of Sephardic style and dated 1898-Calcutta, India.

The ancient scroll was one of several Torahs held in the custody of The Brotherhood Synagogue of New York under the care of Rabbi Irving J. Block, spiritual leader of the Greenwich Village congregation. Presenting the Torah to the Michigan community, however, was a modest, unassuming Sephardic individual by the name of Edward S. Abrahams. Mr. Abrahams' full Hebrew name was Ezra-Shalom ben Abraham Khazzam. His many friends and acquaintances knew him simply as "Eddie."

Abrahams was born on July 7, 1901 in Basra, Mesopotamia (Iraq). As the Jews of Europe in the early 20th century looked upon the United States as the golden land of opportunity, so did the Jews living under the rule of the Turkish Ottoman Empire look upon India as their refuge and a place where their lives could be improved. When he was three years old, his widowed mother took Eddie along with his two brothers to British-ruled India. This was done in compliance with the expressed wishes of his father before Arabs murdered him when the boy was only six months old. Growing up in Calcutta, Eddie was raised in the strong Hebraic tradition of the Bagdadian Jews who formed the bulk of the city's Jewish population.

The strange saga of Abrahams' life began when he left home at an early age to become a seaman. Because of his fluent knowledge of his native Arabic, he posed as an Egyptian to attain employment on a Danish vessel. Arriving in Seattle, he abandoned ship. A stranger in that great Pacific port city, he made his way to HIAS (The Hebrew Immigrant Aid Society) who graciously took him in. He soon found a little synagogue where he was able to observe the Passover celebration. He didn't miss the symbolism in his experience.

Following that Passover in the spring of 1917, Eddie took a job on an American sailing vessel, an old wooden windjammer whose destination was Alaska. A benevolent captain shared the ship calendar and changes of the moon with Abrahams, enabling the young Jewish sailor to keep all the holidays subsequent to the Passover by the guidance of the moon, "that faithful witness in the sky," as the Bible describes it.

On his return to Seattle, Abrahams lost all of his belongings. He tried to join the Army. Too young to enlist in the American Army, he decided to go to the Canadian recruiting station. There he saw a poster inviting men to join the Jewish Legion, a group of volunteers formed after the Balfour Declaration to enable young Jewish men who so desired, to serve in Palestine in a regularly constituted unit of the British army. This, he decided to do.

Abrahams enlisted and was sent to Nova Scotia in 1918. Here came his first real contact with Jews other than those of his own Levantine tradition. At first his fellow Jews looked upon him with suspicion. Many did not believe that he was Jewish, and later some even ridiculed him for saying his morning prayers and donning the phylacteries according to the custom of pious Orthodox Jews. Abrahams' practice of openly observing his religion had been met with respect from the gentile seaman, he had previously encountered. He expected nothing less from members of his own faith. Instead, he was extremely hurt by their condescending behavior.

After training in England, the Jewish Legion unit to which he had been attached was sent to Palestine. After fulfilling his service there in 1919, Abrahams chose to return to the United States. He arrived during the Thanksgiving season in late November 1919.

Again, the temptation of the sea took Abrahams back to American ships, but some three years later came an abrupt change of plans. Desiring to see more of America, he decided to turn to a "hobo life" for a period. Thus, in 1922, starting out from New Orleans, he joined a group of vagabonds and followed the harvest wheat belt arriving finally in New York City in 1923. At this time, Abrahams had to make a vital decision. Either he would have to go back to sea or settle down to a job on land. He decided on the latter.

He took a job at a garage on the Lower East Side. The foreman was so impressed by Abrahams' work that he persuaded the still very young Calcutta Jewish seaman to remain. Eddie remained at this job for fourteen years, working his way up from odd-job laborer to manager of the station.

Striving to start out on his own, Eddie moved to Northern Westchester in 1937 and went into the gas station business for himself. In 1959, after his three daughters had been married, Eddie decided to give up active management of his business and to travel once again.

Intending to go to Israel for a reunion of the Jewish Legion, by a strange coincidence, Abrahams met two Pakistani merchant officers in the lobby of a New York theater. So impressed were they by his Indian command of the Urdu language, they invited Abrahams and his wife to visit them on their ship. A fast friendship resulted and at dinner on board the ship of his newly made friends, the Abrahams' were invited to come to Pakistan as guests of the ship's captain. After a visit to Karachi, the Abrahams left by air for Calcutta, India. Returning to the place where he had grown up, he wasn't prepared for what he would find.

To his amazement, he discovered that most of his friends were either dead or had left India. The old Jewish community had dwindled as a result of emigration to Israel and elsewhere. Synagogues stood almost empty and the priceless Torah Scrolls within the Arks unused. When Abrahams asked friends what had become of the once flourishing Bagdadian Jewish community in Calcutta, he was told that, since the partition, the Jews had lost their former privileged European status and had left the country. Many opted to emigrate to the UK, U.S.,

Canada and Australia, and some to Israel. This rapid movement of people destabilized the tight-knit, religiously conservative community.

Abrahams became greatly concerned about the large number of Sefer Torahs that had adorned the one time flourishing synagogues. He was told that a few of the ancient and beautiful scrolls had been sent to various communities in Israel and other countries where congregations of Calcutta Jews had been formed. Eddie decided to approach the Jewish community officials about bringing some of the unused Torahs to the United States where they would be placed in synagogues in this country that needed Torah Scrolls. The Jewish community leaders of the city, agreeing that it was almost tantamount to sacrilege to allow Torahs to remain unused, agreed to the request. The great task was arranged through Mr. Isaac S. Abraham, an influential and well-respected member of the Jewish community of Calcutta. Abrahams agreed to cover all expenses for repair and transportation.

Back in America with his priceless cargo, a dozen Torahs, Abrahams seemed providentially led to Rabbi Irving J. Block, spiritual leader of The Brotherhood Synagogue in Greenwich Village, New York, who consented to have his congregation act as custodian of the treasured objects. They would remain there until worthy beneficiaries could be determined.

Over time, the ancient Torahs have found new homes. Two were given to an Orthodox Synagogue in Brooklyn whose Ark had been destroyed by vandals after a break-in. Several went to newly-established congregations from Ethiopian (Falasha) Jews to Japanese Israelites. It was announced that one would be donated to a new kind of house of worship officially opening in February 1966: The International Synagogue at John F. Kennedy Airport, bringing the message of the Hebraic faith to all mankind. And one, of course, ended up in a Michigan congregation of United Israel World Union. Eddie Abrahams was present at all the ceremonies. As a messenger of the Faith, he always presented the ancient scrolls as a gift from the Jewish community of Calcutta, India.

Thanks to a Baghdad-born Jew, Edward Abrahams, who had spent his childhood days in Calcutta, India, and then roamed the world as a modern day "Jack London" only to settle finally in the United States as a successful businessman, the richly-ornamented, antique Indian Torah Scrolls, symbols of the quickly dying Jewish community of Calcutta, now live on in the Arks of new houses of worship. The United Israel Scroll resides today at the United Israel-South Center in St. Francisville, Louisiana. On the occasion of its use, one is left to wonder about a past congregation in Calcutta, India who faithfully read from it so many years ago and to also remember the incredible journey of "Eddie" Abrahams who personally placed it in our care.

Today, fewer than fifty Jews remain in Calcutta.

Chapter 20

Countdown to War

On a mid-November day in 1965, while opening his mail, David Horowitz was surprised to receive a letter from Fannie Hurst, the famous American novelist. She was on the mailing list to receive regular issues of the United Israel Bulletins, and recently Horowitz had sent her a copy of *Thirty-Three Candles*.

Fannie Hurst was among the most popular and sought-after writers of the post-World War I era. She was a contributor to *The Saturday Evening Post*, *Century* magazine, and *Cosmopolitan* magazine and was featured in annual editions of *The Best American Short Story*. Her novels and stories were translated into a dozen languages and over thirty of her works were made into movies. Among the best known were *Back Street* (1932, 1941, 1961), *Imitation of Life* (1934, 1959), and *Humoresque* (1920, 1946).

In her handwritten letter to David dated November 13, 1965, Hurst wrote:

My dear Mr. Horowitz,
I read your compelling book with interest and amazement. An astonishing document! By some alchemy your incredible story carries credibility. It almost seems to me that your mind and spirit were subconsciously prepared for this experience before it happened to you.
Thank you for the inscribed copy of the book and for subsequent material relating to your work.
Cordially,
Fannie Hurst

The original copy of the letter is preserved in the historic archives of United Israel World Union.

As 1966 dawned, David Horowitz was elected President of the Foreign Press Association of New York succeeding Edwin Tetlow, former correspondent for London Daily Telegraph. It was quite an honor. At the time, the association had some 450 correspondents on American soil working for the press, radio and television. A correspondent for more than thirty-five years, Horowitz had served as General Secretary for three years and was currently serving as Senior Vice-President.

In March, the President and officers of United Israel World Union announced a new Vice President. Edward S. Abrahams was elected a new officer in the organization. The outstanding humanitarian and champion of the Torah faith had been an active co-worker on behalf of United Israel's universal aims and purposes.

The World Union for the Propagation of Judaism, established in 1955 and based in Tel Aviv, Israel held a special reception on April 27th at the Deborah Hotel to welcome David Horowitz and new Vice President Eddie Abrahams. It was David's eighth visit to the Holy Land. It was Mr. Abrahams' first visit since Israel's statehood.

Among the highlights of the trip were various meetings to honor Abrahams and his renowned work as the donor of rare Indian Torah scrolls to worthwhile congregations, David's reunion with the Eliezer Tritto family in Safad, and revisiting the famous Cave of the Seventy Sanhedrin. Horowitz first visited the Sanhedrin Cave as a young pioneer in 1927. It was his experience there that had inspired him to write *Thirty-Three Candles*.

The situation in the Middle East was beginning to heat up, as if there would be any other way to ever describe it. The Palestine Liberation Organization (PLO), the Arab League's new weapon in its war against Israel, had stepped up both its belligerent rhetoric and attacks. Most of the attacks involved Palestinian guerillas infiltrating Israel from Jordan, the Gaza Strip, and Lebanon. The orders and logistical support for the attacks were coming, however, from Cairo and Damascus. The Syrian army used the Golan Heights, which tower 3,000 feet above the Galilee, to shell Israeli farms and villages forcing families living on kibbutzim in the Huleh valley to sleep in bomb shelters. Israel repeatedly and unsuccessfully protested the Syrian bombardments to the United Nations Mixed Armistice Commission, which was charged with policing the cease-fire. Nothing was done to stop Syria's aggression. Meanwhile, the UN condemned Israel whenever it retaliated.

On a much lighter note, David Horowitz learned that Hollywood actress, Joan Crawford, would be in New York during the time of a planned cocktail reception for members of the Foreign Press Association. In August 1966, he extended an invitation to Ms. Crawford, whom he had met once before, to attend the reception as his guest, and she accepted. Later, on August 22, Horowitz received a warm and thoughtful letter from Ms. Crawford expressing her gratitude to him and his colleagues for honoring her at the reception. She thanked David for giving her such a fine introduction. In closing, she also thanked him for presenting her with a copy of his book, *Thirty-Three Candles*, "so beautifully autographed to me," while also adding a P.S., "Thank you too for the beautiful roses." David seemed always to remember the thoughtful details. Horowitz and Ms. Crawford continued their correspondence between the period of August 22, 1966 and August 6, 1967, exchanging a total of six letters. A couple of the letters from Ms. Crawford were sent from London while on filming location.

An interesting little side story emerged from an unlikely source about an event that took place in November of 1966. As President of the Foreign Press Association, David Horowitz, along with a group of his colleagues, visited General Electric's Space and Technology Center in Valley Forge, Pennsylvania. It was the largest plant in the world manufacturing America's spacecraft and satellites, including the "Nimbus II" that had just been placed into orbit.

The group discovered the amazing fact that for over a year the vital scientific Center had been using the Hebrew word "chay," in Hebrew print, as its main working slogan for "Zero Defects" in its errorless production of spacecraft. All throughout the plant, in the corridors and over the doors, the word "chay" in Hebrew print was prominently displayed on signs and posters. The scientists themselves, including thousands of personnel, were wearing their security badges fastened to their coats with metal pins containing the two-letter Hebrew word.

During a scientific briefing before the group, Mr. J. C. Hoffman, Manager of Product Information, explained why the company had adopted specifically this Hebrew word above any other symbol. He related that at a meeting of officers and scientists many proposals had been put forth, but that the term "chay" had appealed most because it represented "the world's oldest language" and it signified "life." It was felt that it best expressed the company's aims of creating spacecraft to have long-life. Following this explanation, Mr. Hoffman officially presented one of the "chay" pins to Mr. Horowitz and each of the Foreign Press colleagues in the group.

Chapter 21

And After Six Days...

Famous entertainer Sammy Davis, Jr., who had corresponded with David Horowitz and was himself a convert to Judaism, announced his plans to visit Israel along with his Swedish actress wife, May Britt. He was scheduled to appear in two benefit performances on April 1-2. The proceeds of the benefits were to go toward the construction of a rehabilitation center for war victims. In accepting the offer to appear, Mr. Davis stipulated that a certain number of the seats be reserved for war invalids and soldiers.

United Israel World Union Vice President Eddie Abrahams was back in the news when it was announced that an ancient Oriental Torah Scroll would be donated to the Jewish Community of Kansai in the Ohel Shelomoh Synagogue in Kobe, Japan. The Kansai Jewish Community not only serves the religious needs of the Jews residing in the Kobe and Osaka areas but also thousands of Jewish visitors who pass through the busy port of Kobe each year. The unique Torah Scroll was taken to Japan during the Passover season and personally presented by Mr. Eddie Abrahams himself.

The situation in the Middle East seemed to grow worse with each passing day. The number of PLO attacks conducted against Israel totaled forty-one in 1966. The targets were almost always civilians. In an interesting development, King Hussein of Jordan also viewed the PLO as both a direct and indirect threat to his power. Hussein feared that the PLO might try to depose him with Abdul Nasser's (Egypt) help. By the beginning of 1967, Hussein had closed the PLO's offices in Jerusalem, arrested many of the group's members, and withdrew recognition of the organization. Nasser and his friends in the region unleashed a torrent of criticism on King Hussein for betraying the Arab cause. But, the new year was also to bring a dramatic event that would alter the political, strategic, and psychological landscape of the Middle East.

While the Syrian military bombardment and PLO terrorist attacks intensified against Israel, Egyptian President Gamal Abdel Nasser took additional provocative action. On May 15th, Israel's Independence Day, Egyptian troops began moving into the Sinai and massing near the Israeli border. Nasser ordered the UN Emergency Force (UNEF), stationed in the Sinai since 1956, to withdraw on May 16th. UN Secretary-General U Thant complied with the demand. Shortly after the withdrawal of the UNEF, the "Voice of the Arabs" radio station proclaimed on May 18th: "As of today, there no longer exists an international emergency force to protect Israel. We shall exercise patience no more. We shall not complain anymore to the UN about Israel. The sole method we shall apply against Israel is total war, which will result in the extermination of Zionist existence."

Then, several more events happened in quick succession: On May 22nd, Egypt closed the Straits of Tiran to all Israeli shipping and all ships bound for Eilat. This blockade cut off Israel's only supply route with Asia and stopped the flow of oil from its main supplier, Iran. U.S. President Lyndon Johnson expressed the belief that the blockade was illegal but at the same time, called on the Israelis not to take military action. King Hussein of Jordan signed a defensive pact with Egypt on May 30. Nasser then announced: "The armies of Egypt, Jordan, Syria, and Lebanon are poised on the borders of Israel to face the challenge, while standing behind us are the armies of Iraq, Algeria, Kuwait, Sudan, and the whole Arab nation. This act will astound the world. The critical hour has arrived." The Arab rhetoric was matched by the mobilization of Arab forces. Approximately 465,000 troops, more than 2,800 tanks, and 800 aircraft surrounded Israel.

The United States had tried to prevent a war through negotiations, but it was not able to persuade Nasser or the other Arab states to cease their belligerent statements and actions. Still, President Johnson warned, "Israel will not be alone unless it decides to go alone."

By this time, Israeli forces had been on alert for three weeks. The country could not remain fully mobilized indefinitely, nor could it allow its sea-lane through the Gulf of Aqaba to be interdicted. Israel had no choice but preemptive action. To do this successfully, Israel needed the element of surprise. Had it waited for an Arab invasion, Israel would have been at a potentially catastrophic disadvantage. On June 5, 1967, the order was given to attack Egypt.

On June 5, Israel was indeed alone, but its military commanders had conceived a brilliant war strategy. The entire Israeli Air Force, with the exception of just twelve fighters assigned to defend Israeli air space, took off at 7:14 A.M. with the intent of bombing Egyptian airfields while the Egyptian pilots were eating breakfast. In less than two hours, roughly 300 Egyptian aircraft were destroyed. A few hours later, Israeli fighters were sent to attack the Jordanian and Syrian air forces, as well as one airfield in Iraq. By the end of the first day, nearly the entire Egyptian and Jordanian air forces, and half the Syrians had been destroyed on the ground.

The battle then moved to the ground, and some of history's greatest tank battles were fought between Egyptian and Israeli armor in the blast-furnace conditions of the Sinai desert. While most IDF units were fighting the Egyptians and Jordanians, a small, heroic group of soldiers were left to defend the northern border against the Syrians. It was not until the Jordanians and Egyptians were subdued that reinforcements could be sent to the Golan Heights, where Syrian gunners commanding the strategic high ground made it exceedingly difficult and costly for Israeli forces to penetrate. It was not until June 9th, after two days of heavy air bombardment that Israeli forces succeeded in breaking through the Syrian lines.

Jordan's initial involvement had an interesting twist. Just before Israel launched its attack on June 5th, Israeli Prime Minister Levi Eshkol sent a message to King Hussein saying that Israel would not attack Jordan unless he initiated hostilities. When Jordanian radar picked up a cluster of planes flying from Egypt to Israel, the Egyptians convinced Hussein the planes were theirs, Hussein then ordered the shelling of West Jerusalem. Jordan had now entered the war on Egypt's side. It turned out that the planes were Israel's and were returning from destroying the Egyptian air force on the ground.

It took only three days for Israeli forces to defeat the Jordanian legion. On the morning of June 7th, the order was given to recapture the Old City. Israeli paratrooper battalions stormed the city. After fierce resistance and close quarter battles, the Old City was secured. Defense Minister Moshe Dayan arrived with Chief of Staff Yitzhak Rabin to formally mark the Jews' return to their historic capital and their holiest site.

At the Western Wall, the IDF's chaplain, Rabbi Shlomo Goren, blew the shofar (a ceremonial ram's horn) to celebrate the event. A mere twenty minutes after the capture of the Western Wall, David Rubinger shot his signature photograph of three Israeli paratroopers gazing in wonder up at the wall. It is now considered a defining image of the conflict and one of the best-known photographs in the history of Israel.

The short, intense war had ended. The victory enabled Israel to unify Jerusalem while also capturing the Sinai, Golan Heights, Gaza Strip, and West Bank. But Israel's victory came at a very high cost. Over 900 Israelis were killed and 4,517 were wounded. Arab casualties were far greater. Between 9,800 and 15,000 Egyptian soldiers were listed as killed, wounded or missing in action. Jordanian losses were estimated to be close to 6,000 either killed or missing and Syrians were estimated to have had over 2,500 killed. It was a bloody and costly conflict.

Buried in the historical records of the war is an interesting and little-known fact worth mentioning. In recognition of his contributions, Yitzhak Rabin was given the honor of naming the war for the Israelis. From the suggestions proposed, including the "War of Daring" and "War of Salvation" and "War of the Sons of Light," he chose the least ostentatious, the "Six-Day War," evoking the days of creation.

The Six-Day War was a devastating defeat for Nasserist pan-Arabism. The decline of Nasser's brand of secular Arab nationalism left a vacuum that was to be filled by two movements previously marginalized in Arab politics: *Palestinian nationalism* and *political Islam*. And in the decades to come, these two movements would play an increasingly prominent role, creating a situation with which the peoples of the Middle East, and the international community as a whole, continue to grapple.

Chapter 22
Twelve Volatile Months

By any measure, the leap year of 1968 was a remarkable year. Arguably, one of the most historic years in our modern history, it was called "The year that rocked the world" by *New York Times* best-selling author, Mark Kurlansky.

Six days after President Lyndon Johnson delivered the State of the Union address on January 17, North Korean patrol boats captured the *USS Pueblo*, a U.S. Navy intelligence gathering vessel and its eighty-three-man crew on charges of violating the communist country's twelve-mile territorial limit. This crisis dogged the U.S. foreign policy team throughout the year.

At half-past midnight on January 31, the North Vietnamese launched the Tet offensive at Nha Trang. Nearly 70,000 North Vietnamese troops took part in the broad action, taking the battle from the jungles to the cities. The offensive carried on for weeks and was seen as a major turning point for the American attitude toward the war.

United Israel World Union marked its 25th year of global activities. Its publication, the *United Israel Bulletin*, had penetrated practically every corner of the globe, bringing seekers of truth in Africa, Europe, Central and South America, Japan, and the Isles, to the understanding of Israel and her universal philosophy of life as outlined in the Bible. The year would also prove to be one of impressive growth and popularity.

Sheikh Kemal Tareef, one of the outstanding leaders of the Druze communities in Israel was in the U.S. in February on a four-week visit. He was invited to be the honored guest before a number of national Jewish organizations including the N.Y. Board of Rabbis and several synagogues at which he recounted the story of the heroic role his people played in assisting Israel during the Six-Day War in June of 1967.

While in New York, Sheikh Tareef paid a visit to David Horowitz at the UN on February 14th, bringing him the greetings of the Israeli Druze leaders who, in 1965, had welcomed Horowitz in their several villages in the true spirit of biblical fraternity. An account of his visit with the Druze appeared in a previous episode of the *United Israel Bulletin*, entitled "Among Jethro's People."

In early April, Horowitz departed for Israel. This was his 10th visit and his first since the Six-Day War. Among the many items on a busy agenda were a scheduled meeting with leaders of The Israeli World Union for the Propagation of Judaism and an important meeting with Stanley Goldfoot, publisher-editor of a projected new Israeli-English daily that was to be called "*The Times of Israel.*"

On April 4, more tragedy struck our nation. The Reverend Martin Luther King Jr. was standing on the second-floor balcony of room 306 at the Lorraine Motel in Memphis, Tennessee when a bullet struck him at 6:01 p.m. The thirty-nine-year-old civil rights leader was rushed to nearby St. Joseph's Hospital but never regained consciousness. He was pronounced dead at 7:05 p.m.

On the same night King was assassinated, Democratic presidential candidate Robert F. Kennedy arrived in Indianapolis on a campaign stop. Upon hearing the news Kennedy informed a crowd of listeners about King's death. They reacted with gasps and cries. Kennedy urged the crowd against bitterness, hatred, or revenge, calling on them instead to embrace King's message of love, wisdom and compassion toward one another. Kennedy's speech is believed to have prevented rioting in Indianapolis on a night where similar events broke out in major cities across the country. In that speech he quoted his favorite poet, Aeschylus, "In our sleep, pain which cannot forget falls drop by drop upon the heart until, in our own despair, against our will, comes wisdom through the awful grace of God."

Just two months later, on June 5th, Kennedy himself was gunned down by an assassin at the Ambassador Hotel in Los Angeles. The attack took place shortly after Kennedy had wrapped up a speech in the hotel ballroom. As he made his way through a kitchen corridor on his way to another part of the building, a Jordanian-born Palestinian named Sirhan opened fire, striking Kennedy in the head and back. He collapsed and was rushed to the hospital where he underwent brain surgery. Twenty-six hours after the attack he died. Kennedy was forty-two years old.

The year 1968 also marked the 20th year of Israeli statehood in the land of new light and restored glory. According to the newly-released *Israeli Statistical Yearbook for 1968*, seventeen percent of world Jewry were residents in Israel in 1966. The total number of Jews in the world in 1966 was 13.5 million, of whom 2.3 million were in Israel. By contrast, in 1900, Jews in the Holy Land formed one-half percent of world Jewry, and on May 15, 1948, 5.7 percent.

Nineteen-sixty-eight also marked a landmark development in U.S.-Israeli relations. Up until 1967, France had been the main supplier of weapons to the Israeli military. During the Six-Day War, however, French President de Gaulle imposed an arms embargo on Israel which, even after hostilities ended, he refused to lift. In response, U.S. President Lyndon Johnson agreed to a longstanding request by Israel for Phantom jets. Up to this point, the United States had avoided becoming Israel's arms supplier because it wanted to reduce the risk of a U.S.-USSR confrontation in the Middle East. From this point forward, the United States became the principal arms supplier to Israel and adopted a policy of maintaining Israel's qualitative military advantage over its neighbors.

In August 1968, the 21st annual B'nai B'rith Institute of Judaism was held at the beautiful Wildacres Retreat in Little Switzerland, North Carolina. The theme of the Institute was "The State of Israel on its 20th Anniversary: Discussions of its World-Wide Influences." It covered the religious, political and cultural implications of Israel's founding and emergence onto the world stage. One of the keynote speakers was UN Correspondent and President of the Foreign Press Association, David Horowitz. As the UN and U.S. correspondent for Israel's daily *"Hayom,"* Mr. Horowitz lectured on Israel's political influence. Lecture titles included "Retrospect: Behind the Scenes Glimpses of Israel's Statehood," "Israel's Relations with Her Neighbors," and "What of the Future?"

THE BOOK OF DAVID

Former Premier David Ben-Gurion of Israel marked his eighty-second birthday on Wednesday, October 9, by issuing a stern warning from his desert home in the Negev, "that Israelis should cling to the ideals of the ancient Hebrew Prophets by becoming a beacon unto the nations of the world."

On November 5, 1968, America elected a new President. Republican challenger Richard M. Nixon defeated the Democratic candidate, Vice President Hubert Humphrey, and American Independent Party candidate George C. Wallace. Nixon ran on a campaign that promised to restore law and order to the nation's cities, torn by riots and crime.

Finally, in December, the eleven-month *USS Pueblo* crisis that threatened to worsen already high Cold War tensions in the region came to an end. After months of negotiations, North Korea agreed to free the eighty-two *Pueblo* crew members. On December 23, the crew was allowed to safely return to South Korean territory and was home in time for Christmas. However, the United States Navy had lost a highly sophisticated intelligence-gathering ship.

Nineteen-sixty-eight was more than the year of sex, drugs and rock and roll. It was a turning point for a generation coming of age and a nation at war. The social forces that swirled through the turbulent 1960s crested in 1968. We experienced the anti-war movement, the Tet Offensive, assassinations, and riots in the streets. Social demonstrations were in vogue, from volatile student unrest on college campuses to Black Power assertions and feminist demonstrations at the Miss America pageant; tumultuous times indeed.

In a contrasting and uplifting endnote to one of the most turbulent and tragic years in American history, millions around the world were watching and listening as the Apollo 8 astronauts-Frank Borman, Jim Lovell, and Bill Anders became the first humans to orbit another world. Apollo 8, the second human spaceflight mission in the U.S. Apollo space program, was launched on December 21 and was the first manned spacecraft to leave earth's orbit. Apollo 8 took three days to travel to the moon and orbited ten times over the course of twenty hours. It marked the first time that humans had travelled to the far side of the moon and we were given the first photos of earth taken from deep space, including the now iconic "Earthrise." It was Christmas Eve and the crew was about to make a television broadcast to the largest audience that had ever listened to a human voice. The only instructions that the astronauts had received from NASA was "to do something appropriate." They did. The crew of Apollo 8 read in turn from the creation story in the Book of Genesis as they orbited the moon. Anders, Lovell, and Borman recited verses 1 through 10 using the King James Version of the biblical text. Their message appeared to sum up the feelings that all three crewmen had from their vantage point in lunar orbit. Following the reading, Borman stated, "And from the crew of Apollo 8, we close with good night, good luck, a Merry Christmas and God bless all of you—all of you on the good Earth." The amazing and joyous mission was a rare high note in a year filled with historically tragic events. The astronauts received countless telegrams after they returned safely home. But one stood out from all the others. It said simply: "You saved 1968."

"Christmas at the moon" was a good closing act.

Chapter 23

An Unseen Hand

As 1969 dawned, Richard M. Nixon was inaugurated the 37th President of the United States on January 20, succeeding Lyndon B. Johnson. During Nixon's time in office, the United States forged quasi-alliances with Iran, Saudi Arabia, and Israel. These relationships were buttressed by a new policy formulation known as the "Nixon Doctrine." The doctrine called for greater reliance on regional "cops on the beat," powerful pro-Western governments that could protect American interests in various parts of the world, thus obviating the need for direct US military intervention.

Just as Nixon was taking office, Egyptian President Gamal Nasser stepped up Egypt's sporadic artillery attacks and commando raids against Israeli positions in the Sinai. Hostilities in the Six-Day War had barely ended when Nasser resumed fighting. Even though his forces had been routed, he was unwilling to leave Israel alone. Having learned that the Israeli army could not be attacked head-on, Nasser was convinced that because most of Israel's army consisted of reserves, it could not withstand a lengthy war. He believed Israel would be unable to endure the economic burden, and that the constant casualties would undermine Israeli morale. Politically, starting a new war also maintained his standing as the leader of the fight against Zionism. The fighting gradually escalated into what became known as the "War of Attrition," lasting nearly two years until 1970.

In March, United Israel World Union board member Eddie Abrahams left for Japan to deliver a beautiful silver-ornamented, Oriental Torah to the Synagogue in Osaka. It was presented during the

Passover as a gift on behalf of The Brotherhood Synagogue in New York.

After the untimely death of Israeli Prime Minister Levi Eshkol, seventy-one-year-old Golda Meir was elected the fourth Prime Minister of Israel on March 17, 1969. After serving as Minister of Labor and Foreign Minister, Golda Meir became Israel's first and only woman to hold the office of Prime Minister. Born in Kiev, Russia, Ms. Meir grew up in Milwaukee, Wisconsin.

On Passover 5729, (April 1969), it was a time to look back in history and reflect deeply on the events of the Exodus under the guidance of the unparalleled prophet Moses. In describing the ancient, never-to-be-forgotten Red Sea episode over 3,500 years ago, David Horowitz often referred to it as the work of an *Unseen Hand* in bringing Israel out of the land of Egypt.

He also felt that Providence was clearly at work in the recent Six-Day War victory in the face of overwhelming odds. In one of his more reflective moods, Horowitz remarked that he could sense it at work. He repeatedly mentioned the odd and unexplainable developments he had witnessed from his unique vantage point at the UN, having covered the world organization since its inception. His thoughts and reflections on events that took place in that world parliament (He referred to it as the "Parliament of Man") were always viewed through the lens of the divine plan, particularly in the adjudication of issues affecting Israel and her enemies.

The rebirth of Israel as a nation in 1948 was considered a watershed event. Once again, as in biblical times, Israel was very much on the global scene. Horowitz felt that Israel was reborn and thus, so were her enemies. He often said that history does repeat itself in a most uncanny manner and that there is nothing new under the sun. Assyria was still with us but in another guise today. Egypt was Egypt. So too, were Ammon, Moab, Syria, Edom, and Babylon, even the troublesome Philistines. Much of the ancient scene in the Middle East remains the same, and so, too, with the people—the main difference being that they were now wearing 20th century garb. He would say (with emphasis), "Despite all our civilization today, the spirit and the ancient enmities have not changed." He felt he could see this in the debates brought out at the UN.

Horowitz felt that following 1948, we began to see certain biblical elements being brought into play: much like the restarting of an ancient clock. Taking on a prophetic tone, he expressed his Passover sentiments:

Following a bitter 2,000-year-old exile, Israel has returned home, but only after having traversed the earth with the Torah message via Judaism, Islam, and Christianity. But not before having paid the horrendous price of unceasing torture and martyrdom. Papal decrees, Spanish Inquisition, Russian and Polish pogroms, Prussian anti-Semitism and Hitlerian murder: what a price!

And the world is still ungrateful.

The serpent's head once again stands poised to strike against the people of Abraham. But *this time* the Hand will be there. This time the words of the prophets will be heard. The result will not be a Treblinka or a Dachau, but an Exodus. For the rod of Moses is still intact and the Cloud of Sinai is not dimmed.

In June, Rabbi Hailu Moshe Paris, a long-standing board member of United Israel World Union, received his Bachelor of Hebrew Literature degree from Yeshiva University and began graduate work at the University's Graduate School of Humanities and Social Sciences. Rabbi Paris, who also studied at Yeshivat Hadarom in Rehovot, Israel in the late fifties, was a vocal advocate for African Jewry and worked tirelessly on behalf of the Falasha Jews of Ethiopia.

On July 7, a *New York Times* dispatch from Tel Aviv reported that "Israeli soldiers give heroes' burials today to some of the 960 defenders who perished in the historic suicide pact on Masada 1,896 years ago." The report went on to recount the history behind the decision taken by the last Hebrew defenders of Israel on the eve of Passover, A.D. 73. Among the many Israeli officials present was Prime Minister Menachem Begin who, as the *Times* reported, pledged in a graveside oration, "Never another Masada." An interesting aspect to the unique and dramatic ceremony lies in the fact that the burials were made in one of the many compounds at the foot of the mount where the Romans had encamped for the siege.

Recalling his first visit to the ancient fortress during the British Mandate days in the mid-1920s, David Horowitz reflected on the event: "As I reached the summit and viewed the scenes of our ancestors' glorious last stand, I looked down the declivity and saw the ruins of the camps which Flavius Silva had built at the important approaches to the mount. I was moved and emotionally touched to the very heartstrings of my being." Offering a final thought, Horowitz remarked: "Eliezer the Hebrew, and his company had chosen death rather than slavery under the Roman eagle. They laid themselves to rest here. Now here we are, back on Masada again, treading on Roman ruins. Jerusalem is rebuilt, and we are again a nation." But then again, no one ever had to convince David Horowitz of the power of an unseen hand at work in the ever-unfolding march of history.

In December, Horowitz was appointed Managing Editor of the *American Examiner*, one of the leading English-Jewish Weeklies in the United States published in New York City.

Another consequence of Egyptian President Nasser's War of Attrition against Israel was the escalation in terrorist activities by the Palestinian Liberation Organization (PLO) that often provoked Israeli reprisals. Instead of attacking Israel from Syria, the terrorist groups usually mounted their operations from Jordan or Lebanon. In addition, the PLO increasingly chose to attack Israeli targets outside the Middle East as hijackings also increased.

As the page turned on the decade of the '60s, the most serious threat posed by the PLO was *not* to Israel but to the regime of King Hussein of Jordan."

David Horowitz (L) greets Israeli Ambassador Abba Eban following a UN session.

UN Journalist David Horowitz offers a few words of counsel to Israeli Prime Minister Golda Meir.

All Photos provided by United Israel World Union.

Celebrated Hollywood actress Gloria Swanson is seen here addressing a group of UN journalists while an amused David Horowitz is seated to her left.

David Horowitz is seen here posing in front of the Isaiah Wall at the UN compound.

A group of early pioneers in British Mandate Palestine in 1924. David Horowitz is pictured in the center holding the trusty canine mascot.

David Horowitz in his UN office in 1970 preparing another syndicated column before a press deadline.

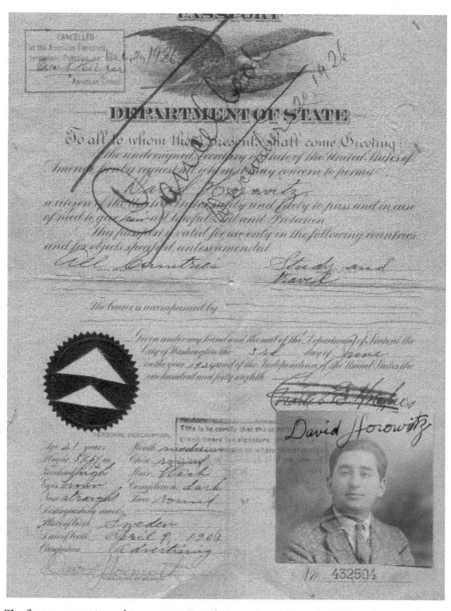

The first passport issued to a young David Horowitz on June 3, 1924, at the age of 21

Israeli Prime Minister Menachem Begin (L) presenting the prestigious Jabotinsky Centennial Award to journalist David Horowitz in 1980.

Journalist David Horowitz and wife Nan seen here greeting a young Menachem Begin during an early 1950's visit to New York.

Young Hollywood actor Kirk Douglas (L) is seen here being interviewed by journalist David Horowitz in 1949.

UN Secretary-General Kurt Waldheim holds a press briefing at the UN. Seated to the right of the vacant chair in the center is journalist David Horowitz reporting for the World Union Press.

Journalist David Horowitz (L) greets Soviet Union leader Nikita Khruschev at the UN in 1960.

Horowitz in a reflective mood after lighting the Hanukkah candles.

Author seen here with David Horowitz in 1999.

Horowitz making a point to author Ralph Buntyn in 1993.

Horowitz is shown here inspecting a Golden Book of the Psalms in 2000 flanked by Professor James Tabor and author Ralph Buntyn.

(L-R) author Ralph Buntyn, David Horowitz, and UIWU associate Gregg Sitrin pictured in Horowitz's cluttered UN office.

Horowitz in a lighter moment with author's wife Rebecca Buntyn. Note the camera flash reflection is not the Shekinah.

Horowitz lighting an antique Jerusalem candlestick in 1996 flanked by Professor James Tabor and author Buntyn.

Veteran journalist Horowitz in 1992, the year the author met him.

Part Three

Chapter 24
Black September

The 28th Annual Meeting of United Israel World Union was held on Sunday, April 12, at the Manhattan home of David and Nan Horowitz. During the meeting it was announced that United Israel Vice President Edward S. (Eddie) Abrahams had received a special award presented by the Israeli Government to former Legionnaires who had fought for the redemption of Palestine during World War I.

It was also revealed that the West Olive, Michigan congregation had sent a memorandum to Michigan Representative Gerald R. Ford requesting him to read into the Congressional Record, a United Israel World Union statement relative to Israel's eternal rights to the Holy Land as decreed in the Scriptures. Congressman Ford would later acknowledge the communication in a letter sent to William Goodin at West Olive. Sending his "warm personal regards," he stated, among other things: "I appreciated your comments and your deep interests in Israel and the Jewish people. I want to thank you especially for sending me the copy of the United Israel Bulletin."

Hostilities in the War of Attrition against Israel would continue until August, ending when a ceasefire agreement was reached. The frontiers remained the same as when the war began and, unfortunately, the agreement produced no real commitment to serious peace negotiations. The War of Attrition, lasting three years, claimed the lives of 1,424 Israeli soldiers and left more than 3,000 wounded. While the number of Egyptian fatalities remained unknown, they were believed to number around 9,000.

A month later, a major crisis occurred that was to have a far-reaching impact on US-Israeli relations. By the late 1960s, the Palestinians in

Jordan had become increasingly militant and powerful. King Hussein of Jordan concluded an agreement in July 1970 with the PLO's new leader, Yasser Arafat, but the ink was hardly dry when Palestinians hijacked TWA and KLM airliners and landed them at the airport in Amman.

The incidents escalated the tension between the Palestinian radicals and King Hussein who saw this as a challenge to his authority. Armed clashes broke out between the king's troops and the PLO, which had established a state-within-a-state in Jordan. On September 1st, an assassination attempt against King Hussein failed. On September 19, a column of Syrian tanks crossed the northern Jordanian border in support of the PLO. King Hussein appealed to the United States to launch air strikes to support his forces. Both logistically and politically however, it would have been extremely difficult for the US to intervene militarily in the Jordanian crisis.

The Israelis were naturally alarmed by a conflict not far from their borders. Concerned that a PLO takeover of Jordan would pose a grave threat to their security, they were willing to intervene on Jordan's behalf. In a menacing gesture, a squadron of Israeli jets flew to northern Jordan and swooped low over the advancing Syrian tanks. The tanks withdrew. King Hussein's forces then turned on the PLO, killing and wounding thousands of Palestinians and forcing the leadership, along with thousands of refugees, into Syria and Lebanon. The defeat of the PLO came to be known by Palestinians as "Black September."

The Black September crisis had a profound effect on US policy-making toward the Middle East. President Nixon was extremely pleased with Israel's behavior in the Jordan crisis and gained a new appreciation for Israel's potential as a strategic ally of the United States. Thus, by the early 1970s, Israel, too, had become an American ally under the terms of the "Nixon Doctrine."

Black September also had a number of other significant repercussions. Israel's willingness to come to King Hussein's aid created warmer relations between Hussein and the Israeli leadership, which facilitated periodic secret meetings to try to make peace. Jordan has never again been involved in military action against Israel. The head of Syria's air force, Hafez Assad, decided not to enter the war in Jordan, thereby dooming the Syrian invasion. The action paved the way for Assad to seize power. The crisis in Jordan had prompted Egyptian President Gamal Nasser to call a meeting in Cairo of Arab heads of state. On September 28, during the talks, he suddenly died of a heart attack. His little-known vice president, Colonel Anwar Sadat, replaced him.

UN Correspondent David Horowitz, in frequent demand as a speaker, addressed five different synagogue bodies on the subject of Israel and the United Nations within the span of six weeks during October and November. In each case he spoke to a capacity crowd.

In early 1971, David Horowitz became vitally interested in another pursuit. It wasn't something that just caught his attention; it demanded a response. It stirred painful memories of personal loss and inflamed a passion to act. The story unfolded with the classic elements of a high-profile Cold Case, a relentless investigative reporter, and an unlikely person-of-interest. The subject of Horowitz's investigation arrived in the United States after World War II under the "Displaced Persons Immigration Law." He was ordained as a priest of the Romanian Church soon thereafter. He rose quickly to the rank of bishop and archbishop. He became the spiritual leader of 35,000 members of the Romanian Orthodox Episcopate, based in Grass Lake, Michigan. He lived in comfort in a twenty-five-room farmhouse on a 200-acre estate maintained by his church.

He was an honored prelate. In 1955, he had given the opening prayer before the United States Senate. He was also appointed to the governing board of the National Council of Churches. His name was Archbishop Valerian D. Trifa, and, despite his many accomplishments and honors, he was a man with a dark past.

David Horowitz became interested in the United Nations agenda item that dealt with the apprehension and punishment of war criminals. After uncovering previous exposes by the late columnist Drew Pearson and broadcaster Walter Winchell, as well as documented evidence from other sources, Horowitz became convinced that the evidence against Trifa had proved to be so absolute, and yet: Why had there not been a breakthrough in the case?

Survivors of the Nazi years, Jewish organizations, journalists and the U.S. Department of Justice had pursued the case against the church leader for more than a decade, but the case against the Archbishop had many twists and turns. The matter rested on the belief that not much could be done in the face of the Immigration Services bureaucracy and negative attitude.

It was at this point that UN Correspondent David Horowitz decided he would become involved in a campaign to have the Justice Department consider reopening the Trifa case. The shocking next step proved only to be an opening salvo in a lengthy campaign for justice. Archbishop Valerian D. Trifa's ecclesiastical life of comfort was about to change.

Chapter 25

Unholy Vows

"War Criminal Remains A Free Man In U.S." blared the bold headline in the March 1971 issue of the *United Israel Bulletin*. Editor David Horowitz opened the article with a bold challenge to all readers:

> A murderer of thousands of Jews, a World War II criminal found guilty of war crimes and sentenced to hard labor for life, today walks the streets of a leading US city as a free man, in the robe of a priest heading a religious body. Unbelievable, you will say. Yes, unbelievable, but it is the truth and only in quick-to-forget America could such a thing happen.
>
> Horowitz continued, "But what is most fantastic of all is the fact that this criminal in the year 1955, in his clerical disguise, was invited to give the opening prayer in the United States Senate. Who exactly is this man who has made Detroit his home base and how, in the face of his World War II record, did he manage to enter the United States?"

Thus, David Horowitz, pulling no punches when a strong voice was needed, launched the first salvo in a campaign to have the Justice Department consider reopening the war crimes charges against Archbishop Valerian D. Trifa, who came to the U.S. in 1950. Valerian Trifa had concealed a past that included membership in a group called the Iron Guard, a fascist movement that was the Romanian parallel of the Nazi storm troopers in Germany. He played a part in provoking the Legionnaires' Rebellion in Bucharest when on January 20, 1941, his anti-Semitic speech touched off four days of attacks in which 300 Jews and others were killed.

After being singled out as a rebel by Ion Antonescu, Romania's "Conducător" and a competitor of the Iron Guard, he spent the final years of World War II in Nazi Germany, as a detainee with privileged status. Romanian authorities tried him *in absentia*, alongside other Iron Guard leaders, and sentenced him to life imprisonment and labor.

Trifa moved to the United States on July 17, 1950, using the "Displaced Persons Immigration Law." According to the Italian weekly *L'Espresso*, this was made possible by the intervention of a "high-ranking (Italian Catholic) prelate." He subsequently became a writer at the *Solia* Romanian language newspaper in Cleveland, Ohio. At the Congress of the dissident Romanian Orthodox Church in America held in Chicago on July 2, 1951, Trifa was chosen bishop and then moved to Grass Lake, Michigan, where the headquarters of the Romanian Orthodox Episcopate was located.

Responsible Romanian-Americans who knew of his true past, including Dr. Charles H. Kremer, President of the Romanian Jewish Federation of America, soon exposed Trifa. Having also exposed the Romanian anti-Semite in his broadcast of May 29, 1955, the late columnist Drew Pearson again laid out the facts of the charges in his syndicated column of June 4, 1955. Walter Winchell, in his broadcast of September 9, 1951, called Valerian Trifa a "murderer" referring to him as being one of the "Nazi leaders who helped Hitler kill American GIs." He urged that the Senate conduct a thorough investigation not only of him but also of his associates.

Following the investigation, Congressman Seymour Halpern (NY) read into the March 1952 Congressional Record a devastating indictment against the former Iron Guard member. Yet, despite all the evidence produced by the genuine Romanian religious authorities, by Chief Rabbi Rosen, by leaders of the World Jewish Congress, and by many other reliable sources, pointing to Trifa's guilt as a war criminal, he managed to evade arrest or extradition. A host of like-minded "friends" in the US and Canada provided aid and support including his acquisition of American citizenship on May 13, 1957.

Nonetheless, despite the secure refuge Trifa enjoyed and the years of slippage into cold case reality, David Horowitz persisted in his belief that it was still not too late for the government to reopen its investigation of the Iron Guard murderer who was admitted to the US and granted citizenship under false pretenses.

With the shocking headline and lengthy article in the March issue of the *United Israel Bulletin*, David launched what would become a five-year campaign in the quest for justice against Valerian Trifa. Yes, *five* years.

During this period, David examined the information in the Winchell and Pearson exposes, the documentary evidence on file in the Anti-Defamation League offices, and consulted with Dr. Charles Kremer who had, for years, been attempting to publicize Trifa's war crimes. David's investigative reporting took him to Romania where he unearthed much of the background information from agency files and personal interviews. He traveled to Israel where he gathered information and interviewed witnesses to Trifa's crimes. He searched databases and made countless phone calls.

The World Union Press syndicate and the *United Israel Bulletin* published well-documented articles, all edited by Horowitz, resurrecting the entire case of the former Iron Guard leader and bringing to light his full background wartime activities. Throughout the years 1971-1973, these publications continuously published feature articles with photographs exposing Trifa as a war criminal. Many of the articles were based on personal interviews with first account witnesses to the crimes, both Jews and non-Jews.

Horowitz communicated with most of the members of Congress, both the House and Senate, alerting them to the criminal background of the Bishop. Among the Senators who took an active interest was Jacob K. Javits. Horowitz also alerted the United Nations Commission on Human Rights, suggesting that the Trifa matter be examined in the light of Assembly Resolution 2840. Jacob T. Moller, UN Officer of the Division of Human Rights, duly acknowledged this latter communication, which included copies of the *United Israel Bulletins*.

Reacting to the article on Bishop Trifa in the March issue of the *Bulletin*, Senator Jacob Javits remarked: "It is important, even a generation after the conclusion of World War II, that war criminals continue to be pursued. There is no statute of limitations on murder..."

A few months after David's first expose, Bishop Trifa wrote him a two-page letter listing 10 points in which he disclaimed all the charges made against him. Accusing Horowitz of making libelous statements, he requested that his response be given the same publicity as the "false allegations" made against him. So, in the July 1971 issue of the *United Israel Bulletin*, Trifa was granted his request. His full letter was published.

Appearing in the same issue however, was a complete dossier of official Romanian documents that clearly substantiated the charges against the Bishop. Included in the evidence were copies of a Trifa anti-Semitic Manifesto, co-signed by four other Iron Guard Nazis, the warrant for Trifa's arrest, and a copy of the court decision sentencing Trifa and others to life imprisonment.

The case of the former Romanian Iron Guard leader was aired over New York's municipal radio station WNYC on Thursday evening, September 30, 1971, in a memorial broadcast honoring the victims of the 1941 pogroms in Jassy and Bucharest. Dr. Charles H. Kremer, President of the Romanian Jewish Federation of America and veteran UN correspondent David Horowitz were guest speakers. Both spoke at length about the case against Trifa. In December 1973, *The New York Times*, following an intensive investigation, published a lengthy article that, in essence, confirmed the charges that David Horowitz had made in his years of relentless pursuit. The long campaign was finally beginning to bear fruit.

At last, following years of intensive efforts on the part of David Horowitz and Dr. Charles Kremer, the US Government took action to bring Bishop Valerian D. Trifa to trial. The US Attorney in Detroit formally charged the Romanian pogromist with having won his naturalization through "false and untrue" denials of membership in the Nazi-inspired Iron Guard and in participation in the murder of Jews and Masons in the year 1941. The US suit, brought against Trifa on July 5, 1975, was the culmination of an extensive review of the Bishop's case by the Immigration and Naturalization Service and was due in large part, to official documents uncovered and published by the *United Israel*

Bulletins, the *World Union Press* and by Dr. Charles Kremer of the Romanian Jewish Federation of America.

In 1980, Archbishop Trifa voluntarily surrendered his citizenship, hoping that would put an end to the government's efforts. Those efforts however, continued and in 1982, in the midst of a trial before an immigration judge in Detroit, the Archbishop voluntarily agreed to his deportation. He did so, he said, because of the financial burden the trial was putting on his church. He was ordered to leave the United States in 1982 but spent two years trying to find a country that would give him refuge. Portugal admitted him in 1984 and he settled in Estoril, east of Cascais. Archbishop Valerian D. Trifa, whom David Horowitz once called "a wolf disguised in a Bishop's robe" died at the age of seventy-two on January 28, 1987 in a hospital in Cascais, Portugal.

Charles R. Allen, Jr., a well-known author who was among the first in the US to expose Nazi war criminals residing in America and Canada, paid high tribute to UN Correspondent David Horowitz for his role in reactivating the case against the Romanian pogromist. Allen wrote: "Mr. Horowitz' investigative reporting aroused national interest in the case. Dr. Charles Kremer, who had made it a life task to publicize Trifa's crimes, was a voice crying in the wilderness until the Horowitz' exposes appeared."

Elements of the Trifa case were the topic of an episode of the documentary series *Forensic Files*, aired by the United States television station *Court TV* in January 2001. The episode, titled "*Unholy Vows*," discussed the case and the forensic evidence gathered from Trifa's correspondence.

Personal Postscript to 1971

The year 1971, closed on a sad note for David Horowitz. His father, Aaron Horowitz, Cantor Emeritus of the United Orthodox Synagogue in Wilkes-Barre, PA, died on December 21, 1971 at the venerable age of 97. Born in 1874 in Dukor, Russia, he had dedicated himself early to the study of theology and cantorial arts, receiving certifications in several fields of study. Moving to Malmo, Sweden in 1900, Cantor

Horowitz was in contact with Theodor Herzl, founder of World Zionism, and was instrumental in establishing one of the first Zionist chapters in the Scandinavian country. Cantor Horowitz and his family, including son, David, who was born in Malmo, immigrated to the United States in 1914. Many of the world's outstanding Rabbis and leaders, among them the renowned Lubavitcher Rebbe, Menachem M. Schneerson, paid high tribute in their messages of condolence to the life-long, devotional career of Cantor Aaron Horowitz.

Chapter 26
Massacre at Munich

The arrival of the year, 1972, brought with it a new Secretary-General of the United Nations. Austrian diplomat and politician Kurt Josef Waldheim became the fourth Secretary-General of the UN on January 1ˢᵗ, succeeding U Thant.

Also in January, David Horowitz was back in Israel. The UN correspondent was honored on Sunday evening, January 23, by the Israeli World Union for the Propagation of Judaism. At a reception held at the Deborah Hotel in Tel Aviv, Mr. Horowitz was hailed as the founder, almost thirty years ago, of the global movement established to propagate the ideals of the Hebraic heritage on a universal scale.

The principal speaker at the reception was Dr. Wolfgang von Weisl, world-famous author, writer, and noted physician. In his address, Dr. von Weisl spoke of Mr. Horowitz' tireless and unselfish work on behalf of the eternal Torah, and of Horowitz being a pathfinder of a movement that had assumed global dimensions. Among the many tributes paid to David was one by Mr. Moshe Maur Schor, editor of the Israeli Romanian weekly *Facla*, who commended Horowitz for his role in exposing Bishop Valerian D. Trifa as a Nazi war criminal.

While in Israel, Horowitz had the rare opportunity to interview a survivor of the murderous Romanian Iron Guard pogrom that took place in Bucharest in January 1941. Horowitz and *Facla* editor Moshe Maur Schor interviewed Rabbi Zvi Guttman, approaching his eighties, at his home in Tel Aviv in late January. During two dramatic hours, Rabbi Guttman, trembling and near tears, recounted in minute detail the unspeakable horrors he, his family, and thousands of other Jews in Romania had experienced during those tragic and horrifying three days of the bitter freezing month of January 1941. The Guttmans were one of the most prominent families in Bucharest where the Rabbi served as the spiritual leader of the Jewish community in the city. The painful details described in the interview, which included Rabbi Guttman's account of witnessing his two sons slain at his side, were published in the February 1972 issue of the United Israel Bulletin.

During his visit in Israel, Horowitz also participated in the second annual conference of the World Federation of Jewish Journalists and attended the opening of the Zionist Congress.

Meanwhile in the Middle East, New Egyptian President Anwar Sadat inherited Gamal Nasser's determination to insure the recovery of the Arab territories lost in the 1967 war. He announced that Egypt would be willing to implement a peace treaty with Israel if Israel fully withdrew from the Sinai Peninsula and from all other Arab territories taken in 1967. Israel rejected Sadat's initiative, insisting that any return of Arab lands would have to take place after the Arab states had made peace with Israel, not as a precondition for peace. In the summer of 1972, Sadat expelled thousands of Soviet advisors from the country and began reforming the Egyptian army for a renewed confrontation with Israel.

Nineteen-seventy-two was the year of the Summer Olympic Games in Munich with the Olympics returning to Germany for the first time since 1936. From the Vietnam War, to racial tensions in the U.S. and continued violence in the Middle East, the world was rife with political unrest. German President Gustav Heinemann welcomed the Olympics "as a milestone on the road to a new way of life with the aim of realizing peaceful coexistence among peoples." Such an elusive ideal.

On the morning of September 5th, with six days left in the Games, the worst tragedy in Olympic history took place. Eight Arab terrorists stormed into the Olympic Village and raided the apartment building that housed the Israeli contingent. Two Israeli athletes were killed and nine more taken as hostages. The Palestinian terrorist group known as *Black September* demanded the release of over 200 Palestinians serving time in Israeli jails along with two terrorists held by Germany.

When it was over, seventeen people were killed during the Black September attack, including six Israeli coaches, five Israeli athletes, five of the eight terrorists, and one West German policeman. Hundreds of journalists from all over the world were covering the 1972 Olympics, so the Black September assault and the murder of Israeli athletes and coaches was, in fact, the very first time that a terror attack was reported and broadcast, in real time, across the globe.

One of five Israeli athletes to narrowly escape the attack was Shaul Paul Ladany; perhaps he could be called the ultimate survivor. Ladany was an Israeli racewalker and two-time Olympian. He set and still holds the world record in the fifty-mile walk and the Israeli national record in the fifty-kilometer walk. As an eight-year-old in 1944, he was captured by the Nazis, along with his parents, and shipped to the Bergen-Belsen concentration camp. Many in his family were killed. One of the few survivors, he was taken to Israel in December 1948 just after Israel had become a nation state. The holder of twenty-eight Israeli national titles and two world records, Ladany returned to the 1972 Olympics in Munich. He wore a Star of David on his warm-up jersey, explaining that he wanted to show the Germans that a Jew had survived. When locals congratulated him on his fluent German, he responded: "I learned it well when I spent a year at Bergen-Belsen."

Shaul Ladany achieved an incredibly accomplished career. He held a B.S. degree in Mechanical Engineering from the Technion-Israel Institute of Technology and his Ph.D. in Business Administration from Columbia University, followed by postdoctoral research at Tel Aviv University. For over three decades he was a Professor of Industrial Engineering and Management at Ben Gurion University of the Negev where he was formerly Chairman of the Department and is now emeritus professor. Author of over a dozen scholarly books and 110 scientific articles, he holds U.S. patents for eight mechanical designs and also speaks nine languages. Speaking of the Munich massacre even today, Ladany contends: "It's with me all the time, and I remember every detail." He visits the graves of his murdered teammates in Tel Aviv every year on the 6th of September.

David Horowitz completed a busy and event-filled year by addressing a meeting of the European Affairs Committee of the Anti-Defamation League of B'nai B'rith at the New York headquarters of the League. "The Jewish Image at the United Nations" was the topic of his detailed report of how Israel had fared in the world organization. He closed by describing how the 27th Session of the United Nations General Assembly held in November had been overshadowed by the murder of the Israeli athletes in the Munich Olympic tragedy.

With no progress toward peace, Egyptian President Anwar Sadat continued to warn of war with Israel. U.S. intelligence and Israeli analysts remained skeptical about his repeated threats. In the coming months, however, the inevitable would happen and trigger another major turning point in America's relations with Middle Eastern states.

Chapter 27

Israel's Day of Infamy

The year 1973 had hardly arrived when Lyndon B. Johnson, our 36th President, died on January 22nd at the age of 64. Johnson, who died two days after Richard Nixon's second inauguration was the second former President to die within the span of two months. Former President Harry S. Truman, whose death made Johnson the only living former President, died less than a month before Johnson did on December 26, 1972.

Also on January 27, 1973, the U.S., North Vietnam, South Vietnam, and the Viet Cong signed the Paris Peace Accords. This led to an immediate cease-fire and the release of all American POWs within sixty days. Mercifully, the long and protracted conflict, that had also created widespread social and political disruption within the United States, was drawing to a close.

The gala 30th Anniversary Dinner of United Israel World Union was held at Congregation Rodeph Sholom in Manhattan on May 12th. General Lucius D. Clay, whose very first act after being appointed Governor of West Berlin after World War II was to prevail upon the Bavarian regime to rebuild the Munich Synagogue destroyed by the Nazis, was one of the outstanding personalities heading the 30th Anniversary Committee. The event honored the life of noted humanitarian Harry Leventhal.

Founded in 1943, United Israel World Union preceded the establishment of the United Nations by two years and the State of Israel by five. David Horowitz saw the three great events in the order of their sequential emergence as significant and providential. Often stressing the universal philosophy of life as blueprinted in the Bible, he named the organization "United Israel World Union" *five* years before the Jewish State was proclaimed "Israel."

In 1947, United Israel had played a vital role at the UN in urging the world organization, through a memorandum, to recognize the rights of Israel in the Holy Land. This memorandum, distributed among UN delegations, was officially acknowledged and recorded in the United Nations archives.

The 30th Annual Meeting of United Israel World Union was held on June 27th at the home of David and Nan Horowitz. David gave a detailed report on the overwhelming success of the 30th Anniversary Dinner. At the meeting, Horowitz read a lengthy letter he had just received from entertainer Sammy Davis, Jr. Mr. Davis began his inspiring letter by stating:

> Many thanks for your kind invitation to be with you on the 30th anniversary of the United Israel World Union. I am familiar with your great work emphasizing the universality of the Hebraic Heritage, and I wish from the bottom of my heart that I could be with you in person. Unfortunately, I will be out of the country on that May weekend, so I can only do the next best thing by extending to you my heartiest felicitations on this auspicious occasion and my best wishes for a successful continuation of your program in the decades that lie ahead.

Davis continued with a full-page explanation of his own motivation for conversion to the Jewish faith, concluding his moving message with: "I wanted to be a part of this people." The full content of Sammy Davis, Jr's letter to David Horowitz appeared in the summer, 1973 issue of the *United Israel Bulletin*.

During a late summer luncheon sponsored by the American Zionist Federation, Horowitz met with world famous Nazi Hunter Simon Wiesenthal. The two discussed the case of Bishop Valerian D. Trifa and other World War II criminals still at large in the US. On a brief visit to America on behalf of his Vienna Institute, Mr. Wiesenthal's dedicated efforts had been instrumental in the arrest of over 1,100 war criminals. Wiesenthal made it a special point to note that *eleven million* civilians were murdered by the Nazis, among whom were six million Jews. "It is incumbent upon Jewish leaders," he emphasized, "to mention the fact that almost an equal number of non-Jews were murdered and that it is therefore not only a Jewish issue but a Christian one as well." At the time Wiesenthal was working on 330 additional cases.

In the Middle East, Egyptian President Anwar Sadat was again threatening war with Israel unless the United States forced Israel to accept his interpretation of UN Resolution 242 and calling for total Israeli withdrawal from territories taken in 1967. Still, most observers remained skeptical of his rhetoric—and for good reason.

On October 6, 1973 on Yom Kippur, the holiest day in the Jewish calendar (and during the Muslim holy month of Ramadan), it happened. Egypt and Syria opened a coordinated surprise attack against Israel. The equivalent of the total forces of NATO in Europe were mobilized on Israel's borders. On the Golan Heights approximately 180 Israeli tanks faced an onslaught of 1,400 Syrian tanks. Along the Suez Canal, 600,000 Egyptian soldiers backed by 2,000 tanks and 550 aircraft attacked fewer than 500 Israeli defenders with only three tanks. Nine Arab states, including four non-Middle Eastern nations actively aided the Egyptian-Syria war effort. The Soviets gave wholehearted political support to the Arab invasion while pouring weapons into the region.

This led to the October 12th emergency airlift order of supplies and arms by US President Richard Nixon. Between October 14th and November 14th, the United States provided 22,000 tons of equipment transported to Israel by air and sea. The airlift alone involved 566 flights. To pay for this infusion of weapons, Nixon asked Congress for and received $2.2 billion in emergency aid for Israel.

Thrown on the defensive during the first two days of fighting, Israel mobilized its reserves and began to counterattack. What followed, history tells us, was an epic period of intense engagement. In the greatest tank battle since the Germans and Russians fought at Kursk in World War II, roughly 1,000 Israeli and Egyptian tanks massed in the western Sinai from October 12th until the 14th. On the 14th, Israeli forces destroyed 250 Egyptian tanks in the first two hours of fighting. By late afternoon the Israeli forces had routed the enemy accomplishing a feat equal to Montgomery's victory over Rommel in World War II.

By October 18th, Israeli forces marched with little opposition toward Cairo. About the same time, Israeli troops were on the outskirts of Damascus. This reversal of fortune brought us to the brink of nuclear war. The Soviets began to panic and on October 24th threatened to intervene in the fighting. Responding to the Soviet threat, President Nixon put the US military on alert, increasing its readiness for deployment of conventional and nuclear forces. The danger of a US-Soviet conflict was real. In fact, this was the closest the superpowers had come to a nuclear confrontation since the Cuban Missile Crisis in 1962.

What followed was an intense period of diplomatic efforts to gain a cease-fire with which Israel reluctantly complied, largely because of U.S. pressure and because the next military moves would have been to attack the two Arab capitals, actions few believed to be politically wise. At the end of the fighting 2,688 Israeli soldiers had been killed. Combat deaths for Egypt and Syria totaled approximately 7,700 and 3,500, respectively. Ironically, the United States had helped save Israel by its resupply effort and then rescued Egypt by forcing Israel to accept the ceasefire. Egyptian-Israeli disengagement talks began on October 28th. It was the first time in twenty-five years that Egyptian and Israeli officials formally communicated with each other. In January 1974, Israel and Egypt negotiated a disengagement agreement thanks to U.S. Secretary of State Henry Kissinger's shuttle diplomacy. Over the next two years, Kissinger brokered a series of bilateral agreements between Egypt and Israel, setting the stage for the Camp David peace process of the late 1970s.

Professor Abraham Kotsuji, the noted Japanese scholar who discovered his faith through the Torah and who, in 1959, was officially inducted into traditional Judaism in Jerusalem, died on October 31st in Japan following an illness while in New York. He was seventy-four years old. A Bible scholar and researcher, Professor Kotsuji was the author of several books including a textbook on Hebrew grammar and a biographical work entitled: *From Tokyo to Jerusalem*. Professor Kotsuji, who was credited with having saved many Jewish refugees in World War II, was first welcomed to America some twelve years earlier by United Israel World Union at a reception given in the home of Dr. Paul Riebenfeld. Throughout his many visits to America, Professor Kotsuji was featured in numerous articles published in issues of the *United Israel Bulletin*. According to his wishes, Dr. Kotsuji was flown to Israel and interned in the Holy City of Jerusalem on November 9, 1973.

Chapter 28

I am Joseph, Thy Brother

Ms. Pelpina W. Sahureka, Foreign Minister of the Republic of the South Moluccans, whose Government-in-Exile is headquartered in Holland, addressed a special meeting of United Israel World Union held at the Mount Nebo Congregation in Manhattan on February 3, 1974. Ms. Sahureka reported on the background history of the heroic South Moluccan people and their unceasing struggle to regain their independence. The Republic of the South Moluccans is a self-proclaimed republic in the Maluku Islands, a part of the vast Indonesian archipelago. Indonesian forces seized the main Maluku Islands in November 1950. The American South Moluccan delegation submitted a memorandum to the United Nations stating its case for recognition of independence. Correspondent David Horowitz was among the many UN supporters of the three million South Moluccan people in their struggle to regain their independence.

The political fallout in Israel following the Yom Kippur War was well underway. The fact that the Arabs had succeeded in surprising the IDF and inflicting heavy losses in the early part of the war against the Israeli army was a traumatic experience for Israel. The government reacted to the public's calls for an inquiry by establishing a commission chaired by Shimon Agranat, the president of Israel's Supreme Court. The Agranat Commission published its preliminary findings on April 2, 1974, holding six people particularly responsible for Israel's failings. Although it absolved Prime Minister Golda Meir and Defense Minister Moshe Dayan of all responsibility public calls for their resignations intensified. On April 11th, Golda Meir resigned. Her cabinet followed suit including Dayan. A new government was seated in June, and

Yitzhak Rabin, who had spent most of the war as an advisor to IDF Chief of Staff David Elazar in an unofficial capacity, became Prime Minister.

It seemed the fallout from the war's result even reverberated in Moscow where Soviet leader Leonid Brezhnev pitched the classic "hissy fit." According to historian Anatoly Chernyaev, on November 4, 1973, Brezhnev unloaded:

> We have offered them (the Arabs) a sensible way for so many years. But no, they wanted to fight. Fine! We gave them technology, the latest, the kind even Vietnam didn't have. They had double superiority in tanks and aircraft, triple in artillery, and in air defense and anti-tank weapons they had absolute supremacy. And what? Once again, they were beaten. Once again, they screamed for us to come save them. Sadat woke me up in the middle of the night twice over the phone saying, "Save us!" He demanded that we send Soviet troops, and immediately! No! We are not going to fight for them.

Brezhnev's tirade sounded more like an enraged fan whose team had just suffered another unbearable loss than that of statesman speak.

In the summer 1974 issue of *United Israel Bulletin*, an announcement was made that Holt, Rinehart and Winston, Inc. had published the book believed to have influenced Pope John XXIII and the Second Vatican Council to reject the charge of collective Jewish guilt for the crucifixion in English translation. Entitled *Jesus and Israel,* it is the work of the noted French historian Jules Isaac who, as a result of the Nazi occupation of France in 1940, was led to delve into the origin and widespread development of anti-Semitism. The writing was begun in 1943 and finished in 1946, during which period his wife and daughter were killed in a concentration camp. It chronicles the martyrs, killed by Hitler's Nazis, simply because their name was Isaac. The book was dedicated to them.

In his volume, Professor Isaac, who died in 1963 at the age of eighty-six, charges that "anti-Judaism will retain its virulence as long as the Christian churches and peoples do not recognize their responsibility to correct the latent anti-Semitism being taught in all its forms, an interpretation of which I am absolutely convinced is contrary to the truth and love of him who was the Jew, Jesus." *Jesus and Israel* was translated into English by Sally Abeles, and contains an interpretive forward by Claire Huchet Bishop, a writer and lecturer on social and spiritual movements in France, to whom Isaac entrusted the responsibility for the American editions of his works. First published in France in 1949, and in a revised edition there in 1959, it "rocked European Christians' complacency, particularly in France and in Rome," Mrs. Bishop declared. Two of the direct results it produced, she stated, were the revision of French catechisms and textbooks, and Jules Isaac's private audience with Pope John XXIII in 1960.

The incredible story of Angelo Giuseppe Roncalli who became Pope Saint John XXIII and reigned from October 28, 1958 until his death in 1963, is one of a dedicated servant of God. One of the most popular Popes of all time, he inaugurated a new era in the history of the Roman Catholic Church by his openness to change, shown especially in his convoking of the Second Vatican Council. Though Pope John XXIII did not live to see the Vatican Council to completion, he was responsible for the creation of several important documents that pertained to Catholic reconciliation with Jewish people.

In 1960 a delegation of American Jewish leaders presented the Pope with a Torah Scroll to express gratitude for the Jewish lives he had saved during the holocaust. He replied to the group: "We are all sons of the same heavenly Father. Among us there must ever be the brightness of love and its practice." He concluded: "I am Joseph, your brother." By quoting the biblical self-revelation of Joseph to his brothers in Egypt, he was making a statement pregnant with theological implications.

In October of 1960, Pope John XXIII received French scholar Jules Isaac, whose personal family losses during the holocaust had caused him to study the origins of anti-Semitism in Christianity's ancient "teaching of contempt" against Judaism. The Pope had read his book, *Jesus and Israel.* The Pope responded positively, placing the issue on the Council's agenda and paving the way for long overdue changes in establishing a new, positive understanding of the Jewish People in covenant with God. The man known affectionately as "Good Pope John" died on June 3, 1963. His life's example and the changes he fostered live on. So also, is the following haunting indictment he left behind to a church in need of righting an ancient wrong.

In 1965, the Catholic Herald newspaper quoted Pope John XXIII as saying:

> We are conscious today that many, many centuries of blindness have cloaked our eyes so that we can no longer see the beauty of Thy chosen people nor recognize in their faces the features of our privileged brethren. We realize that the mark of Cain stands upon our foreheads. Across the centuries our brother Abel has lain in blood, which we drew, or shed tears we caused by forgetting Thy love. Forgive us for the curse we falsely attached to their name as Jews. Forgive us for crucifying Thee a second time in their flesh. For we know not what we did.

The first of a series of articles abridged from the late Oscar S. Straus' book, *The Origin of the Republican Form of Government* appeared in the 1974 summer edition of United Israel Bulletin. Mr. Straus (1850-1926) served as Minister Plenipotentiary to Turkey under Presidents Grover Cleveland Alexander and William McKinley. Out of print at the time, the Jewish Publication Society first published the volume. The series of articles sought to reveal that the Founding Fathers received their inspiration in the establishment of the American Republic from precedents of government by and for the people as set forth ages ago by the ancient Hebrews under Moses, Joshua and the Judges. In his brilliant essays, Mr. Straus makes it clear that the Republic established by Moses constituted a perfect pattern for the form of government instituted by the Continental Congress. He reveals that the Republic of Moses had its (1) Chief Executive in the Judge or Shophet; (2) an elected Senate of seventy elders, usually referred to as the Sanhedrin, and (3) an Assembly or "Congregation" as distinct from "all Israel." The democratic spirit of the Mosaic Republic, he shows, is borne out by the fact that the people themselves "selected" or "appointed" their leaders. The Levites, however, were separated from the other tribes, thus keeping the priesthood apart from the State government.

As the year wound down, The Brotherhood Synagogue had found a new home. It had been forced by the acts of a new strong-willed pastor, to abandon its Greenwich Village sanctuary they had shared with a Presbyterian Church in a venture of brotherhood for nearly twenty years. The former "Friends Meeting House" at twenty-eight Gramercy Park South, an imposing structure that, in 1965, was designated as a landmark building by the Landmark Preservation Commission of the City of New York, was to be their new location. Rabbi Irving Block, founder of the Synagogue and who, together with the late Reverend Jesse Stitt had functioned in harmony and genuine brotherhood for some nineteen years until the new reactionary pastor took over the church, expressed great pleasure in having the landmark building as the new home of his Brotherhood Synagogue. Rabbi Block was a great friend and supporter of United Israel World Union. In later years, United Israel held several of its annual meetings at the Brotherhood Synagogue's new location in Gramercy Park.

On August 9, 1974, Richard M. Nixon became the first President of the United States to resign from office, an action taken to avoid being removed by impeachment and conviction in response to his role in the Watergate scandal. Vice President Gerald R. Ford became our 38th President.

Chapter 29
Waging a New Diplomatic War

On November 29, 1974, David Horowitz wrote a letter to King Hussein of Jordan on the question of Jordanian-Israeli relations. In the letter, Mr. Horowitz referred to the past correspondence he had with Hussein's late grandfather Abdullah Bin al-Hussein that dealt in detail with the common heritage shared by both peoples based on the Bible and the Koran. A few copies of the past exchanges were included in the letter to the King. Horowitz concluded the letter by saying: "I hold the strong view that Allah-Jehovah would surely want you to assert yourself, not as a bystander, but to seek a common understanding for a settlement on the whole Palestinian question with the children of Jacob-Israel. My prayer is that Allah inspires you to act according to His will, as based upon the written word."

In less than two weeks, Mr. Horowitz received a response dated December 11, 1974 written on the Jordanian royal stationary. The message read:

Dear Mr. Horowitz, upon personal instruction from His Majesty King Hussein I, I have the honor to write you conveying a message of thanks and gratitude for your thoughtfulness and sincerity shown to His Majesty in your letter of November 29, 1974. Your genuine concern for peace and justice is very much shared by His Majesty and under his leadership Jordan continues to strive towards that goal. With my highest regards and very best wishes, yours sincerely, (signed) Marwan Kasim, Secretary-General of the Royal Hashemite Court.

In October 1974, the Arab states decided at the Rabat Conference to recognize the PLO (Palestinian Liberation Organization) as the sole legitimate representative of the Palestinian people. This gave the organization an immediate political authenticity that was further bolstered by its international recognition by the United Nations, who invited PLO leader Yasir Arafat to address the General Assembly on November 13th.

The Israelis certainly weren't thrilled with this shift in strategy. Now it would be necessary to fight the PLO on two fronts: military and political. With this shift from strictly terrorist activities to waging a diplomatic war against Israel it became fashionable to refer to the Arab-Israeli conflict as the cause of all instability in the Middle East. Policymakers, the press, and pro-Arab scholars all repeated the mantra that it was the root of all evil in the region, as did the Arabists at the State Department. The problem with this view was that it was patently false as anyone familiar with Middle Eastern affairs could plainly see. Multiple conflicts were brewing or exploding that had nothing whatsoever to do with Israel or the Palestinians.

David Horowitz, the old-school journalist who wasn't afraid to speak his mind and who covered the 29th session of the UN General Assembly when Arafat spoke, called it "a shameful spectacle of a gangster chief being honored as a head of a legitimate state." Horowitz further called it "scandalous that the terrorist organization leader would be allowed to vent his poisonous venom at a reborn Judea within these halls originally created for peace and justice."

In another key Middle Eastern event on March 25, 1975, King Faisal of Saudi Arabia was assassinated by his nephew Faisal bin Musaid. Enormously popular, King Faisal was credited with rescuing the country's finances and implementing a policy of modernization and reform. He was honored in many ways: foundations, mosques, cities and highways were renamed in his honor. He was even eulogized by lyricist Robert Hunter in the title track of the Grateful Dead's 1975 album, *Blues for Allah*.

Mr. Yosef Tekoah, one of Israel's foremost diplomats and the chief delegate to the United Nations for the past seven years announced he was leaving the post to return to Israel. He had served during the stormy period of 1968-1975 and would be remembered for his sharp debates on the Palestinian question. Speaking of Tekoah's time as Israel's Ambassador to the UN, David Horowitz remarked: "None can compare in brilliance and greatness of statesmanship to the dynamic and forthright Yosef Tekoah, whose seven years as the clarion voice of Israel reborn here in this world organization has now come to an end." In departing his post as ambassador, Tekoah also offered high praise for correspondent David Horowitz. In a letter to Horowitz dated April 25, 1975, ambassador Tekoah wrote among other things: "May I take this opportunity to express to you my heartfelt gratitude for your sympathy and cooperation and my high esteem of your important work in the cause of the Jewish people and the Jewish State."

Yosef Tekoah returned to Israel and became president of Ben-Gurion University of the Negev. The university was established in 1969 with the purpose of promoting the development of the Negev desert that comprises more than sixty percent of Israel. He was elected chancellor of the university in 1981. Yosef Tekoah and David Horowitz remained friends and continued to communicate after Tekoah's return to Israel.

Having entered its fourth decade of global activities in championing the Torah faith and supporting Israel, United Israel World Union held its 32nd Annual Meeting on June 1, 1975 at the Horowitz home in Manhattan. Special guest at the meeting was the renowned radio commentator and journalist, Shelomo ben Israel, whose widely acclaimed broadcasts were heard each Sunday over New York's radio station WEVD. Key items on the agenda were an update on United Israel's past year activities, a review of current UN issues and the latest update on the South Moluccans progress toward attaining independence.

The Suez Canal finally reopened on June 5, 1975; it had been closed since the Egyptian blockade of the canal during the 1967 Six Day War.

In July 1975, David Horowitz exchanged letters with an old friend, Menachem Begin, updating him on various items of interest on the political front at the UN. Knowing also that Begin had been an admirer of the Revisionist Zionist, Ze'ev Jabotinsky in his youth, Horowitz included a tribute he had previously written about Jabotinsky. Begin immediately responded in a letter dated August 1, 1975, thanking David for the political material. He also remarked: "Your tribute to Ze'ev Jabotinsky based on Mr. Gilioni's book is very touching." Vowing to continue his efforts to convince the people to take a firm stand against the pressures being exerted against them in Israel and thanking Horowitz again for his good work, Begin included his best wishes for continued success. Few could have predicted the degree of his huge political success that lay just ahead, included a crowning achievement very few could have imagined at the time.

On August 25, 1975, the Brazilian Academy of Humanities Executive Council, at a session held at San Paulo, Brazil, voted unanimously to award UN correspondent David Horowitz with the *"Pro Mundi Beneficio"* medal along with a special diploma for his humanitarian activities and for his lifelong battle against bigotry and former Nazi war criminals.

September had arrived, and it was an especially tough month for President Gerald Ford when his agenda included California stops. While in Sacramento on September 5, 1975, he survived an attempted assassination by Charles Manson follower Lynette "Squeaky" Fromme, who fired a Colt .45-caliber handgun at the president. As she pulled the trigger, Larry Buendorf, a secret service agent, grabbed the gun and Fromme was taken into custody.

Seventeen days later, as President Ford was leaving the St. Francis Hotel in downtown San Francisco, Sara Jane Moore, standing in a crowd of onlookers across the street, fired a single round from a .38-caliber revolver at Ford, missing because of a faulty gun sight. Just as she fired a second round, retired Marine Oliver Sipple grabbed at the gun and deflected her shot. The bullet struck a wall about six inches to the right of President Ford's head. President Gerald Ford had somehow miraculously survived two assassination attempts within three weeks of each other in the same state.

Chapter 30
Doing the Right Thing in the White House

At 9:00 a.m. on June 27, 1976, 228 passengers boarded Air France flight 139 from Ben Gurion Airport in Israel to Charles De Gaulle Airport in Paris, with a stopover in Greece. After takeoff from Athens, four Palestinian and German terrorists hijacked the plane. The plane was diverted to the warm welcome of Ugandan despot Idi Amin in Entebbe. Soon afterward, the hijackers freed the French crew and non-Jewish passengers while retaining 105 Jewish and Israeli hostages. The hijackers had the stated objective to free forty Palestinian and pro-Palestinian militants imprisoned in Israel, along with thirteen other prisoners held in four other countries, in exchange for the hostages. They threatened to kill the hostages if their prisoner release demands were not met. The threat led to the planning of a rescue operation including preparation for armed resistance from Ugandan military troops, if all attempts at a diplomatic solution failed.

On July 4, 1976, as the United States observed its bicentennial year with coast-to-coast celebrations of the 200th anniversary of the Declaration of Independence, Operation Entebbe took place. Israeli transport planes carrying 100 commandos had flown over 2,500 miles to Uganda for the rescue operation. A twenty-nine-man crack commando unit led by Lt. Colonel Yonatan Netanyahu had been assembled for the actual assault and rescue attempt. The entire operation, which took place at night, lasted fifty-three minutes. All the hijackers, three hostages, and forty-five Ugandan soldiers were killed. One hundred and two hostages were rescued. Five Israeli commandos were wounded and only one, the unit commander; Lt. Colonel Yonatan Netanyahu was killed.

The operation at Entebbe, which had the military codename "Operation Thunderbolt," was renamed officially by the government of Israel as "Operation Yonatan" in memory of the unit's leader. Thirty years of age and a former student at Harvard University and the Hebrew University of Jerusalem, Yonatan, the older brother of Benjamin Netanyahu the current Prime Minister of Israel, was a brilliant military commander and tactician. As a result of the operation, the United States military developed rescue teams modeled on the Entebbe rescue. One notable attempt to imitate it was "Operation Eagle Claw," a failed rescue of fifty-three American embassy personnel held hostage in Tehran during the Iranian hostage crisis.

The Bicentennial Year Was Also an Election Year.

On November 2, 1976, America elected the relatively unknown former governor of Georgia, Jimmy Carter, the Democratic candidate, over the incumbent President Gerald Ford the Republican candidate. Becoming president upon Richard Nixon's resignation on August 9, 1974, Ford thus became the only sitting president who had never been elected to national office. Carter narrowly won the election, becoming the first president elected from the Deep South since Zachary Taylor in 1848.

In a little-known political oddity, on December 10, 1976, the first F-15 fighter aircraft arrived in Israel from the United States. The fact that they landed in Israel on a Friday evening, after the start of the Sabbath, caused a political crisis prompting the religious parties in the Knesset to topple the first Yitzhak Rabin government.

In 1977, David Horowitz was back in the Holy Land. The occasion marked a conference of the World Federation of Jewish Journalists held in the capital of Israel. The group also met with Israel's President Ephraim Katzir, himself a world-renowned scientist, during a visit to the stately presidential mansion in Jerusalem. Horowitz later had a brief private meeting with Katzir, updating him on the state of UN affairs.

Following the conference, Horowitz remained in Israel and, as usual, scheduled a busy agenda. Among many appointments were meetings with leaders of the "Friends of Converts in Israel," a Tel Aviv based organization, with authors, Dr. Israel Ben Zeev and Mordecai Alfanderi, and he was the guest of the noted newspaperman, Moshe Ben Shachar, the *World Union Press* correspondent in Israel. Horowitz also made a quick trip to Safad and Biria in the Galilee to visit his devoted friends, Esther and Eliezer Tritto and family, who were among the many former Italian Catholics who had embraced the Torah faith and migrated to Israel.

When Jimmy Carter was sworn in as 39th President of the United States, on January 20, 1977, the time appeared ripe for a new peace initiative. Carter, a deeply religious man, felt a connection to the Holy Land and he believed he could do what all others had failed to accomplish—to bring peace to the Middle East. Immediately after taking office, he became actively involved in Middle Eastern politics.

In the light of recent U.S. State Department maneuverings taken by Secretary of State Cyrus Vance regarding Israel, correspondent David Horowitz was inspired to write directly to the new president on February 22, 1977. In the lengthy message, David congratulated Carter on his election win and his selection of Mr. Andrew Young as the White House spokesman at the United Nations. He mentioned the fact that both President Carter and Mr. Young were blessed with a strong biblical background, the president as a Sunday school teacher and Mr. Young as a minister.

Moving directly to the main point of the letter, David stated:

Since you and Mr. Young, as contrasted with so many others in government, firmly believe in the biblical blueprint and in its prophecies, I would like to set forth as a reminder some of the promises made in the Bible with respect to the resurrection of Israel in her ancient homeland. You are undoubtedly familiar with them.

After mentioning a recent UN column that he had written regarding Ambassador Young's first appearance at the UN, Horowitz continued:

> Indeed, President Carter, you and I know that the biblical mandate for Israel's presence in the land of the Prophets, according to the boundaries set forth by our Creator, is absolute and beyond dispute. So too is the mandate adjudicating the borders of Israel's cousins, the Arabs.
>
> The children of Esau and Ishmael were allotted and blessed with vast territories to the east and south of the land of Canaan, territories that the Bible holds inviolate. Thus, the borders of the territories for all the children of Abraham, including the Arabs, were clearly defined in the biblical blueprint. But the promise relative to the deed to Palestine as "an everlasting possession," was passed down from Abraham to Isaac and then only to Jacob-Israel.

After quoting key verses to support this position, Horowitz continued his appeal:

> My dear President Carter, as you must certainly be aware, all the biblical Prophets predicted the return of the children of Israel to their homeland. That we have lived to see this happen in our lifetime is proof of the veracity of these prophecies. This is exactly what we have seen happen in the reborn State of Israel where, since the end of World War II, the Hitlerian escapees have been and are still being healed.
>
> The present-day descendants of Ishmael and Esau, Israel's cousins, the Arabs, already possess the vast territories promised them in the Bible. It might be wise for them not to begrudge their kin, the children of Jacob, their very tiny little land but to welcome them back to the Holy Land and live in peaceful coexistence with them to the benefit of the entire crescent region.

Mentioning what he had witnessed at the UN during his thirty years of coverage, Horowitz stated that it was clear to him that a higher power was at work in the affairs of men and nations. Citing Israel as the best proof of this, he said: "we are all witnesses."

The fearless writer then summed up his message to the new President:

Surely it is this higher power that placed you, Jimmy Carter, a man of spirit and justice, into the most exalted office in the world. Why did this happen at this critical period in mankind's history? The answer to this will have to become manifest in tests and challenges that will face the White House. As Harry Truman, in 1948, stood up against his own advisors in the State Department and shocked the world by his recognition of Israel it is my belief that Jimmy Carter will likewise do and follow the dictates of his own heart with what he thinks is right in the way of God's justice and ordained plan.

The three-page letter to President Carter read like the oracle of a modern-day prophet and it was not the first time that David Horowitz was moved to challenge a sitting president to "do what is right" regarding the biblical blueprint.

The first, of course was Harry Truman himself, who was the first leader among the nations to formally recognize the nation of Israel reborn. Like another key piece in the puzzle, on May 17, 1977, The Likud Party, led by Menachem Begin, won the election in Israel, ending almost thirty years of rule by the left-wing alignment and its predecessor, Mapai.

Whatever forces might indeed be at work in the affairs of men and nations, the bombshell event that was to follow later in the year could only be described as historic and stunning. David Horowitz would refer to it as "a touch of the messianic."

Chapter 31

It Happened in the City of David

It was high summer 1977. New President Jimmy Carter was settling into office and determined to bring peace to the Middle East. Initially, Carter favored a comprehensive approach, whereby all the outstanding issues of the Arab-Israeli conflict could be addressed simultaneously at an international conference. Such a conference would include Israel, the Arab states, and the key powers of the world. Carter proposed holding the conference in Geneva.

The Soviets and most Arab states welcomed the Geneva formula, but Israel strongly objected to it. Israel feared it would be outnumbered at a multilateral conference and forced to make bigger concessions than it wished. It also preferred to deal with the Arab states individually. Israel was also determined to keep the Soviet Union out of Arab-Israeli diplomacy.

Israel's objections, and strong domestic pressure within the U.S., caused Carter to begin backing away from his own proposal. President Anwar Sadat of Egypt also became convinced that no Geneva conference would be possible and decided to return to a bilateral process approach.

David Horowitz heard from an old friend when he received a letter from former Ambassador to the UN, Yosef Tekoah. At that time the president of the Ben Gurion University in the Negev, Tekoah expressed deep appreciation for clippings of a review Horowitz had written about his last book, *In the Face of the Nations: Israel's Struggle for Peace*, published by Simon and Shuster. He also thanked David for the issues of the *United Israel Bulletin* he received.

In late August, David Horowitz welcomed the Reverend Vendyl Jones, a former Baptist minister who left the ministry to study Hebraica and engage in excavations in Israel. The two-hour interview was conducted at David's UN office. Discussing the newly elected Prime Minister, Menachem Begin, Jones called the former Irgun leader a "military and political genius and a true statesman." Justifying Begin's heroic struggle against the British in Palestine during the Irgun underground days, Jones said, "It is totally unfair to categorize him as a terrorist. If he were, so were Chaim Salomon and George Washington who did the same thing to the same British government on different soil." Jones expressed his belief that with Begin, peace was closer than ever before.

As the notion of a Geneva conference faded, Anwar Sadat grew increasingly impatient. Through a variety of secret contacts, many conducted in Morocco with the assistance of King Hassan, the Israelis conveyed to Sadat the message that they were prepared to trade land for peace. Sadat decided to make a bold gesture and announced to the Egyptian parliament on November 9th that he was prepared to go to Jerusalem and speak directly to the Israeli parliament, the Knesset, if that would help bring peace.

A key to building trust between Begin and Sadat was the Israeli decision to pass on intelligence that the Mossad (the Israeli government's intelligence agency) had collected of an assassination plot against Sadat. The would-be killers were Palestinians backed by Libya. Based on the Israeli information, Sadat had all the conspirators arrested and launched an airstrike against Libyan targets. Sadat was indeed grateful, and the incident helped to pave the way for the peace negotiations.

Realizing the opportunity, Menachem Begin formally extended an invitation. Sadat accepted and in an unprecedented move for an Arab leader, traveled to Jerusalem on November 19, 1977 where he met with Israeli Prime Minister Begin and spoke before the Knesset. The bold move stunned the international community and was met with outrage in most of the Arab world.

It is difficult to understate the impact of Sadat's gesture. His presence in Israel broke an Arab policy of not dealing publicly with the Jewish state since its creation in 1948. He had achieved a remarkable psychological breakthrough that could not have been accomplished with regular diplomacy. For the first time, Israelis saw an Arab leader extend his hand in friendship, and in their capital.

Meanwhile, the radical Arabs: the PLO, Syria, Libya, Yemen, Iraq and Algeria, were fuming over the bombshell event of Egyptian President Anwar Sadat's world-shaking visit to Israel. Stunned by the unbelievable happening, Israel's enemies at the UN were thrown off base. David Horowitz reported that the embittered and bewildered Syrian Ambassador described the Egyptian visit in a speech before the General Assembly as a bad dream. In an anxious tone, the Ambassador lamented "People all over the world rub their eyes in disbelief. They listen in amazement. Are we truly awake or are we dreaming? Is this one of a series of science-fiction illusions or are we still on earth?"

In one of his regular columns, Horowitz provided a response:

Indeed, it was not a dream. It happened in the City of David, in Jerusalem of biblical and prophetic renown. A descendent of the Pharaohs, spiritually imbued, communed with a son of Israel, mighty in the Torah-faith of Moses when Anwar Sadat and Menachem Begin found common ground in their common ancestor Abraham.

In a beautifully poetic style, Horowitz described the scene and its implications;

The great Prophet Isaiah came back to life in the modern setting of the Knesset as the speaker, introducing the noted Egyptian visitor, read out before the eyes and ears of the world the famous peace-passage describing the final redemption of mankind. There was something truly biblical to what the world witnessed in the Holy City, a touch of the messianic.

Horowitz continued, "Throughout the weekend visit, people everywhere saw and heard via satellite, the son of the Torah and the disciple of the Koran gave voice to the will of the Almighty for peace among brethren as they both invoked Providence for guidance and prayed for a successful outcome of the mission."

Leading commentators and columnists were moved to put special emphasis on this Biblical-Koranic theme. Noted journalist and radio commentator, Shelomo ben-Israel, broadcasting over radio station WEVD in New York, called the Jerusalem event "one of the miracles of our times, the significance of which only the future would reveal." Both the Libyan and Iraqi spokesmen, bemoaning the "tragedy" that had befallen the Arab Nation, later outdid the Syrian Ambassador's reaction at the UN in vehemence and vituperation. Calling it "painful to see," the Libyan delegate cited the "serious damage" Sadat had inflicted on the Arab cause of destiny.

On December 2, 1977, representatives from Syria, Iraq, Libya, Algeria, South Yemen and the PLO met in Libya to discuss ways of stopping the Israeli-Egyptian peace process. Three days later, Egypt cut diplomatic ties with Syria, Iraq, Libya, Algeria and South Yemen. That didn't take long. Sadat had made it very clear that he would not be deterred. Sadat's historic trip to Jerusalem caused enormous excitement throughout the world.

President Carter himself was greatly encouraged by this development. He dropped his plans for an international conference and threw his support behind Sadat's bilateral initiative. Menachem Begin and Anwar Sadat met again in Ismailia, Egypt on Christmas Day in 1977, but the meeting did not produce an agreement. The Egyptian president was holding out for more territory and wanted to give less than full peace in return. But, little progress was made over the next several months. President Carter also met personally with Sadat and the two men began to develop a close personal relationship that helped bring the countries together.

The 34th Annual Meeting of United Israel World Union was held in the Empire State offices of Vice President Harry Leventhal on February 19, 1978. Key reports were given on the activities of the organization and the state of UN affairs regarding the Egypt-Israel peace initiative.

In the opening months of 1978, Egypt and Israel still had little to show for their efforts to achieve peace. To jump-start the process in the summer, Carter, ignoring his advisors' counsel, invited Sadat and Begin to come to Camp David for a summit meeting and negotiate directly with each other, with Carter himself serving as intermediary. Carter felt that by getting them to Camp David, away from the press and out of the glare of publicity and away from their own political constituencies, he had a better chance to bring them to an understanding of each other's positions. Egyptian President Anwar Sadat and Israeli Prime Minister Menachem Begin both accepted President Carter's invitation. What had begun in the City of David was about to continue in the United States at a Camp called David.

Chapter 32
Counsel for the Defense

During the spring of 1977, David Horowitz ran into an old friend, Paul O'Dwyer, at the screening of *Operation Thunderbolt,* the account of the dramatic Entebbe rescue operation. At that time, O'Dwyer was president of the City Council of New York. A prominent attorney in the law firm of O'Dwyer and Bernstein, he had known Horowitz since the days of the Jewish underground when Prime Minister Menachem Begin headed the Irgun. Both Paul and his late brother William O'Dwyer, a former mayor of the city of New York, were active on the American scene in dedicated support of the Jewish struggle for independence. Little did Horowitz know, at the time, how important the chance meeting and warm visit was to become later on.

David Horowitz's relentless battle against Nazi war criminals was fueled with profound personal emotions. He had been instrumental in reactivating the case against the notorious Romanian Nazi war criminal Bishop Valerian D. Trifa, resulting in his deportation. Now, based upon information supplied by a Romanian-American Christian, Dean Milhovan, Horowitz was attempting to expose yet another Hungarian-Transylvanian with a Nazi past who was living in the US.

While living in Palestine in 1927, he married a Polish Jew, Pola Kleinowa. After spending six months with her parents in Poland, where a son Emmanuel was born, Horowitz then returned alone to the U.S. with plans for his family to follow. But Pola delayed departure several times, eventually remaining in Poland for ten years until she died of a cancerous tumor in 1938. Horowitz wrote to his father-in-law, Loeble Klein, and contacted the American Consulate General in efforts to have Emmanuel sent to him in America. The boy's grandfather refused, choosing instead to wait until he was older. Emmanuel never got the chance to grow up. His life ended at Auschwitz.

On April 29, 1977, Horowitz wrote a letter to Congressman Edward I. Koch of New York to inform him about Hungarian community issues and a suspected troublemaker with a Nazi-fascist past. Horowitz wrote, among other things,

> The purpose of my letter to you at this time is to alert you to the fact that in the U.S. today are a number of Hungarian emigres, old-time fascists, who are stirring up much trouble in the legitimate Hungarian and Romanian-American communities. One of these troublemakers resides in New York City. His name is Ferenc Koreh.

Ferenc Koreh did indeed have such a past. He was a member of the Hungarian "Arrow and the Cross" Nazi party. During the years 1941-1944, he was the chief editor of *Szekely Nep,* the largest provincial newspaper in Axis Hungary. During that period, the propagandist published over 200 racist articles that created a climate in Hungary that helped to make Nazi persecution of Jews acceptable.

David Horowitz, the consummate journalist, had begun his expose. In addition to his letter to Congressman Koch, he petitioned many others, including Mario Cuomo, American Jewish Congress, Haifa University, and his UN colleague in Budapest. He also wrote letters to Yad Vashem in Jerusalem and to noted Nazi hunter Simon Wiesenthal. As credible evidence began to surface, Horowitz released expose' articles in issues of the *United Israel Bulletin* and syndicated in other Anglo-Jewish newspapers.

In the summer of 1977, David Horowitz received some shocking news. Hungarian Ferenc Koreh had filed a $3 million libel suit against him. Koreh's suit was based upon a story that appeared in the spring issue of the *United Israel Bulletin* in which he was accused of World War II pro-Nazi activities. The story was based upon charges previously published in the American-Romanian publication *Dreptatia* (The Justice), edited by the Romanian-American Christian writer Dean Milhovan, who was also being sued.

The high-powered Wall Street law firm of Cadwalader, Wickersham and Taft represented Koreh. Horowitz, not having that kind of money for a libel defense lawyer, appealed to several Jewish organizations in vain. Then David happened to remember old friend Paul O'Dwyer. O'Dwyer had just run for a second term as president of the New York City Council, a post in which he had served for five years but lost his bid for re-election to Carol Bellamy. He returned to his law practice. One of his first calls was from his old pal David Horowitz. O'Dwyer recalls the phone conversation in his autobiography, *Counsel for the Defense*:

> "I know you didn't want to lose the election," David said, "but I think God has made you available to me."
> "What's up, David?" I asked.
> "I need you. I'm being sued for libel."
> "Do you have a defense, David?"
> "The best in the world."
> "What is your defense?"
> "Truth! He was a Nazi bastard. I want you to make him eat the ton of papers he served on me. But I want to tell you he's got Cadwalader, Wickersham and Taft on his side."
> "All right, David," I said. "Come right down and tell me again the story of David and Goliath."
>
> It was if I had never been away.

When Horowitz met with O'Dwyer, the entire Koreh episode was recounted to him. After patiently listening to Horowitz, Paul O'Dwyer's response was: "David, let me handle this case. We'll get this guy." Without mentioning money or costs, Paul O'Dwyer took the case. The Horowitz-Milhovan defense, as presented by O'Dwyer of the Wall Street law firm O'Dwyer and Bernstein, proclaimed that the facts contained in the article were true and would be proven at the trial. Horowitz says he confirmed and substantiated the facts through an official of the Romanian government who claimed that written documents proving the charges were in the possession of the government.

On April 26, 1978, David Horowitz wrote another letter to Dr. H. Rosenkranz, Director at Yad Vashem in Jerusalem. After thanking Rosenkranz for directing him to Professor Bela Vago at Haifa University, who was an expert historian on the fascist regime in Hungary, Horowitz related the results of a personal meeting he had with Vago recently at his UN office in New York. David also included copies of key incriminating documents against Koreh in his possession, "for use in the Yad Vashem archives." Horowitz closed his letter to Rosenkranz by stating:

> No doubt thousands of Jews faced their death as a result of Koreh's activities and the time has come for him to be exposed. For some 30 years here in America no one knew that he had been a Nazi. It is important now that Ferenc Koreh be exposed.
>
> At the age of 14, my son Emanuel was butchered at Auschwitz.

Horowitz then wished Mr. Rosenkranz a "Happy Passover."

In June 1978, Nazi-hunter, Simon Wiesenthal provided additional information to attorney Paul O'Dwyer that Koreh had been found guilty by the People's Court of Budapest in 1947 of war crimes that espoused the Nazi cause. What transpired next was two years of depositions, two years of battles between Paul O'Dwyer, the tough Irishman and the equally tough law firm for Koreh. But the incriminating evidence was mounting against Ferenc Koreh.

A trial date was set for July 1, 1979 in Federal Court but was postponed until later in the year. At a pre-trial hearing, attorney Paul O'Dwyer was confronted with a request for a summary judgment from the judge in the presence of Koreh's lawyer. Realizing that O'Dwyer now had the proof of Koreh's guilt, they sought to avoid a public trial.

The civil action suit was settled without trial after a year's proceedings in U.S. District Court in New York. Judge Joseph Griesa read a statement saying Koreh was responsible for the mass murder of Jews. A New Jersey Federal Judge, Maryanne Trump Barry, finally revoked Koreh's citizenship on a summary judgment. Koreh immediately appealed the decision to the 3rd Circuit Court.

In a process that took years, Ferenc Koreh was stripped of his American citizenship by a U.S. District Court in Newark in June 1994 and was ordered deported. A federal appeals court upheld that decision in February 1995.

Ailing Nazi war criminal Ferenc Koreh died on April 1, 1997 at the age of eighty-seven after undergoing surgery. The U.S. government had agreed at the time of the court order that it would not act to remove Koreh from the U.S. unless his rapidly deteriorating health improved. In summary, the thirty-page ruling that contained most of the facts, which the Office of Special Investigations of the Justice Department had taken years to check and verify, had been supplied by David Horowitz and by the Paul O'Dwyer law firm files. The law firm of O'Dwyer and Bernstein donated a major portion of their services to "pursue this case to a positive conclusion" as was stated by Paul O'Dwyer.

Chapter 33
Breakthrough at Camp David

After being expelled from Jordan in 1970 following the "Black September" conflict with Jordanian government forces, the PLO relocated the center of its activities to South Lebanon. In the area adjacent to Israel's northern border, the PLO effectively established a "state within a state" and the region became a staging point for infiltration into Israel and rocket attacks on Israeli towns. By 1978, terrorist infiltrations from Lebanon had become intolerable. After a PLO terrorist attack on two buses near Tel Aviv in which thirty-seven civilians were murdered and seventy-six wounded, Israel decided to act, invading Lebanon on March 14th and advancing to the Litani River.

In response to the invasion, the UN Security Council passed resolutions calling for the withdrawal of Israeli forces. Under pressure from the U.S. and the UN, Israel agreed to withdraw. The UN created a multinational peacekeeping force (UNIFIL) to enforce the mandate and to act as a buffer zone.

Citing a 100-year-old article that appeared in *The Jewish Chronicle* in London on May 2, 1879, David Horowitz published the first of his three-part series on the Ten Northern Tribes in the 1978 summer edition of the *United Israel Bulletin*. Titled "The Jews Are Not Alone," the exposition became one of his most popular compositions.

In the winter edition of the 1978 *Bulletin*, it was revealed that United Israel World Union had established contact with a group of black Jews in Ghana. In a letter from the founder and leader of the Ghana group, Aaron Ahomtre Toakyurufah, to David Horowitz, he reaffirmed their faith in the Torah and expressed sincere gratitude to United Israel for reaching out to them. In his letter, Toakyurufah stated that their community was established on June 22, 1975 at Sefwi-Sui in the Republic of Ghana, and that "We obey the Law and other Jewish customs as expressed in the Torah of our Lord God of Israel and we also cling to the Sabbath." In a touching expression of gratitude, he also indicated that the Jewish community of Ghana observed Saturday, July 1, 1978 as "the Sabbath of Good News" because "it was on that day that we received a letter and literature from the United Israel organization." Further stating, "We lack assistance such as training in Hebrew education and customs," Toakyurufah promised they would be "studying all the literature that United Israel sent to them."

David Horowitz and United Israel would become instrumental in assisting the Ghana community in many ways including educational material they so badly needed and the gift of Siddurim (prayer books) donated by Rabbi Irving Block and the Brotherhood Synagogue in Manhattan. Thirty-eight years later, the Sefwis community in Ghana, West Africa became the subject of a documentary film produced by Canadian film-maker Gabrielle Zilkha titled: "Doing Jewish: A Story from Ghana." Included in the production was the role United Israel played in the community's journey of self-discovery and growth.

"Have we not all one father? Hath not One God created us? Why then do we deal treacherously every man against his brother?" With this challenging universalistic biblical passage from the Prophet Malachi, Yehuda Z. Blum, Israel's new Ambassador to the United Nations, opened his UN maiden speech delivered at a specially arranged press conference after presenting his new credentials to Secretary-General Kurt Waldheim. An escapee of the Bergen-Belsen concentration camp where, at the age of thirteen, he had undergone his Bar Mitzvah, the forty-seven-year-old Blum was taking his place as the latest Israeli spokesman to tackle the vexing perennial problems facing the Jewish State in this parliament of man.

Attending the press conference, David Horowitz reported that the youthful former professor of law delivered a moving message that resonated throughout the room. Calling it "an honor to serve my country and my people in this organization," Blum offered a challenging reminder to the members to "bring the UN back to its very own charter of which espouses those universal principles which were first proclaimed over 3,000 years ago by the prophets of Israel."

Still, a state of war had existed between Egypt and the State of Israel since the establishment of Israel in 1948. Prior to Anwar el-Sadat becoming Egypt's president in 1970, three Arab-Israeli wars had been fought with Israel decisively defeating Egypt in each. As a result of the 1967 war, Israel occupied Egypt's Sinai Peninsula, the 23,500-square-mile peninsula that links Africa with Asia. In October 1973, Egyptian and Syrian forces launched a joint surprise attack against Israel that became known as the Yom Kippur War. Although Egypt had again suffered military defeat against its Jewish neighbor, the initial Egyptian successes greatly enhanced Sadat's prestige in the Middle East and provided him with an opportunity to seek peace.

Following Anwar Sadat's dramatic journey to Jerusalem in November 1977 where he spoke before the Israeli Knesset (Parliament), US President Jimmy Carter invited Sadat and Israeli Prime Minister Menachem Begin to the presidential retreat at Camp David to attempt to negotiate a peace agreement. On September 5, 1978, the three heads of state and their aides arrived at Camp David. A news blackout was subsequently imposed for the duration of the talks. They argued, they haggled and, at one point, personal relations became so badly strained it appeared that the talks might collapse. In the end there were breakthroughs and the framework of a successful peace treaty between Israel and Egypt. Two agreements were signed on September 17, 1978 that came to be known as the Camp David Accords.

The agreements represented a monumental shift in Middle East relations. Menachem Begin had made the startling concessions of not only the entire Sinai, with its settlements and military bases, but also agreed to withdraw from parts of the West Bank and grant the Palestinians a measure of self-rule. In exchange for these tangible compromises, Israel received nothing more than Egyptian promises of a new peaceful relationship. But those commitments were the fulfillment of a thirty-year dream.

Hundreds of thousands of Egyptians lined Cairo's streets when Sadat returned from Camp David. He was hailed as the "hero of peace" and called a Pharaoh by some, but in the rest of the Arab world, not so much. Seventeen hardline Arab nations, reacting to the separate peace with Israel, adopted political and economic sanctions against Egypt. For his willingness to make peace with Israel, Sadat became a hero in the United States. For his willingness to cut a deal that benefited Egypt alone while leaving the Palestinians under Israeli occupation, Sadat was seen as a traitor in the Arab world. For the risks he took to dare seek peace with the Jewish nation, paying the high price of peace was now on the clock.

A little over a month after the conclusion of the Camp David talks, which laid the foundation for a later formal Peace Treaty, Egyptian President Anwar Sadat and Israeli Prime Minister Menachem Begin were jointly awarded the 1978 Nobel Peace Prize for their efforts in bringing about peace between Israel and Egypt. The award was presented in a ceremony on December 10, 1978. The award of the Prize to Anwar Sadat and Menachem Begin could be called historical in the wider sense, in that we only know of one previous peace agreement between Egypt and Israel. This, as Israeli scholars have revealed, took place some 3,000 years ago; it was the peace concluded between King David's son, wise King Solomon, and the Egyptian Pharaoh.

On December 8, 1978, Golda Meir died in Jerusalem at the age of 80. Serving as the fourth Prime Minister of Israel (1969-1974), Meir was in office during the Yom Kippur War, the last with Egypt before peace finally came.

Chapter 34
Takeover in Tehran

Spring was in the air when United Israel World Union held its 35th Annual Meeting at The Brotherhood Synagogue, Gramercy Park South in Manhattan, on March 8, 1979. Rabbi Israel Mowshowitz, former president of the New York Board of Rabbis opened with these remarks: "We gather here in celebration of the 35th anniversary of United Israel World Union which has, throughout the years, been a beacon of light to our people and to the world, a mighty champion of the State of Israel and a disseminator of the spiritual and moral light of Torah to all men."

Speakers at the historic meeting included President David Horowitz, the honoree Harry Leventhal, Bernard G. Sharrow, and Irving J. Block, spiritual leader of The Brotherhood Synagogue. A longtime friend of United Israel, Rabbi Block paid high tribute to the noble work of the movement and to its president and officers.

Following the historic Camp David Accords in September 1978, the months dragged on with additional shuttle diplomacy and grudging compromises between Egypt and Israel. Finally after six months the deal was completed. On March 26, 1979, in a ceremony hosted by U.S. President Jimmy Carter at the White House, Israeli Prime Minister Menachem Begin and Egyptian President Anwar Sadat signed the Israel-Egypt Peace Treaty, the first peace treaty between Israel and an Arab country.

The Arab world reacted angrily to the peace treaty, as it had to the Camp David Accords, which it saw as a "betrayal of the Arab cause." As a result, the Arab League suspended Egypt.

David Horowitz published the last of a three-part series titled: "The Jews are Not Alone" in the spring edition of the *United Israel Bulletin*. The riveting series on the existence and identity of the Ten Lost Tribes was one of his most popular compositions and would inspire widespread interest and response.

Iran was in a state of revolution beginning with a wave of anti-government demonstrations in the summer of 1978. In January 1979, the shah of Iran fled the country, ultimately ending up in Mexico. The Iranian army quickly collapsed, clearing a path for the revolutionaries to seize state power. In February 1979, the exiled Ayatollah Khomeini, whose fundamentalist supporters gained dominant positions in the revolution, triumphantly returned to Iran. It set the stage for a later crisis involving the United States.

In the month commemorating the Balfour Declaration, the UN Partition Vote, and Anwar Sadat's world-shaking visit to Jerusalem, an unusual biographical work titled: *Counsel for the Defense* (Simon and Schuster, New York) was published. Significant, first of all because the author was the staunch friend of Israel, attorney Paul O'Dwyer, former president of the City Council of New York. Additionally, because this was the same Paul O'Dwyer, who had taken on the defense of David Horowitz in a libel suit, filed against him by the former Hungarian Nazi war criminal Ferenc Koreh.

And just who was this fellow O'Dwyer, the spirited liberal voice in New York politics and the friend of UN correspondent David Horowitz? O'Dwyer's amazing story is one which deserves a brief review. The eleventh child of rural schoolteachers, Paul O'Dwyer was born in County Mayo, Ireland. He immigrated to New York at the age of eighteen. He attended Fordham University and St. John's Law School at night while working as a packer, elevator operator, and cargo checker on the Brooklyn waterfront.

A lifelong fighter on behalf of human rights in all spheres of life, O'Dwyer had known David Horowitz since the days of the Jewish Underground when Prime Minister Menachem Begin headed the Irgun. Both Paul and his brother William O'Dwyer, a former mayor of the City of New York, were active on the American scene in dedicated support of the Jewish struggle for independence. In a little-known fact, it was during William O'Dwyer's incumbency as Mayor of New York that the United Nations decided to set up its headquarters at its present site selected from several under consideration. Thanks to Mayor O'Dwyer's considerable skill in negotiating the grant by the Rockefellers, this former slum and slaughterhouse region fronting the East River became the permanent home of the United Nations. David Horowitz attended the UN groundbreaking ceremony and later "watched the UN compound go up brick by brick."

During the critical years of 1946 and 1947 when leaders of Jewry were struggling for recognition of Jewish statehood, Paul O'Dwyer took on the chairmanship of the Lawyers' Committee for Justice in Palestine. He also served as the director of the American League for a free Palestine, in which capacity he came before the United Nations and pleaded for the establishment of a sovereign Jewish state in Israel.

From his humble beginning, O'Dwyer labored to become one of New York's leading defenders of the underclass, fighting for the labor movement and embattled immigrants in the 1940's, against McCarthyism and racial segregation in the 1950's, and against the Vietnam War in the 1960's.

Counsel for the Defense is a terrific book, one resembling a Horatio Alger story with an idealistic theme. An immigrant succeeded in the new country and fought uncompromisingly against human rights abuses and became an advocate for those less fortunate. O'Dwyer, the Irish-born defender of justice, closed his classic autobiography by recounting the case whereby he successfully defended friend and UN Correspondent David Horowitz against the libel suit brought against him by former Nazi war criminal Ferenc Koreh.

An article titled "From Rome to Jerusalem," written by Alexander Schindler, appeared in the winter 1979 edition of the *United Israel Bulletin*. The article was a biographical sketch of Aime Palliere (1875-1949), the former French Jesuit whose spiritual odyssey led him to accept a form of universal Torah faith. Although he never made a full conversion to Judaism, Palliere lived the life of an ardent and ascetic Jew. He became a spiritual guide to the Paris Liberal (Reform) Synagogue and the French Reform movement. He was much sought after as a lecturer and became president of the World Union of Jewish Youth. Aime Palliere's autobiography, *The Unknown Sanctuary: A Pilgrimage from Rome to Israel*, was first published in 1930 by Bloch Publishing Company, New York. David Horowitz and Palliere once corresponded. The original copy of Aime Palliere's historic 1947 letter to Horowitz remains a part of the United Israel archives.

David Horowitz was pleasantly surprised when he received another letter from Aaron Ahomtre-Toakyirifah, spiritual leader of the House of Israel in Ghana. United Israel had assisted the community group by sending educational and study materials, including prayer books, they so badly needed. Ahomtre-Toakyirifah reported on recent activities and a renewed effort to trace their past. He stated, "I have taken upon myself the task of tracing the early settlements of the House of Israel in the Ivory Coast." Ahomtre-Toakyirifah revealed that most of the Jews in the north were taken as slaves and brought to Ghana, the Gold Coast at the time, and to other parts of West Africa. The Arabs conquered those that remained north of the Ivory Coast. A few lucky ones managed to escape and establish settlements in the eastern part of the state. He included a photograph of his grandmother who was 99 years of age and whose mother was taken to Ghana as a slave.

As the decade of the seventies drew to a close, the diplomatic crisis between Iran and the United States would only intensify. Ayatollah Ruhollah Khomeini's religious fundamentalists were poised to seize power in Iran. All they needed was an opening. In the fall of 1979, it was given to them. President Carter had allowed the Shah of Iran to enter the United States to receive advanced medical treatment for cancer. Khomeini's student supporters suspected that the reports of the Shah's illness were a cover story, concocted to get the Shah into the U.S. where he could meet with U.S. intelligence officials and plot his return to Iran. Convinced that the CIA was using the U.S. Embassy as a headquarters for plotting the Shah's return, on November 4, 1979, Iranian students seized the U.S. Embassy in Tehran and took more than sixty American diplomats and citizens hostage. Khomeini, sensing opportunity to consolidate his power in Iran, publicly endorsed the seizure of the embassy, ensuring a protracted captivity for the American hostages.

There was little informed understanding in the United States government about the political implications of this new, fundamentalist regime. Gary Sick, who was on the National Security staff, recalled a meeting in which Vice President Walter Mondale asked the Central Intelligence Agency director Stansfield Turner, "What the hell is an Ayatollah anyway?" Turner said he wasn't sure he knew.

On that reassuring note, we boldly entered a new decade.

Part Four

Chapter 35
Talking Torah with the Prime Minister

In January 1980, David Horowitz, accompanied by his wife Nan, departed to Israel for a two-week sojourn. After a brief stay in Jerusalem, they traveled to Haifa where they were the guests of the Israeli veteran, Jule Amster, heroic commander of the lower city of Haifa during the War of Independence. While in Haifa, the two had lunch with Abraham ben-Schachar, famous author and lecturer. From Haifa, they traveled to the town of Beria, adjacent to historic Safad where they met with old friends Elizer and Esther Tritto and family. The Trittos, close friends of Horowitz for over 30 years, represent a group of Italian Catholic converts who immigrated from the South Italian town of San Nicandro over three decades ago.

Arriving at the northern town of Metulla the next day, Horowitz was driven by the Israeli Government Press Office guide, Samuel Becker to the border crossing where Israeli guards escorted them into Lebanon, their final destination. Sam Becker had agreed to escort Horowitz into Lebanon to meet with Francis Rizk, spokesman for Major Saad Haddad, the founder and head of the South Lebanon Army (SLA) during the Lebanese Civil War. For years Haddad was closely collaborating and receiving arms and political support from Israel against Lebanese government forces, Hezbollah, and the Syrian army. Rizk reported that Major Haddad had lost total respect for the UN. The United Nations Interim Force in Lebanon (UNIFIL) had failed to prevent infiltration of terrorists into the south and according to Rizk, the PLO had established over forty bases of operation.

Haddad's militia badly needed the UN and UNIFIL to take action against the terrorist infiltration. Haddad's message, conveyed through

Rizk, was that "had it not been for the support of Israel, we would have been exterminated. The Israelis understand our problem and we are grateful to them. The Jewish people are the only ones in the world who are standing with us."

Unfortunately, the terrorist buildup continued, resulting in repeated attacks on the Israeli Defense Forces and Israeli citizens in the north. The attacks and counter-attacks triggered a later invasion by the IDF into southern Lebanon in 1982.

But the new year also brought brighter news that helped balance the continued strife difficulties along Israel's northern border and in Lebanon. On February 26, 1980, a historic event occurred: Full diplomatic relations between Egypt and Israel were established with foreign embassies opening in Cairo and Tel Aviv.

Before returning to the United States, Horowitz and his wife, Nan, experienced what would be the highlight of their visit to the Holy Land. The opportunity arose to spend "Motzei Shabbat" (the first evening after the Sabbath) as guests in the home of Israeli Prime Minister Menachem Begin and his wife Aliza. It had been the Begin's custom for many years to invite friends for a late Sabbath afternoon tea at their home in Tel Aviv. Horowitz, having known Begin for years, had been blessed with several such visits in the past. The Prime Minister greeted them warmly with an embrace before graciously passing around a tray with cookies to go with the tea. Two other invited couples seemed equally thrilled with this personal encounter with the Prime Minister and First Lady.

Prime Minister Begin, who had just concluded the historic Peace Agreement with Egypt and had a Nobel Peace Prize (co-recipient with Anwar Sadat) to show for it spoke openly about his faith and heritage. He revealed that following the weekly Motzei Shabbat teas, he experiences something that gives him the greatest joy. In the quietude of his home, he meets with several outstanding scholars and rabbis in a Bible session discussing the weekly Torah portion. Begin said that nothing else in the world gives him greater pleasure that these weekly Bible sessions: "They serve as a relaxing tonic, a welcome relief from the day-to-day political tensions which the office of Prime Minister imposes upon me." As it was during his days with the Jewish underground, the Tanach (Bible), which Begion always carried with him, continues to serve as his guide and textbook. Horowitz offered this explanation: "It is in this spirit, his devotion to Israel's eternal Torah-heritage, that Providence prepared the road for him towards the highest office in the land."

Meanwhile, the disturbances in Iran had disrupted oil shipments to the West, resulting in a sixty percent hike in oil prices and a steep rise in inflation. These problems led to an increased sense of vulnerability and fear that the Soviet Union might take advantage of the West's distress. Such fears appeared vindicated in December 1979 when 80,000 Soviet troops invaded Afghanistan.

As the Iranian hostage crisis lingered, President Carter faced growing domestic pressure to do something about the situation. In April 1980, the President authorized the U.S. military to proceed with a complex and daring plan to rescue the hostages. "Operation Eagle Claw" was supposed to send an elite rescue team into the embassy compound. However, a severe desert sandstorm on the day of the mission caused several helicopters to malfunction, including one that veered into a large transport plane during takeoff. Eight American servicemen were killed in the accident and "Operation Eagle Claw" was aborted. The constant media coverage of the hostage crisis in the U.S. served as a demoralizing backdrop for the 1980 presidential race.

During the course of the summer, Horowitz received high tributes from several notable people for the publication of his recent series of articles entitled, "The Jews Are Not Alone." Senator Frank Church of Idaho, chairman of the important Senate Committee on Foreign Relations and a long-time friend of Israel, called the Horowitz exposition, "brilliant and historical." In a letter to Mr. George Caudill, who had sent the articles to him, Senator Church wrote: "Mr. Horowitz brilliantly details the origins and genealogy of the Jewish people, and I was very impressed by his historical accounting. I am having copies of his articles forwarded to the B'nai Brith organization in Washington, perhaps for their own use in preparing overviews of the roots of Jewish civilization." Senator Donald W. Riegle, Jr. of Michigan also called the series "fascinating articles concerning the ancient Hebraic Republic and should, therefore, be pursued." A former Mormon, George Caudill, aware of the Mormon's longstanding claims of a genealogical link to the peoples of ancient Israel, had also sent Mormon President Ezra Taft Benson copies of the Horowitz articles. David later received a warm, personal letter from Benson thanking him and calling the exposition "fascinating and excellent material." He also said that he hoped to meet Horowitz in the future.

A military conflict broke out between Iraq and Iran in September. Open warfare began on September 22, 1980, when Iraqi armed forces invaded western Iran along the countries' joint border. The roots of the war lay in a number of territorial and political disputes between the two nations. It became a long and brutal eight-year confrontation with consequences that still resonate to this day.

On Tuesday, November 4, 1980, Republican and former California Governor Ronald Reagan defeated incumbent Democrat President Jimmy Carter and Independent candidate John B. Anderson, to become our nation's 40th President. The election, coming one year and two days after the hostage crisis began, resulted in a landslide victory for Reagan. Americans had lost confidence in Carter, whose popularity had plunged to twenty percent, even lower than Nixon's during the Watergate scandal. Many historians believe the hostage crisis cost Jimmy Carter a second term as president. Carter spent his final weeks as president trying desperately to get the hostages freed before he left office. Using Algeria as an intermediary, he worked out a deal with the Iranian government. The U.S. would release about $12 billion in Iranian assets frozen in American banks and pledge not to interfere in Iran's internal affairs and in turn, Iran would release the hostages. The Iranians, however, refused to release the hostages while Carter was still president. On January 21, 1981, 444 days after the crisis began and just hours after President Ronald Reagan delivered his inaugural address, the hostages were set free. The republic rejoiced.

It had been quite a year for David Horowitz. A year that began at the home of Prime Minister Menachem Begin in Tel Aviv would be concluding in the hotel suite of the Prime Minister in New York, receiving one of Israel's most prestigious awards. Horowitz received a telegram from Eryk Spektor, General Chairman of the Jabotinsky Centennial Dinner to be held in New York on November 11, where, he learned, he was to receive the Jabotinsky Centennial Citation Award. Conferring the award would be none other than Israeli Prime Minister Menachem Begin at a special reception to be held in Begin's suite at the Waldorf-Astoria Hotel. Horowitz, who had devoted a lifetime to the cause of Israel and Jewry, was one of several recipients from all phases of professional life to receive the award "in recognition of their distinguished service to the State of Israel and the Jewish people."

In the next episode, we take a closer look at the Jabotinsky Centennial and the gala event that David Horowitz called "unlike any celebratory function I've ever attended."

Chapter 36

The High Cost of Peace

Veterans Day, November 11, 1980. It was the day of the Centennial Dinner celebration at the Waldorf-Astoria Hotel in New York City, commemorating the 100th anniversary of the birth of Zeev Jabotinsky. And what a celebration it was!

Vladimir (Zeʾev) Jabotinsky (1880-1940) was a towering figure in the history of Zionism. He was a Zionist activist, orator and writer who founded both the Betar Movement (a Revisionist Zionist youth movement) and the Jewish Legion of the British army during World War I. Fascinated by Zionist leader Theodor Herzl, he was elected as a delegate to the 6th Zionist Congress. As a young disciple of Jabotinsky, Menachem Begin rose rapidly within the Betar ranks becoming the active head of Betar's Polish branch in 1937. In 1942, Begin joined the Irgun (a Zionist paramilitary organization that operated in Mandate Palestine between 1931 and 1948). He assumed the organization's leadership in 1944.

Now Prime Minister of Israel, Menachem Begin, was present in New York to honor his heroic mentor. He was welcomed by an enthusiastic audience composed of leaders from every segment of life within the American Jewish community, including a number of well-known non-Jewish political figures, among them some of President-Elect Reagan's top aides. More than 2,000 people jammed the Ballroom and an additional audience filled the Starlight Roof of the Waldorf-Astoria. The evening offered an impressive procession: the presentation of colors by the U.S. Military Academy at West Point; the Veterans of the Jewish Legion; American Veterans of Israel and the Honor Guard of Betar. Large portraits of Jabotinsky and of Herzl flanked the stage. The highlight of the evening, of course, was the address by Prime Minister Begin, who gave a studious and detailed record of Jabotinsky's life work. "Without him," he declared, "without his vision, his suffering, his faith, and his fight, the State of Israel would not have come into being. Our generation and all the generations to come, owe a debt of gratitude to him who led us and them from bondage to liberty."

To David Horowitz and his wife, Nan, the Jabotinsky Centennial held a special meaning. Both of them—Nan even before they were married over thirty years ago—had been active on the American scene eliciting support for the underground Irgun fighters. They were fully aware of the hectic struggle Jabotinsky and later his successor, Begin, endured in order to gain recognition for Jewry's liberation. It was here that David Horowitz was awarded the coveted Jabotinsky Centennial Award Medal and Citation, presented personally by Prime Minister Begin. An obviously moved David Horowitz remarked, "I have attended many vital functions through the past several decades. None could in any way be compared with this fabulous gala event. It has been both spell-binding and thrilling from the beginning to the end."

As 1981 dawned, we watched as a one-time movie star and president of the Screen Actors Guild became our 40th President. Former California Governor, Ronald Reagan was sworn in on January 20, 1981.

The New Year brought another very special achievement to the career of David Horowitz. For the first time in UN history, a correspondent representing Jewish media was elected president of the United Nations Correspondents Association (UNCA), consisting of correspondents from all over the globe. Following a three-day election campaign, David Horowitz, editor of the *World Union Press* and the *United Israel Bulletin* and who also writes for the *Jewish Press*, won the election over two formidable opponents.

Little-known details behind the historic election add a measure of special significance. Horowitz was opposed for the presidency by an Arab woman, Raghida Dergham, a Lebanese correspondent for *Al Nahar*, and Eugene Forson of the Ghana News Agency. Horowitz tallied fifty-seven votes, Ms. Dergham thirty-seven, and Forson thirty-five. The election was noteworthy, not only had the first correspondent representing Jewish media and Israeli newspapers who was also a strong partisan of Israel, won, but, in doing so, he had also defeated an Arab and a Third World candidate to boot. Fellow correspondent Richard Yaffe cryptically added, "It might be the first time that the Arab-Third World-Soviet bloc cartel has not prevailed. It's nice to know that's one area, at least, at the UN that has remained democratic—the UNCA ballot box."

Upon assuming his new prestigious role, Horowitz stated, "It is not so much a victory for me but for all Jews around the globe, that in this house of contention, even Arabs and members of the Third World voted in favor of a Jew." David received numerous letters and notes congratulating him on becoming president of UNCA. Among the many well-wishers were Baron Rudiger von-Wechmat, President of the UN General Assembly and Secretary-General Kurt Waldheim.

Horowitz's role in exposing former Nazi war criminals living in the U.S., such as Romanian bishop Valerian Trifa and Hungarian Fenrec Korah, was honored by The Committee to Bring Nazi War Criminals to Justice in the United States who awarded him the *Zehor (Remember) Award* on March 31, 1981. Recognized for his dedication to justice and respect for truth, it read: "Your courage gives courage to others."

On June 7, 1981, a surprise Israeli air strike, known as "Operation Opera," effectively destroyed an Iraqi nuclear reactor under construction ten miles southeast of Baghdad. In a well-planned and rehearsed operation, the attack squadron of eight F-16A planes left Etzion Airbase, flying unchallenged into Jordanian and Saudi airspace. To avoid detection, the Israeli pilots conversed in Saudi-accented Arabic while in Jordanian airspace and told Jordanian air controllers that they were a Saudi patrol that had gone off course. While flying over Saudi Arabia, they pretended to be Jordanians, using Jordanian radio signals and formations. The attack lasted less than two minutes, completely destroying the Osirak reactor complex. According to Ze'ev Raz, the leader of the attack force, the Israeli pilots radioed each other and recited the biblical verse Joshua 10:12 as they were returning to the base.

The attack was universally criticized, and the U.S. voted for a Security Council resolution condemning Israel. American and coalition forces however, might have faced a nuclear-armed Iraq during the Persian Gulf War in 1991 and again during the U.S. invasion of Iraq in 2003 had Israel not destroyed Iraq's nuclear reactor in 1981.

On October 6, 1981, Anwar Sadat sat in a reviewing stand in Cairo, a commanding figure in gold-braided hat, starched dress uniform and green sash. As the Egyptian President watched an extravagant military parade celebrating his 1973 surprise attack on Israel, a junior lieutenant in crisp khakis stepped from a truck and walked toward him. Sadat rose, expecting a salute. Instead the young officer tossed a grenade and a band of accomplices scrambled from the truck and opened fire. Sadat fell mortally wounded, leaving the Middle East facing a dangerous political void and the world without one of the few leaders whose bold imagination and personal courage seemed to have made a difference to history.

Throughout the long process of pursuing peace, Anwar Sadat and Menachem Begin, himself, viewed as a grizzled hardliner, became close. Close enough to exchange personal notes about family events such as the birth of a grandson or Jihan Sadat receiving her master's degree. They addressed extremely difficult political issues, shared moments of humor, and developed an enormous measure of mutual respect one for the other. In 1978 Anwar Sadat and Menachem Begin were both awarded the Nobel Peace Prize.

In Jerusalem, Begin's sorrow at Sadat's death "went beyond matters of state" said an Israeli policymaker. "Begin mourned the death personally." When official word of the assassination reached Jerusalem, Begin immediately instructed his staff to organize a trip to Cairo to attend Sadat's funeral on Saturday. The decision was more complicated than it seemed. As a religious Jew, Begin could neither fly nor ride on the Jewish Sabbath. Thus, he was forced to fly to Cairo a day early and spend the night, multiplying the security risks. He wanted to demonstrate his respect, both for Sadat and for his successor.

Anwar Sadat was buried in a muted ceremony under tight security in the Unknown Soldier memorial in Cairo, across the street from the stand where he was assassinated. New President Hosni Mubarak led the funeral procession, taking the hand of Sadat's son, Gamal. Sadat's body was entombed under a black marble tombstone inscribed with the simple epitaph: "President Mohammed Anwar Sadat, hero of war and peace. He lived for peace and he was martyred for his principles."

Not far away lay the Giza Plateau, where stood the timeless pyramids and the great Sphinx. The Sphinx, sitting as if guarding the tombs of past Pharaohs, with a weathered face and an empty stare, like one who had already seen too much.

Chapter 37

Broken in Beirut

In April 1982, the evacuation of the Israeli settlement of Yamit in the Sinai Peninsula began and on April 25, Israel completed its withdrawal from the Sinai in accordance with the Egyptian-Israeli peace treaty of 1979.

On April 24-25, David Horowitz appeared as one of the keynote speakers at the 32nd anniversary celebration of the proclamation of independence of the South Moluccans people, held in Utrecht, Holland. In his address, Mr. Horowitz called upon the large gathering of South Moluccans to never to give up in their continuing struggle for independence based on pledges of original treaties recorded in United Nations documents. Following the departure of the Dutch from the Indonesian archipelago over three decades ago, the South Moluccas, one of the sixteen federated states, proclaimed independence on April 25, 1950. Its people have continued to struggle against Indonesians who repeat acts of aggression against the neighboring people of East Timor. Jakarta was condemned at the UN for such acts.

Horowitz declared that the case for South Moluccans' independence "is based on historical facts and from the international point of view, the South Moluccas' case is still on the agenda of the Security Council of the United Nations." "Dating back to the year 1950, it has never been removed," Horowitz stated. Horowitz has been an advocate and tireless worker on behalf of the South Moluccans people in their struggle for independence since 1950.

Tension along Israel's northern border increased during the course of 1981, following the lobbing of Katyusha rockets at Israeli settlements by terrorist organizations in southern Lebanon. The ceasefire declared in July 1981 was broken and the attacks against Israeli targets in Israel and abroad became unbearable. The final provocation occurred on June 3, 1982, when a Palestinian terrorist group led by Abu Nidal attempted to assassinate Shlomo Argov, Israel's Ambassador to Great Britain. Three days later, on June 6, 1982, the IDF launched "Operation Peace for Galilee," in an effort to drive out the terrorists. The Israeli Defense Forces moved 80,000 troops into Lebanon. The invasion took the Israelis all the way to Beirut in an attempt to expel the PLO. The siege of Beirut ended in August when an agreement was reached that allowed a multi-national force of U.S., French and Italian troops to enter Beirut to aid in the evacuation of PLO and Syrian fighters while the Israelis pulled back their troops.

On August 21, 1982, Palestinian fighters began to withdraw as the French contingent of the multi-national force arrived. Over the course of twelve days, approximately 14,000 Palestinian and Syrian combatants were evacuated. This led to Yasser Arafat and his PLO fighters being unceremoniously forced to depart to Tunisia. Though the IDF succeeded in driving the PLO out of Lebanon, the action did not end the terrorist threats from that country. The war was also costly: 1,216 soldiers died between June 5, 1982 and May 31, 1985.

During its 51st annual convention on June 10, the world-renowned Yeshiva University honored David Horowitz by bestowing upon him the prestigious *Mordecai ben-David Award* for his services to world Jewry. In presenting the award, Rabbi Dr. Leo Jung, chairman of the Mordecai ben-David Award Committee, paid high tribute to Mr. Horowitz for his integrity and life-long dedication to the ideals of the Torah-faith and for his leadership in the United Israel World Union movement. He was also cited as a distinguished Jewish correspondent at the United Nations. The Commencement also marked the presentation of an honorary degree to Senator Bob Packwood of Oregon who delivered the Commencement address.

In July, following the "Operation Peace for Galilee" war in Lebanon, *World Union Press* editor, David Horowitz, at the invitation of the Israeli Embassy in Washington, joined a group of fourteen editors of English-Jewish newspapers published in various sections of the country on a fact-finding tour of Lebanon and Israel. After ten days of intensive talks with Lebanese civilians, both Christian and Muslim, as well as interviews with soldiers on both sides of the border, and with officials involved with the war on the scene, Horowitz prepared his report. It was written in Jerusalem and syndicated to the publications that carried his columns. A full copy of his report appeared in the summer 1982 edition of the *United Israel Bulletin*.

In an interesting and coincidental development, David ran into Hollywood entertainer Sammy Davis Jr. in the El Al lounge at JFK airport on July 13, as he prepared to depart on the fact-finding mission to Israel and Lebanon. As it turned out, Davis flew on the same plane as Horowitz and the group of Jewish editors. Having corresponded in the past, Davis and Horowitz had ample time to enjoy a warm visit. Sammy Davis Jr. was a convert to the Jewish faith in 1961.

On August 23, 1982, the Lebanese Parliament elected leader Bachir Gemayel as president of the Lebanese Republic. A Maronite Catholic, he was a senior member of the Phalange party and the former supreme commander of the Lebanese Forces militia during the early years of the Lebanese Civil War (1975-90). With the PLO having been ousted, maybe now the prospects for Lebanon to return to stability would be brighter. Gemayel was clear on his vision and purpose as leader. He explained, "We are looking for the liberation of our country. We are looking that all the foreigners leave, Syrians, Palestinians and Israelis, and even UNIFIL. We don't need any foreign, armed presence in this country." He, of course, never mentioned the covert relationship he had established with Israel.

On September 1, 1982, Gemayel visited Netanya in Israel to meet with Israel's Prime Minister Menachem Begin. The Israeli premier requested the start of immediate negotiations toward a peace treaty between the two countries. Gemayel asked instead for a respite of six to nine months to establish his authority. He did concede, however, to an agreement to "normalize" relations between the two countries. On September 12, Bachir Gemayel also met secretly with Israel's Ariel Sharon in Bikfaya.

But Lebanon's youngest president-elect would never be able to fulfill his promises. He was assassinated two days later on September 14, along with twenty-six others, when a bomb exploded in the Beirut

Phalange headquarters. Habib Shartouni, a member of the Syrian Social Nationalist Party and also a Maronite Christian, was arrested for the assassination. He later confessed to the act, saying he had done this because "Bachir had sold the country to Israel." A reporter was overheard telling him: "You didn't kill a man, you killed a country." With a light of hope now extinguished, Israel continued to have difficulty escaping the morass in Lebanon. Even the U.S. was soon drawn into the Lebanese quagmire.

During the weekend of November 20-21, 1982, David Horowitz was afforded the opportunity to recall the horror of the Holocaust. He was invited to appear as the guest speaker at a gala banquet sponsored by the American Congress of Jews from Poland and Survivors of Concentration Camps, held at the Ambassador Hotel in Los Angeles. The event was in tribute to its long-time president, Benjamin Grey, with the occasion marking his eightieth birthday. Grey's life story depicts a saga replete with heroic deeds both during and after the Holocaust that one-day must be fully told in book and film.

In his address, Horowitz presented a detailed account of the on-going battle Israel was waging against the rabid Soviet-Arab-Third World automatic majority, which was dominating the UN on almost every issue of its agenda. He noted, however, that Israel enjoyed a few friends at the UN, most prominent of whom was Jeanne Kirkpatrick, the U.S. Ambassador to the UN. Thanks to her, he stated, the Arabs failed in their attempt to oust Israel from the Assembly. Horowitz also paid tribute to Israeli Ambassador Yehuda Z. Blum who in his brilliant and eloquent rebuttals gained him respect and admiration from both friend and foe.

A unique Hanukkah kindling ceremony was held at the United Nations on December 15, 1982, in the late afternoon in the *World Union Press* bureau office of David Horowitz. Approximately twenty people crowded into the bureau office to participate in the joyous, festive occasion. It was the first of many more to come.

In a *Jerusalem Post* article appearing later in 1996, writer Naomi Farrell-Golan reflected on the Hanukkah celebrations:

The celebration of Hanukkah at the UN began in the office of David Horowitz in 1982, and this paved the way to an awakening of the Jews working at the UN. The annual Hanukkah party that started in his small crowded office is now a great elaborate celebration held in a hall, with lots of good food, entertainment and Israeli folk dancing.

On September 21, 1982, the National Assembly elected Amine Pierre Gemayel President of Lebanon to replace his brother Bachir Gemayel, who had been elected the previous month but was assassinated before taking office. A multinational force, composed of U.S. and European military personnel, remained stationed in Lebanon to help the Lebanese government maintain stability during the civil war.

Chapter 38
A Legend says Farewell

Nineteen-eighty-three arrived, bringing David Horowitz a new personal milestone. He became an Octogenarian. On April 9th, he celebrated his eightieth birthday doing what he always does, faithfully manning his post at the UN while covering the affairs of the world body. Eighty years on earth is a long time. David Horowitz had witnessed the Great Depression and World War II, but he was quick to remind those around him that the great lawgiver, Moses, was eighty when he began his main work in the redemption of Israel. The best was yet to come.

In the spring 1983 issue of *United Israel Bulletin*, United Israel approached its fortieth year by restating the mission and purpose of the organization while listing many of its accomplishments during that period. Calling United Israel World Union "a pathfinder" David Horowitz urged Jewry once again to recognize Israel's universal mission and thus take the lead in answering the cry of humanity for social justice, peace, freedom and human dignity.

Perhaps stirred by his vantage point at the United Nations, David seemed to be issuing a new warning to those with ears to hear by stating, "United Israel insists that the Torah faith message to the world be such that the great challenge of the new prophets be met now; that bold, new leadership must assert itself in order to meet the perils posed by the Nuclear Age."

On April 18, 1983, a suicide bomber crashed a truck into the front of the U.S. Embassy in Beirut, Lebanon, detonating approximately 2,000 pounds of explosives. The massive blast killed sixty-three people, including seventeen Americans, some of whom were CIA officers. One month later, Lebanon, Israel and the United States signed an agreement on Israeli withdrawal from Lebanon. The Israeli Cabinet later voted to withdraw troops from Beirut but to remain in southern Lebanon as a buffer against acts of terrorism.

Major-General Chaim Herzog became the 6th President of Israel on May 5, 1983. Born in Belfast and raised predominantly in Dublin, he was the son of Ireland's Chief Rabbi Yitzhak HaLevi Herzog. Migrating to Mandatory Palestine in 1935, he served in the *Haganah* Jewish paramilitary group. Later serving as an officer in the British Army during World War II, he received the nickname "Vivian" because the British could not pronounce "Chaim." To our knowledge, he was never called Vivian during his ten years as Israel's president.

David Horowitz appeared as the guest speaker at the 87th annual convention of the Federation of Jewish Women's Organizations, held on May 4 at the Minskoff Cultural Center in New York City. The theme of the convention was "Ethics Today" and Mr. Horowitz spoke on "Ethics in Journalism."

David Horowitz received a formal note of thanks from new UN Secretary-General Javier Perez de Cuellar on July 27th, expressing his appreciation for sending him a copy of his book, *Thirty-Three Candles*, and for including a copy of the late Spanish General Franco's letter to Horowitz from 1964. Peruvian diplomat Javier de Cuellar became the fifth Secretary-General of the United Nations in 1982.

On August 28, 1983, a tired and embattled Menachem Begin resigned as Prime Minister of the State of Israel, telling his colleagues that "I cannot go on any longer." Begin had lost his beloved wife, Aliza, who died in November 1982 while he was away on an official visit to Washington. He descended into a deep depression. He also became very disappointed by the war in Lebanon because he had hoped to sign a peace treaty with President-elect Bachir Gemayel, who was assassinated before taking office. Mounting Israeli casualties, political protests to end the war and ill health were other factors that continued to plague Begin. He subsequently retired to an apartment overlooking the Jerusalem Forest and spent the remaining years of his life in seclusion.

The Jerusalem Forest is a special place; a pine forest located in the Judean mountains west of Jerusalem. The forest more or less surrounds Yad Vashem, the official memorial to the victims of the Holocaust. The Jewish National Fund, financed by private donors, planted the forest during the 1950s.

Rarely leaving his apartment, except to visit his wife's gravesite, Begin spent most of his days reading, watching movies, and keeping up with world events by continuing his life-long habit of listening to the BBC each morning and maintaining a subscription to several newspapers.

On the 10th of October, Israeli politician and former Mossad member Yitzhak Shamir succeeded Menachem Begin as the 7th Prime Minister of the State of Israel.

At 6:22 AM on October 23, 1983, a suicide bomber crashed a pickup truck carrying 2,000 pounds of explosives into the Marine compound in Beirut, killing 241 U.S. service personnel. At the same time, a second suicide bomber struck a building housing French paratroopers, killing 58 French soldiers. With the second attack within six months after the U.S. Embassy bombing, the Beirut blues continued.

There were 1,800 Marines stationed in Beirut at the time as a part of the multi-national peacekeeping force with units from France, Italy and the United Kingdom. The bombing was traced to Hezbollah, a militant and political group that originated in Lebanon in 1982. Syrian and Iranian involvement was also suspected. It was the deadliest attack against U.S. Marines since the battle over Iwo Jima in February 1945.

The eight flames of the Menorah again brightened a corner of the UN when over seventy people gathered on December 7, 1983 to celebrate Hanukkah 5744. Arranged and hosted by David Horowitz, the historic event was held in the UN Correspondents Association Club in the Secretariat building. Among the attendees was Israeli Ambassador Yehuda Blum who had left one of the many conferences to attend the event. Ambassador Blum addressed the jubilant audience on the significance of Hanukkah. Even the new president of the UN Correspondents Association for 1983, Ifthikar Ali of Pakistan stopped by for a brief visit and offered his best wishes.

As 1983 drew to a close, it was apparent that Syrian president Hafiz al-Assad was making life miserable for the Americans in Lebanon. He was providing support to the militant Shiite group Hezbollah, which along with other Lebanese groups, continued sniping, shelling, and harassing the U.S. Marines. Hezbollah was deeply hostile to the United States because of America's support for Israel during its invasion of Lebanon and because the U.S. had an antagonistic relationship with Iran, from which Hezbollah drew both inspiration and material aid.

Following the tragic October attack on the Marine barracks in Beirut, members of Congress began demanding that the Marines be pulled out of Lebanon. The Reagan administration bowed to reality and on February 26, 1984, withdrew the Marines from Lebanon, essentially abandoning it to the Syrians and their radical Shiite allies.

On March 5, 1984, the Lebanese government, seeing the chaos that had resulted from the peace treaty with Israel, formally repudiated the treaty. It was a final blow.

The abduction of Lebanon continued.

Chapter 39
Bibi's UN Debut

Nineteen-eighty-four arrived and United Israel World Union was turning forty. The annual meeting of the biblically inspired body was held on April 25th in the home of President David Horowitz. Among those in attendance at the historic meeting were Ms. Dorothy Adelson, author of the historic volume, *Operation Susannah*, recounting Jewry's struggle for statehood at the UN; Rene Shapshak, renowned sculptor; and Martin J. Warmbrand, Secretary of the Board of Governors of the City University of New York. Executive Vice President of United Israel, Barnard G. Sharrow, reported on the organization's progress through recent years in Ghana, the Philippines, Mexico, and units within the United States. It was also announced that the Chief Rabbi of South Africa, Dr. Bernard Casper, former Dean of the Hebrew University, and Dr. Heskel M. Haddad, MD, President of the World Organization for Jews from Arab Countries, had both joined the *United Israel* Editorial Board.

In news from Rome, the Vatican and the U.S. had agreed to exchange diplomats after a 116-year hiatus, and though it took a few hundred years, Italy and the Vatican agreed to end Roman Catholicism as a state religion.

On June 28, 1984, Yigael Yadin, Israeli archaeologist, soldier and politician, died at the age of sixty-seven. Yadin, the son of renowned archaeologist Eleazar Sukenik, was educated at Hebrew University, became a member of the Haganah (military organization) and served as chief of the general staff of the Israeli Defense Forces from 1949 to 1952. He was also Deputy Prime Minister from 1977 to 1981. He is best remembered for his role in acquiring and interpreting the Dead Sea

Scrolls, and for his excavation of King Herod's mountain palace at Masada. Commenting on the timing of the scrolls discovery, Yadin once remarked:

> I cannot avoid the feeling that there is something symbolic in the discovery of the scrolls and their acquisition at the moment of the creation of the State of Israel. It is as if these manuscripts had been waiting in caves for two thousand years, ever since the destruction of Israel's independence, until the people of Israel had returned to their home and regained their freedom.

During a Friday evening Sabbath Service at New York's Beth Achim, Rabbi Irving J. Block, longtime spiritual leader of The Brotherhood Synagogue, presented a Torah Scroll to Rabbi and Mrs. Samuel S. Lerer for use in the newly established Beth Shmuel house of worship at Vera Cruz, Mexico. After expressing his gratitude to Rabbi Block and his congregation for the beautiful endowment of the Torah Scroll, Rabbi Lerer offered this moving tribute to United Israel President David Horowitz: "You were the source and fountain from which I drew my inspiration, my conviction, and my dedication to work hand-in-hand with you to bring the multitudes into the fold of our God, our faith and our people." The fast-growing congregation of Beth Shmuel in Vera Cruz, Mexico now had their very own sacred Torah Scroll to use and cherish as a part of their Hebraic faith.

As a UN correspondent, David Horowitz's incisive coverage and tough-reporter mentality continued to earn widespread respect and admiration. An example came from well-known journalist and author, Dr. Hillel Seidman. In an article published in the Israeli Daily *Hatsophe* on August 3, 1984, Dr. Seidman had this to say:

> Mr. Horowitz knows the UN inside out, keeping an eye on everything that goes on there. As the author of a widely circulated political column appearing in a number of papers, he has won admirers among many delegations. He knows everyone. More than that, there's no one like him as an expert

in the workings of all the UN elements. He keeps a watchful eye on the maneuverings of the delegations that aim their venom at Israel. Thus, Horowitz fulfills a vital task as both a watchman and champion of Israel.

Dr. Seidman further cited Horowitz as a long-time friend of former Prime Minister Menachem Begin. This was, indeed, high praise coming from the homeland of Israel.

Although the U.S. Marines had been pulled out of Lebanon earlier in 1984, it was not to be the end of the Reagan administration's troubles in Lebanon. On September 20, 1984, the Shia Islamic militant group Hezbollah, with support and direction from the Islamic Republic of Iran, carried out a suicide bombing targeting the U.S. embassy annex in East Beirut, Lebanon, killing twenty-four people. Hezbollah had also used suicide car and truck bombs in the April 1983 U.S. embassy bombing and the October 1983 Beirut Marine barracks bombing.

In the American presidential election held on November 6, 1984, Republican Ronald Reagan was elected to a second term, defeating Democrat Walter Mondale, a former U.S vice president. Reagan won forty-nine states en route to amassing 525 electoral votes to Mondale's thirteen. It was one of the biggest landslide victories in U.S. election history. The election was also notable for being the first time a major party had a woman on its ticket. Geraldine Ferraro was Mondale's running mate.

On November 21, 1984, a seven-week clandestine operation to bring Falash Mura Ethiopian Jews to Israel was underway. The unprecedented undertaking, code-named "Operation Moses," was a three-way collaboration between the Mossad, the CIA and Sudanese State Security (SSS) to smuggle nearly 8,000 Falash Mura out of refugee camps in Sudan in a massive airlift to Israel. Operation Moses turned out to be the beginning of large-scale, official Israeli efforts to facilitate a Falash Mura Aliyah that continued in some form for years.

Every night, except the Sabbath, from November 21, 1984, until January 5, 1985, buses picked up groups of about fifty-five Ethiopian Jews from the refugee camps and took them to Khartoum, where they boarded Boeing 707s. Altogether, thirty-six flights carrying approximately

220 passengers flew first to Brussels and then to Tel Aviv. All told, "Operation Moses" brought 8,000 Jews to Israel, 1,500 of them children and young people who arrived without their parents. The operation was halted as the result of leaks to the press and the fears from the Sudanese government of a backlash from Arab countries.

The next wave of Ethiopian emigration did not take place for another six years when "Operation Solomon" (which brought an additional 14,000 Falash Mura) was finally made possible by a regime change in Ethiopia in 1991. Columnist for *The New York Times*, William Safire, wrote: "For the first time in history, thousands of black people are being brought into a country, not in chains, but as citizens."

As the year 1984 faded into history, a new UN Envoy burst onto the scene. The State of Israel had a new Ambassador to the United Nations, the youthful and handsome Benjamin Netanyahu, whose previous post was that of deputy to the Israeli Ambassador in Washington. Benjamin Netanyahu (known to his friends as "Bibi") was born in 1949 in Tel Aviv, Israel. Initially raised and educated in Jerusalem, he lived in the United States from 1963 to 1967. After graduating from high school in 1967, young Benjamin returned to Israel to enlist in the Israeli Defense Forces. He trained as a combat soldier and served for five years in an elite Special Forces unit of the IDF.

Netanyahu fought in the 1967-70 War of Attrition, rising to become a team leader in the unit. He was wounded in combat on multiple occasions. He led Operation Inferno (1968) and in the rescue of the hijacked Sabena Flight 571 in May 1972, in which he was shot in the shoulder. After completing his army service in 1972, Netanyahu returned to the United States to study at the Massachusetts Institute of Technology (MIT), but was interrupted to return to Israel in October 1973 to serve in the Yom Kippur War. While there he fought in special raids along the Suez Canal against the Egyptian forces, before leading a commando attack deep inside Syrian territory, whose mission remains classified today. Finally able to return to his studies in the U.S., he earned both his bachelor's degree (SB) and his master's degree (SM) from MIT, graduating near the top of his class, while simultaneously completing a thesis in a graduate course at Harvard.

In making his debut during the 39th session of the General Assembly, Israel's new Ambassador to the UN injected a fresh dynamism into the world body, deeply impressing both the press and the assembled delegations. The occasion of his debut marked an assembly debate during which the Iranian spokesman, supported by the radical Arabs, sought to oust Israel from the organization with an amendment questioning its credentials. Netanyahu's maiden speech was a remarkable defense of both Israel's credentials and the UN's very fundamental principle of universality. David Horowitz would later remark that "Bibi's words struck the assembled delegations like a thunderbolt and his message resonated throughout the assembly." Thanks to a quick countermove by the Danish Ambassador, on behalf of the five Nordic states, the anti-Israel action was killed by assembly vote.

Having David Horowitz, the grizzled veteran journalist who was referred to as "the watchman and champion of Israel," and Bibi Netanyahu, the war hero and brilliant new spokesman, both representing and protecting Israel's interest at this world organization, it couldn't have been in better hands.

Chapter 40
The Storytellers

In a pre-publication fete announcing the release of his new book, *Heritage: Civilization and the Jews,* Israeli Minister Abba Eban hosted a reception on the sailing yacht "Caravan" which took the guests to Ellis Island for a briefing and later a sail up the Hudson River. Also aboard was journalist David Horowitz, who had known Eban since his days as a Representative to the UN.

During the reception, Horowitz introduced Eban to another friend and author, Dr. Rochelle Saidel, whose new book about the pursuit of Nazi war criminals in America was soon to be released. Dr. Saidel's 239-page volume entitled, *The Outraged Conscience: Seekers of Justice for Nazi War Criminals in America,* was published in December 1984 by the State University of New York Press, Albany, N.Y. The brilliant work by Dr. Saidel produced the most comprehensive research yet done on the subject of Nazi hunters in America. Famous Nazi hunter Simon Wiesenthal commented about the masterful volume: "For this book I have waited a long time."

Dr. Saidel dedicated an entire chapter of the book to David Horowitz's role in exposing Nazis who somehow had managed by fraud and bribery to find haven in America. Her chapter about David was called, "Always a Man with a Cause." One of the first copies of Dr. Saidel's new book was later sent to Minister Abba Eban in Jerusalem.

United Israel World Union commemorated its 40th Anniversary on Saturday, April 27, 1985 in the small Michigan township of Ottawa and the town of West Olive, situated between the "Dutch" city of Holland and Grand Haven along the coast of Lake Michigan. A special outdoor service was held at the former township with an evening gala banquet at an inn in the Tulip Festival city of Holland. Among the special guests participating in the historic anniversary was Congressman Mark Siljander, a member of the House Foreign Affairs Committee and who also served on the Middle East subcommittee. The delegation from New York included United Israel President and Mrs. David Horowitz and Vice President Eddie Abrahams. Also in attendance was Dola Ben-Yehuda Wittman, daughter of the renowned founder of Modern Hebrew, Eliezer Ben-Yehuda. Ben-Yehuda was a Jewish Litvak lexicographer of Hebrew and newspaper editor. He was the driving spirit behind the revival of the Hebrew language in the modern era.

The highlight of the gala banquet was a spellbinding message by Congressman Siljander who spoke of falling in love with Israel and the Jewish people to the extent of being inspired to study the sacred language, Hebrew, and to accept the Torah faith as part of his own religion. Congressman Siljander also paid high tribute to David Horowitz, the local unit leaders, and United Israel World Union for having pressed forward through forty years, the very biblical principles on which our own country was founded and for propagating prophetic truths to the world. Local newspapers in Grand Haven and Holland, Michigan devoted special articles to the event.

Following the 1982 Lebanon War, the PLO moved its base to Tunisia. After continued PLO hijackings and terrorist activities, Israel chose to retaliate directly against the Tunis headquarters of the PLO. Operation "Wooden Leg" was launched by Israel against the Palestinian Liberation Organization headquarters in Hammam Chott, near Tunis, Tunisia, on October 1, 1985. With a target 1,280 miles from the operation's starting point, this was the most distant action undertaken by the Israeli Defense Forces since Operation "Entebbe" in 1976. The PLO headquarters was completely destroyed, although Yasser Arafat, the head of the organization, was not there at the time and escaped unharmed. Interestingly, intelligence supplied to Israel by Jonathan Pollard on the Tunisian and Libyan air defense systems greatly facilitated the raid. Pollard, a former intelligence analyst for the United States government would later plead guilty in 1987 to spying for and providing top-secret classified information to Israel.

During October and November of 1985, David Horowitz delivered lectures on the global situation as it affected Israel from the vantage point of the UN to three congregations: Beth Ahm, Springfield, NJ; Sons of Israel, Woodmere, NY; and Temple Emanuel, Manhattan. He was also the guest speaker at the "Fortieth Annual Religious Service and Breakfast, Nassau Masonic Districts" on October 27th.

Also in October, Mr. Horowitz received a special guest. Mr. Lowell Gallin, Director of the Israeli headquartered "Root and Branch Association," which has as an affiliate "The Noah Institute," stressing the universal values of the Seven Noachide Principles, paid a visit to David at his UN office. The discussion centered on common interests of activities.

As 1985 drew to a close, David Horowitz announced the publication of a new book. The Philosophical Library of New York, a long-established publishing firm known for publishing some of the most important historical works on Science, Philosophy and Religion, had just released the new volume. The new work, *Pastor Charles Taze Russell; An Early American Christian Zionist*, was compiled and written by Mr. Horowitz to chronicle one of America's staunchest Christian supporters of the Zionist cause at the turn of the century. The renowned Christian preacher and Bible scholar, Charles Taze Russell (1852-1916) was the first President of the Watchtower Society and is known to many as the founder of Jehovah's Witnesses. But few realize that Pastor Russell was an early advocate of Zionism and that he boldly predicted the imminent return of the Jewish people to Israel.

Researching the fascinating enigma of Pastor Russell for over fifteen years, Horowitz dedicated the new volume to the late John J. Hoefle of the Epiphany Bible Association, who was a life-long devotee of Pastor Russell. Horowitz credited Mr. Hoefle's widow, Emily, for providing inspiration and valued assistance to his efforts.

David Horowitz immediately received two prestigious endorsements for his new book. Israel's Ambassador to the UN, Benjamin Netanyahu, having seen and read an advanced copy, offered these comments:

> David Horowitz sets the record straight about the beliefs and achievements of Charles Taze Russell. Recognition of Pastor Russell's important role as an early American Christian

advocate of Zionism is long overdue. Mr. Horowitz has performed an admirable service in restoring to public knowledge the story of this important Christian Zionist.

Ambassador Netanyahu's good friend, the former U.S. Ambassador to the UN, Jeanne Kirkpatrick, having also read an advanced copy of the historic volume, had this to say: "This is a fascinating account of a neglected man and a neglected chapter in the history of Zionism. David Horowitz's well-written book on Pastor Charles Taze Russell makes for extremely interesting reading. I definitely recommend it."

Among the many literary contributions of 1985, the works of Eban, Saidel and Horowitz provided important historical volumes that inform, enlighten and provide important linkages between past and present.

Chapter 41

A Century of Liberty's Light

As 1986 arrived, eighty-two-year-old David Horowitz wasn't about to slow down. In the first quarter of the New Year he delivered five weekly lectures at the Herzl Institute of New York on the "Behind the Scenes" activities at the UN. Horowitz' new book about the late Pastor Charles Taze Russell, the early Christian Zionist, was also receiving widespread attention. The book was the topic of two half-hour radio programs in the New York area. Mr. Horowitz also appeared on the "Richard Roffman & Friends" Cable WNWC Television Show. In an interesting note of timing, the release of the Horowitz book also marked the 100th anniversary of the publication of Pastor Russell's first comprehensive biblical exposition under the title, *The Divine Plan of the Ages*. It constituted the initial work of six volumes. During the past 100 years some ten million copies of "The Divine Plan" have been distributed around the world.

On a somber note, renowned sculptor and veteran United Israel World Union member, Rene Shapshak, passed away on April 8, 1986. A large gathering of family and friends attended special services held at the Gramercy Park Chapel in New York. Rabbi Irving J. Block, spiritual leader of The Brotherhood Synagogue and a long-time friend of United Israel, lead the services with an inspirational eulogy. David Horowitz also spoke at the service.

Eddie Abrahams, long time vice president of United Israel and a founder of the famous International Synagogue Chapel at JFK Airport, to which he had donated an oriental Torah Scroll, was honored at the 11th Annual Breakfast Forum on May 18th. The guest speaker was

Malcolm Hoenlein, Director of the Jewish Community Relations Council of New York.

Amid the flurry of activities, the United Israel organization held its 43rd Annual Meeting at the home of its president on May 18, 1986. Among the newcomers present at the meeting were Lowell Gallin, visiting from Israel, where he directs the "Root and Branch Association" and local author Raymond Solomon.

On April 5, 1986, a bomb exploded in a discotheque in Berlin frequented by U.S. service personnel. Of the 200 injured, sixty-three were American soldiers; one soldier and one civilian were killed. Citing "irrefutable proof" that Libya had directed the terrorist bombing, President Ronald Reagan authorized the use of force against the country. During the evening of April 15 and early morning of April 16, under the code name *El Dorado Canyon,* the U.S. launched a series of military strikes against ground targets inside Libya. It was more than just a message to Colonel Muammar Gaddafi and his ability to export terrorism. Gaddafi's residential compound took a direct hit that resulted in one death. The Colonel was not at home at the time.

Secretary-General Perez de Cuellar of Peru took the oath of office at the UN to begin a second term. As a lawyer and career diplomat with the foreign ministry of Peru, Mr. Cuellar had held several high-level posts at the UN before becoming Secretary-General in 1982. David Horowitz had a friendship and warm working relationship with Mr. Cuellar, who had read David's autobiography, *33 Candles,* in 1983 and knew the details of Horowitz's personal exchanges with the late General Francisco Franco of Spain in 1964.

In October, it was announced that the 1986 Nobel Peace Prize would be awarded to Elie Wiesel, one of the world's leading spokesmen on the Holocaust. The Jewish author, philosopher, and humanist made it his life's work to bear witness to the genocide committed by the Nazis during World War II. The Norwegian Nobel Committee referred to Wiesel as a "messenger to mankind." However, mankind would never have heard the Wiesel message except for a little-known reason. For ten years after the war, Wiesel refused to write about or discuss his experiences during the Holocaust. He began to reconsider after a meeting with the French author Francois Mauriac, the 1952 Nobel

Laureate in Literature, who eventually became Wiesel's close friend. Mauriac was a devout Christian who had been with the French Resistance during the war. He compared Wiesel to "Lazarus rising from the dead," and saw from Wiesel's tormented eyes, "the death of God in the soul of a child." Mauriac persuaded him to begin writing about his harrowing experiences. Elie Wiesel's memoir, *Night*, sold over ten million copies in the United States and was eventually translated into 30 languages and now ranks as one of the bedrocks of Holocaust literature.

America's "leading lady" celebrated her 100th birthday on the 28th of October. The Statue of Liberty is a colossal sculpture on Liberty Island in New York Harbor in New York City. The copper statue, designed by Frederic Auguste Bartholdi, a French sculptor, was built by Gustave Eiffel, (yes, *that* Eiffel) and dedicated on October 28, 1886. It was a gift to the United States from the people of France. The statue is of a robed female figure representing *Libertas*, the Roman goddess, who bears a torch and a *tabula ansata* (a tablet evoking the law) upon which is inscribed the date of the American Declaration of Independence, July 4, 1776. A chain and the broken shackles of oppression and tyranny lie at the feet of the statue. Lady Liberty is more than a monument. She has become a universal symbol of freedom and democracy to millions around the world. After all, the actual name of the statue is "Liberty Enlightening the World." The Statue of Liberty is only a nickname.

For many years, Israeli master photographer Isaac Berez provided United Israel World Union with professional photographs that enriched the pages of the *United Israel Bulletins*. He did so without charge and it was time to recognize this outstanding professional and his many contributions.

Born in the western Ukraine (a part of Poland at the time), Isaac grew up in an affluent family and was well on his way toward attaining a law degree when the invading German army interrupted it. Unable to unite with his family Isaac fled along with hundreds of students and professors to Tashkent (in the Soviet Union's Central Asia) where a friendly Jewish family there helped him establish residence for educational purposes. Isaac entered the local university. He could delay military service as a student while supporting himself with part time work at a factory. By 1944, he had his law degree which fate decreed he would never use. Isaac returned to Poland to seek out the remnants of his family. Only his sister had survived who had been taken in and aided by a kindly Czech family. With the help of the Joint Emergency Committee for Jewish affairs he moved to Italy. Here he studied photography. While attempting to enter Palestine in 1946, he was apprehended by the British and interned in Cyprus. By 1947, he was in Palestine, friendless, without knowledge of Hebrew, and penniless. Again, he became embroiled in war, but this time it was for Israel's independence. Soon, Isaac was speaking Hebrew and practicing photography.

Following his excellent work in Israel where he provided historic coverage of the late David Ben-Gurion, Golda Meir, and other founders of the State, Berez came to the United States as the full-time photographer of the Israel Symphony Orchestra while also serving as a foreign correspondent for press photos for Israeli news outlets. Berez' skills brought him to the attention of several major organizations that made him their exclusive photographer, including the Conference for Soviet Jewry and the Lubavitch World Zionist Organization.

Isaac Berez met journalist David Horowitz while covering events at the UN. They both shared a common personal odyssey of being immigrants and losing family members in the holocaust. Their friendship grew and over the course of many years, Isaac Berez contributed his superior photographic skills in support of United Israel World Union and its mission.

Chapter 42
An Unheeded Holocaust Warning

The response to David Horowitz's book recounting the activities of the late, pro-Zionist Pastor Charles Taze Russell, who preceded Thedor Herzl in calling upon the Jewish people to return and rebuild their ancient homeland, continued to receive favorable reactions. Among prominent Jewish leaders who found the book to be valuable were the Chancellor of Bar Ilan University in Israel, Rabbi Emanuel Rackman and B'nai B'rith International's UN representative, Dr. Harris O. Schoenberg. Thanking journalist Horowitz for the book, Dr. Schoenberg wrote this warm tribute:

> I have been privileged to know you for close to two decades and to visit many times your 'Jewish corner" at the UN. I have also noted the spiritual quality you bring to your work. Very few at the UN these days remember the teaching that humans were created in the image of God. It is, of course, a Jewish teaching, but within its parameters a philosophy of sanctification of the human spirit and dedication to human rights is set out.

At United Israel's 44th Annual Meeting on April 19, 1987, Horowitz also reported on the enthusiastic reception given the volume by other outstanding leaders in both the Jewish and non-Jewish worlds. The widespread circulation of the book brought many new subscribers to the *United Israel Bulletin*.

A proposal was made at the meeting that United Israel establish a Youth Unit to "serve as a sort of watchdog body of trustees based upon its Constitution and by-laws, to continue unabated and that it perpetuate its activities year-in and year-out." The new United Israel Youth Unit "Shomre Ha'Agudah" (Guardians of the Union) held its first meeting on August 17, 1987.

On June 12, 1987, U.S. President Ronald Reagan, while standing at the Brandenburg Gate in West Berlin, uttered his famous line "Mr. Gorbachev, tear down this wall!" calling on the leader of the Soviet Union, Mikhail Gorbachev to open up the barrier which had divided West and East Berlin since 1961. Two months later, on August 17th, Nazi war criminal Rudolf Hess died at Berlin's Spandau prison. He hanged himself. Hess was Adolf Hitler's National Socialist party leader deputy. Rudolph Walter Richard Hess was tried at the Nuremberg war crimes trials, convicted, and given a life sentence. He served his sentence at Spandau prison in Berlin, where from 1966 he was the sole inmate. Soon thereafter, the Spandau prison was demolished to prevent it from becoming a neo-Nazi shrine.

In late 1987, the first Palestinian *intifada* (uprising) against Israeli rule in the West Bank, Gaza Strip, and East Jerusalem erupted in Gaza. Violent from the start, the insurrection lasted until the convening of the Madrid peace conference in 1991. During the four-year period, the Reagan administration, convinced that the status quo was untenable, responded to a bold PLO diplomatic initiative by opening a political dialogue with the PLO, much to the dismay of the Israeli government. The U.S.-PLO dialogue, failing to yield any tangible results, was later suspended by the Bush administration in mid-1990.

The year 1988 arrived, marking two significant anniversaries. The front page of the 1988 summer edition of the *United Israel Bulletin* carried the message from Prime Minister Yitzhak Shamir for *Yom Ha'atzmaut* 5748, celebrating the 40th anniversary of the State of Israel. In the forty years of the State's existence, there was no respite from violence. The wars, taking many forms, all had one thing in common; they all targeted Israel's very existence. The message from the Prime Minister stressed that in the midst of the present trying times, all Israelis join hands and continue to display the courage, and unity and determination that had brought them back to Zion. He then called on everyone to celebrate the unity and solidarity of the Jewish people restored as a nation in their ancient homeland.

The Annual Meeting of United Israel World Union held that year on April 24, 1988 in New York marked its 45th anniversary. David Horowitz opened the meeting by calling for a moment of silent prayer for Rabbi Leo Jung, who had passed away a few months earlier. Dr. Jung was a long-time member of United Israel's Consultative Board and an ardent supporter of the movement. Recognized as one of the world's outstanding orthodox scholars and spiritual leaders, Dr. Jung was instrumental in selecting Mr. Horowitz as the annual commencement recipient of the prestigious Yeshiva University Mordecai ben-David Award in 1982. Rabbi Israel Mowshowitz, another member of United Israel's Consultative Board and then currently an aide to Governor Mario Cuomo of New York, gave the invocation. Among first-time attendees were the acclaimed Israeli piano virtuoso, Amiram Rigai and Israeli playwright Marshall Ross. Other special guests included Lowell Gallin, founder of Israeli-based "Root and Branch Association" and Mijael Garcia, spiritual leader of Congregation Beth Shmuel at Xalapa, Veracruz, Mexico, along with his associate Josef Tamariz. In a special announcement, David Horowitz informed the attendees that Mr. Gregg Sitrin had joined the *United Israel Bulletin* staff as an Associate Editor. Mr. Sitrin previously had assisted the late Dr. Charles H. Kremer in exposing Nazi war criminals living in the United States. President Horowitz cited a number of responses received on the occasion of the 45th anniversary. Too many to mention, special greetings were conveyed from many people and organizations around the world, including Israel, India, France, Canada and Mexico, hailing United Israel as a "Light Unto the Nations."

It was in 1988 that the militant Sunni Islamist multi-national organization *Al-Qaeda* ("the Base") was founded by Osama bin Laden, Abdullah Azzam, and several of their aides. The United Nations Security Council, the North Atlantic Treaty Organization (NATO), the European Union, the United States, Russia, India, and other countries designated it as a terrorist group.

On August 20, 1988, the long Iran-Iraq War mercifully came to an end. The armed conflict, lasting almost eight years, resulted in over one million casualties and billions of dollars in damages. Viewed from a historical perspective, the protracted war was the latest phase of the ancient Persian-Arab conflict throughout the ages.

David Horowitz and Israeli consul Colonel Assad-Assad, an Israeli Druze currently serving in the Israel Mission to the UN, co-authored a feature article entitled, "The Druze and the Jewish People: Why Such Close Affinity?" The comprehensive work is based on *Sefer HaYashar*, a lost book of the Bible, which unveils the mystery behind Jethro's link to Moses. The lost book is mentioned in two places in the Bible; Joshua 10:13 and II Samuel 1:18. Jethro, the father-in-law of Moses, is the central figure of veneration among the Druze people.

During the Hanukkah Season 5748, Reuven Raymond Solomon of the *Solomon Press* published a sixteen-page pamphlet entitled, "Rav Kook's 1929 Holocaust Warning." It contained the English translation of pre-state Israel's two Chief Rabbis' proclamation warning the world in 1929 of a holocaust to befall the Jewish people. Seryl Gellerman, daughter of distinguished Torah teacher, Dr. Yisrael Gellerman, translated the warning. Resurrected by Reuven Solomon, it was being published in English for the first time. There's a background story to the unusual event and it involved David Horowitz.

Horowitz recalled in *Thirty-Three Candles* (1949) that in 1929, a warning was issued and distributed throughout the Jewish world by the two Chief Rabbis of pre-state Israel. In the proclamation, Rabbi Abraham Isaac Kook and Rabbi Jacob Meir warned of a great tragedy that was to be visited upon the Jewish people and calling for intense prayer and repentance. This warning was issued as a result of four strange dreams experienced by Turkish Cabbalist Emanuel Ben-Nisan. He had the strange and troubling dreams after having prayed intensely for an answer concerning the long and bitter exile of the Jewish people. Rabbi Kook and Rabbi Meir incorporated these dreams into the warning pronouncement that was issued.

Among the people who took notice of this warning was the world-renowned sage, writer, and Cabbalist of Warsaw, Poland, Hillel Zeitlin. David Horowitz and Zeitlin became friends during Horowitz's six-month stay in Poland during 1928 and they continued to correspond after Horowitz returned to America. Much of their correspondence dealt with this warning declaration that had come to their attention.

Was this warning the result of a preposterous premonition or something more?

In his letters to Horowitz, written in Hebrew, Zeitlin expressed the view that God would not allow more suffering to come upon his people Israel who, he insisted, had suffered enough through the ages. Horowitz disagreed. In his correspondence, Horowitz appealed to Zeitlin to consider the "manifestation" as a message not to be taken lightly. Citing the words of the prophet in Amos 3:7, Horowitz wrote that "the Divine Presence is at all times evident everywhere."

When the Nazis began liquidating Polish Jewry in 1942, Hillel Zeitlin was seventy-one years old. He was killed by Nazis in the Warsaw ghetto while holding a book of the Zohar and wrapped in a prayer shawl and phylacteries. His family was also killed, with the only survivor being his eldest son, Aaron. David Horowitz wrote the Introduction to *"Rav Kook's 1929 Holocaust Warning"* at his United Nations office on Hanukkah 5748 (1988).

United Israel owes a debt of gratitude to Reuven Raymond Solomon for his work in bringing the English translation of this historical document into the light of day. Copies of the original proclamation in Hebrew and Reuven Solomon's publication remain a part of the United Israel World Union archives.

Chapter 43
An Historical Presidential Oath

The inauguration of George H. W. Bush as the 41st President of the United States was held on January 20, 1989. The oath of office carried a special historic significance and a little-known United Israel connection. The occasion marked the 200th anniversary of the Presidency and was observed as George Bush took the executive oath on the very same Bible that George Washington used in 1789. The ceremony occurred on the west front terrace of the Capitol with Chief Justice William Rehnquist administering the oath.

The inauguration of America's first President took place on the historic day of April 30, 1789, when the stately figure of George Washington, the father of our country, stood before a huge crowd gathered to witness the grand occasion on Wall Street in New York City. Washington took the oath of office holding his right hand on the Bible and his left hand over his heart, symbolic of the prayer for protection of this first democracy of a great nation and a pledge for his supreme efforts to preserve it. Chancellor Robert R. Livingston administered the oath.

The famous Bible, printed in 1767, had been held in the possession of the St. John's Lodge #1 of the Masonic Order in Manhattan. A three-man delegation of leading Masons was selected to bring the priceless heirloom to the swearing-in ceremony for President Bush's Inauguration. Chosen to officially convey the original Bible and attend the ceremony were Louis Warter, long-time United Israel World Union member and supporter; R.W. Clifford Green, Master of St. John's Lodge #1, and R.W. Charles Clement, Chairman of the Bible Committee for the George Washington Bible. As part of the celebration of the 200th

239

anniversary of the grand historic occurrence, the Bible was placed on display in a special glass enclosed case in the White House where it was viewed by thousands of visitors over a period of ten weeks.

The 46th Annual Meeting of United Israel World Union was held on April 30, 1989 at the home of its President, David Horowitz, in New York City. The day chosen for the meeting was symbolic: it was Yom HaShoah (Holocaust Remembrance Day), and the 200th anniversary to the very day of George Washington's inauguration as the first President of the United States.

In key appointments, Dr. Heskel Haddad, M.D., noted Sephardic leader and head of the World Organization of Jews from Arab Countries, along with Ms. Joy Malka, great granddaughter of the late Chief Rabbi of the Sudan, Solomon Malka, were elected members of the Board of Directors of United Israel. Mr. Gregg Sitrin was also elected to the position of Secretary-Treasurer. Dr. Haddad spoke to the group about the symbolism of the day, Yom HaShoah, and his plans to work closely with Nobel Laureate and Holocaust survivor, Elie Wiesel, for the establishment of a Holocaust Memorial in Washington, DC. United Israel veteran Louis Warter, one of the three leading Masons chosen to convey the Washington Bible to the Bush inauguration, also spoke of their personalized tour of the White House and opportunity to meet the new president.

On June 3rd, Grand Ayatollah Ruhollah Khomeini, Supreme Leader of Iran died at the age of eighty-six. Founder of the Islamic Republic of Iran, he was the leader of the 1979 Iranian revolution that saw the overthrow of the Pahlavi monarchy and Mohammad Reza Pahlavi, the Shah of Iran. Khomeini was named "Man of the Year" in 1979 by American news magazine *Time* for his international influence. This "Man of the Year" would later be known for his support of the hostage takers during the Iran Hostage Crisis, when fifty-two American citizens were held hostage for 444 days, and his later fatwa calling for the murder of British Indian novelist Salman Rushdie, and for referring to the United States as the "Great Satan." Khomeini called democracy the equivalent of prostitution.

In June, Edward Ezra Shalom Abrahams, long-time vice president and active supporter of United Israel passed away at his Los Angeles residence following a brief illness. He was eighty-eight years old.

Those familiar with United Israel most likely know the incredible story of Eddie Abraham's life and his role as donor of rare Indian Torah Scrolls to worthwhile congregations around the world, including one to the United Israel World Union organization. He was elected a Vice President of United Israel in 1965.

A formal review of U.S. Persian Gulf policy, finalized in National Security Directive 26 that was signed by President Bush in 1989, reaffirmed the existing view that Iran, and not Iraq, posed the greater threat to U.S. interests in the region. As a result, President Bush supported a policy of trying to build a political and commercial relationship with Iraq, in the hopes of moderating its behavior and offsetting Iranian power. The Middle East juggling act was on full display.

During the summer, David Horowitz met with Israeli Knesset member Rabbi Elizer Waldman, who also heads Yeshivat Kiryat Arba located in Hebron. Rabbi Waldman served as a reserve captain of a tank unit that aided the liberation effort in the 1967 Six-Day War. He was one of the original pioneers who returned to Hebron and established the Hesder Yeshiva.

Iraq possessed the largest and most powerful Arab military force, it had substantial oil reserves, and it served as a counterbalance to Iran in the region. The U.S. provided Iraq with tens of millions of dollars in agricultural credits, gave them satellite intelligence information on the position of Iranian forces, and provided naval protection in the Persian Gulf to Kuwaiti tankers, whose oil shipments financed the Iraqi war effort. Equally important, President Bush encouraged friendly Arab regimes; Saudi Arabia, Egypt, Jordan and Kuwait to "transfer" U.S. supplied arms to Iraq.

But soon after the Iraq-Iran War had ended in late 1988, tensions began to rise between Iraq and Kuwait. Kuwait demanded repayment of the fifteen billion dollars Iraq had borrowed from Kuwait to wage the war. Saddam Hussein refused, saying that Iraq had already paid its debt in blood. Saddam then charged that Kuwait was producing too much oil, driving the price down and reducing Iraqi oil revenues. He also charged that Kuwait was extracting oil from Iraqi oil fields on the Iraqi-Kuwaiti border. By the end of the year, the U.S. effort to work with Iraq was deterred by the reality of Saddam's bad behavior.

The Middle East has been called many things including volatile and complex, and maybe another thing can be said: It is never *boring*.

Part Five

Chapter 44

Invasion Kuwait

As we entered a new decade, the United Israel World Union organization was approaching middle age and David Horowitz was about to celebrate his eighty-seventh birthday. Neither was about to slow down. In January of 1990, it was announced that a revised edition of David Horowitz's book, *Pastor Charles Taze Russell, An Early American Christian Zionist,* was to be published by Shengold Publishers of New York City. The first edition, published by the Philosophical Library in 1986 and praised by many notables including Ambassadors Jeanne Kirkpatrick and Benjamin Netanyahu, sold out and an on-going demand called for re-publication.

On April 23rd Paul O'Dwyer, prominent attorney and a devoted friend of Israel was sworn-in by Mayor David Dinkins as the New York City Commissioner for the United Nations. The New York Mayor recalled O'Dwyer's contributions to the creation of the new State of Israel: "When those seeking to create the miracle we call Israel needed him, he was there. As the Director of the American League for a free Palestine, he was there to argue the case for a Jewish State before the UN. And, he was there to help arm the heroic freedom-fighters who made the State a reality." The proud Irish Catholic's fight for justice would later earn him the Jerusalem Medal from the Israeli Government.

The 47th Annual Meeting of United Israel was held on April 29, 1990 at the historic landmark Brotherhood Synagogue in New York City. The synagogue was originally a Quaker Meeting House built in 1859 and contained a network of underground tunnels that were used to assist slaves fleeing their owners. Rabbi Irving J. Block, spiritual leader of the synagogue, has been a long-time advocate and participant in the work of United Israel.

At the meeting, Secretary-Treasurer Gregg Sitrin reported on a new monumental work entitled, *The Word: The Dictionary That Reveals the Hebrew Source of English,* by Isaac E. Mozeson and published by Shapolsky Publishers in New York City. The unique reference text traces the vast majority of English words back to their ultimate origins in Biblical Hebrew. Researcher and author of several books, Isaac Elchanan Mozeson teaches English at Yeshiva University. Mozeson also co-authored, along with Monroe Rosenthal, the significant historical volume, *Wars of the Jews: A Military History from Biblical to Modern Times,* published in March of 1990 by Hippocrene Books.

On May 16, 1990, entertainer Sammy Davis Jr., died in Beverly Hills, California at age sixty-four. The highly popular actor, comedian, singer and dancer was also part of the "Rat Pack" with Frank Sinatra and Dean Martin, with whom he starred in several films. As previously noted, the famous entertainer and legend formally converted to Judaism in 1961 and was a regular reader of the *United Israel World Union Bulletin* and communicated often with David Horowitz during the 1960s.

In the Middle East, the Iraqi-Kuwaiti situation was deteriorating rapidly. In July, Saddam Hussein demanded that Kuwait hand over to Iraq the islands of Bubiyan and Warba, located at the head of the Persian Gulf. He also claimed that oil overproduction by Kuwait and the United Arab Emirates amounted to "economic warfare" against Iraq. The United States was concerned about the developments in the Gulf but was led to believe that Saddam's threats were all bluster. The U.S. ambassador to Iraq, April Glaspie, reported that Hussein would not use force against Kuwait. Later, the Egyptian President gave President Bush the same assurance. Despite these promises, Iraq amassed nearly 30,000 troops on Kuwait's border in an effort to coerce the emirate to reduce oil production.

On August 2, 1990, Iraq invaded Kuwait. More than 100,000 Iraqi soldiers backed by over 700 tanks quickly overwhelmed the tiny, oil-rich neighbor, forcing the Kuwaiti ruling family into exile. Hussein announced that Kuwait was being permanently annexed to Iraq. The seizure of Kuwait now gave Saddam control of over twenty percent of the world's oil reserves and a substantial coastline on the Persian Gulf.

The Bush administration worked closely with the UN Security Council to pass a resolution condemning the invasion and demanding an immediate withdrawal from Kuwait. The Security Council also imposed economic sanctions against Iraq.

On November 5, 1990, American-Israeli Orthodox Rabbi Meir David Kahane was assassinated following a speech at Manhattan's Marriott East Side Hotel. El Sayyid Nosair, an Egyptian-born American citizen, shot him to death. Rabbi Kahane was the founder and national chairman of the Jewish Defense League and an outspoken activist for Jewish causes. Nosair was later convicted for his role in the 1993 World Trade Center bombing.

Beginning with the Winter 1990-91 issue of *United Israel World Union Bulletin*, Dr. James Tabor, author and noted Professor of Religious Studies at the University of North Carolina at Charlotte, began a series of articles contributed to the United Israel publication. Tabor's two articles—"B'nai Noach: The Reappearance of the God-Fearers in Our Time," and "The Restoration of All Israel"—centered on the major themes of the Biblical Prophets of the restoration of all Israel in the last days. Dr. Tabor first met David Horowitz in New York City in July of this year, before flying to Israel.

In December, David Horowitz was again the recipient of one of Israel's most prestigious awards. He was chosen as one of 100 outstanding individuals to be honored as "Defenders of Jerusalem" at the 10th Anniversary Dinner of the Jabotinsky Foundation on December 10th at New York's Grand Hyatt Hotel. A special private reception for the honorees was held with Israeli Prime Minister Yitzhak Shamir before the dinner. In 1977, David Horowitz had been among the recipients of the "Defenders of Jerusalem" Award for the first time. Prime Minister Menachem Begin personally awarded him the Medal.

Following the seizure and annexation of Kuwait, Iraqi forces seemed capable of moving on into Saudi Arabia, which contained an additional twenty percent of the world's oil. The Saudis formally requested U.S. assistance on August 7. Under UN authorization, a massive international military force began materializing in Saudi

Arabia. President George Bush ordered the launch of *Operation Desert Shield* under the command of General Norman Schwarzkopf to establish U.S. troops in Saudi Arabia as a part of the coalition of nations prepared to reverse Saddam Hussein's action by force if necessary. Over the course of five months, President Bush succeeded in building a coalition of three-dozen nations, which contributed a combined 670,000 troops. The bulk of the forces however, were American, British and French. In late November 1990, the UN Security Council passed a resolution demanding that Iraq withdraw from Kuwait by January 15, 1991. The council authorized the use of force against Iraq should it fail to withdraw by that date.

In an interesting twist to the entire affair, Saddam Hussein tried to link the Kuwait crisis to the Palestine issue in an attempt to break up the anti-Iraq coalition. Saddam said that he would consider withdrawing from Kuwait if Israel also withdrew from the territories it had occupied in the 1967 war. Saddam's proposal was enthusiastically received throughout the Arab world. President Bush however, refused to consider any direct *quid pro quo* and rejected any such linkage.

The power of oil politics as a geopolitical game was in full vogue in 1990. Closing the tense year on a lighter note, it seems fitting to offer the wisdom of Rashid bin Saeed Al Maktoum, the Emir of Dubai, commenting on their oil-centric economy from 1958 to 1990: "My grandfather rode a camel, my father rode a camel, I drive a Mercedes, my son drives a Land Rover, his son will drive a Land Rover, but his son will ride a camel."

The world seemed to pause for that brief year-end period of holidays, New Year's celebrations and momentary peace; that glorious moment in history when everybody stands around reloading. After all, the deadline for Iraq to withdraw from Kuwait was fast approaching.

Chapter 45

A Storm in the Desert

Nineteen-ninety-one began with Iraq on notice. The UN Security Council had authorized the use of force against Iraq should it fail to withdraw from Kuwait by the January deadline date. Both houses of Congress had also approved the use of force. The January 15th deadline passed without any Iraqi withdrawal from Kuwait. It was time to act.

On January 16th, the United States and its coalition partners launched "Operation Desert Storm." In the first twenty-four hours, allied planes flew more than 1,000 sorties, wiping out Iraq's command and control capability as well as its anti-aircraft batteries. The coalition also attacked industrial and infrastructural targets inside Iraq. The massive U.S.-led air campaign continued throughout the war. Despite the beating Iraq was taking from the air, it still refused to withdraw.

On February 23rd, the coalition forces launched a ground war to directly expel Iraqi forces from Kuwait. Within three days the massive allied ground offensive had retaken Kuwait City in the face of crumbling Iraqi resistance. By the time U.S. President George Bush declared a cease-fire on February 28th, Iraqi resistance had completely collapsed.

During the war, Saddam Hussein hoped to provoke a military response from Israel. Thirty-nine Iraqi Scud missiles caused extensive damage in Tel Aviv and Haifa, two of Israel's three largest cities. The Iraqi government hoped that many Arab states would withdraw from the coalition, as they would be reluctant to fight alongside Israel.

Israel prepared to retaliate, however, President Bush pressured Israeli Prime Minister Yitzhak Shamir not to do so, fearing that if Israel attacked Iraq, the other Arab nations would either desert the coalition or join Iraq. The Israelis grew increasingly impatient, warning that if the U.S. failed to stop the attacks, they would. At one point, Israeli pilots boarded their aircraft prepared to fly into Iraq before aborting the mission. In response to the Scud attacks, the U.S. rapidly deployed Patriot missile air defense batteries to Israel.

Military operations ceased on February 28th, after forty-three days of fighting. On April 6th, Iraq accepted a cease-fire and agreed to pay reparations to Kuwait. Even though it stayed out of the fighting, Israel had helped guarantee Jordan's security by warning that it would take military measures if any Iraqi troops entered Jordan. The war had ended with Saddam Hussein still in power and much of his army intact; it would only prolong the international confrontation with Iraq to another day.

On March 20, 1991, President George Bush signed into law a Joint Resolution of both houses of the United States Congress which recognizes the Seven Noahide Laws as "the bedrock of society from the dawn of civilization." The historical resolution urges a return of the world "to the moral and ethical values contained in the Seven Noahide Laws." The Joint Resolution also proclaimed that March 26th, 1991, the 90th birthday of Rabbi Menachem Schneerson, leader of the worldwide Lubavitch movement, be designated as "Education Day, USA"

United Israel World Union celebrated its 48th year in the Manhattan home of David Horowitz. The annual meeting featured keynote speakers Professor Aaron Lichtenstein of City University of New York; Dr. Heskel Haddad, President of the World Organization of Jews from Arab Countries; and Rabbi Hailu Paris, reporting on the movement to bring Ethiopian Jews to Israel. Greetings and messages were acknowledged from members and supporters around the world, including Israel, Ghana, The Philippines, England, and France. The Officers and Board approved the proposal to add Professors Aaron Lichtenstein and Dr. James Tabor to United Israel's Consultative Board.

On May 24-25, 1991, Israel launched "Operation Solomon," a covert military operation to airlift Ethiopian Jews to Israel. Non-stop flights of 35 Israeli aircraft, including Israeli Air Force C-130s and El Al Boeing 747s, transported 14,325 Ethiopian Jews to Israel in 36 hours. Aircraft seats were removed to accommodate as many people as possible, while Prime Minister Yitzhak Shamir authorized the Israeli airline, El Al to fly on the Jewish Sabbath. "Operation Solomon" rescued twice the number evacuated in the winter of 1984-85 during "Operation Moses" and "Operation Joshua," in a fraction of the time. Yet again, Israel had pulled off a bold, successful mission to bring Jews back to their homeland.

The winter edition of the *United Israel Bulletin* reviewed *The Seven Laws of Noah,* an instructive 122-page book, first published in 1981 and reissued in 1986 by Berman Books, Brooklyn, NY. Authored by Professor Aaron Lichtenstein of the City University of New York, the work presents an historic background detailing the evolution of the Seven Laws of Noah, how they were accepted within both the Jewish and Non-Jewish worlds, and what each of them means on the basis of the Talmud and the Bible. The *Bulletin* also included part II of Dr. James Tabor's articles: "B'nai Noach: The Reappearance of God-Fearers in Our Time," and "The Restoration of All Israel."

The Madrid Peace Conference of 1991 was held from October 30 to November 1. Hosted by Spain and co-sponsored by the U.S. and the Soviet Union, it was an attempt by the international community to revive the Israeli-Palestinian peace process. The Madrid conference was a watershed event. For the first time, Israel entered into direct, face-to-face negotiations with Syria, Lebanon, Jordan, and the Palestinians. The three-day conference achieved little by way of substantial agreement, but it was an historic breakthrough in Arab-Israeli diplomacy. It became a link between the end of the 1991 Gulf War and later signing of the 1993 Oslo Accord.

In early December, the UN Judaica Book Club honored David Horowitz at the United Nations for his "Lifelong Dedication to the Highest Ideals of Judaism and of the United Nations." The Club's President, Dr. Harris O. Schoenberg, Director of the B'nai B'rith International UN Affairs Division, presented the "Achievement Award" to Horowitz during the Club's well-attended annual Hanukkah celebration on December 5, 1991. On hand for the presentation, among other notables, were Israel's UN Ambassador, Mr. Yoram Aridor and Ambassador Arthur Liveran, one of the earliest Israeli Mission delegates. Also attending were many of Horowitz's stalwart allies and friends at the UN, among them veteran UN staff member, Abraham Weinstein.

Dr. Schoenberg credited Horowitz as having originally sowed the seeds at the UN for the Hanukkah and other holiday observances, which action had given birth to the creation of the club. Ambassador Liveran paid high tribute to David's manifold historic endeavors throughout his coverage of the United Nations since 1947. The United Nations Judaica Book Club is an officially recognized club with more than 100 active Jewish members at the New York Headquarters.

In other UN news, on December 16th, the United Nations General Assembly voted overwhelmingly to revoke the bitterly contested statement it approved in 1975 that said, "Zionism is a form of racism and racial discrimination." The 1975 UN Resolution No. 3379 was part of the Soviet-Arab Cold War anti-Israel campaign. Applause broke out in the General Assembly as the result flashed on the big electronic voting board high on one side of the hall. Delegates leapt up from their seats and rushed to congratulate Israel's Foreign Minister, David Levy, who led his country's delegation at the session. In the history of the UN, this is the only resolution that has ever been revoked.

A new year was about to arrive, one in which "Remembering David Horowitz" would take on a new and personal dimension for this writer.

Chapter 46

A Personal Involvement

April 2, 1992. It was a clear and crisp spring morning in Manhattan when I arrived at the United Nations Headquarters on the Upper East Side. After clearing a security check, I proceeded to the information desk where an official UN Press Pass as a guest of World Union Press was waiting for me. Accompanied by a security attendant, I was escorted to room 373 of the busy press section, situated on the 3rd floor of the stately glass and marble Secretariat building.

The little office was piled high with books and papers. Covering the walls were many photos of David Horowitz with dignitaries from all over the world depicting his participation in the history of the UN. There were shelves of Jewish memorabilia: a mezuzah, an Israeli flag, Kiddush cups and an embroidered kippah, a Hanukkah menorah and a photo of Jerusalem. Many of the items were gifts from visiting delegates and dignitaries. It was truly a Jewish-Israeli niche at the United Nations.

Rising from behind his desk to greet me was the slightly built, silvered haired dean of UN correspondents. It was the first time I met David Horowitz. Little was I aware at the time of the impact this appointment of destiny would bring to my life.

On March 9th, all Israel received the news of the death of one of its founding heroes. Menachem Begin was an Israeli politician, founder of Likud and the sixth Prime Minister of Israel. Before the creation of the State of Israel, he was the leader of the Zionist militant group Irgun. His most significant achievement as Prime Minister was the signing of a peace treaty with Egypt in 1979, for which he and Anwar Sadat of

Egypt shared the Nobel Prize for Peace. Begin was seventy-nine-years-old.

Menachem Begin was buried in a simple ceremony in the Jewish Cemetery on the Mount of Olives. He had asked to be buried there instead of Mount Herzl, where most Israeli leaders are laid to rest, because he wanted to be buried beside his beloved wife Aliza. As has been mentioned previously, David Horowitz and Menachem Begin had had a long friendship. Horowitz's wife Nan had actually been a friend and active supporter of Begin's efforts with the Irgun before she and David were married. David and Nan were guests in the Begin home in Israel on several occasions and there were many written exchanges between Horowitz and Begin over the years. Those letters remain a part of the United Israel archives.

On April 23, 1992, David Horowitz appeared as the main speaker at a special Passover Party sponsored by the Sofrim Society of New York, a body composed of employees of the offices of the Comptroller, the Department of Finance and affiliated agencies of the City. Held at the Municipal Building, the subject of Mr. Horowitz's address was "Israel, the United Nations and the World."

The 49th Annual Meeting of United Israel took place on May 3, 1992, in the Manhattan home of David Horowitz. One of the items discussed was the composition of a special universal prayer for redemption than could be offered on the beginning of each new moon. The "New Moon Prayer," based on the words of the Prophets "Return to Me, says Jehovah, and I will return to you," an idea originally conceived by Horowitz, was composed in consultation with United Israel Consultative Board Member Dr. James Tabor. The inspiration and idea behind the New Moon Prayer deserves a reflective look.

David Horowitz had long worked passionately in promoting the vision of a universal Torah faith based on the faith of Abraham and the prophetic vision of the Prophets. He asked Dr. Tabor to compose a prayer for redemption, based entirely on Biblical concepts and vocabulary, which would be appropriate for Jews or Gentiles. It was to be a prayer applicable for any and all who share the faith in Jehovah God, his Way and His Plan for the world. It was suggested that the monthly time of prayer be set on the evening of the last day of each

Jewish month, before the New Moon (Erev Rosh Chodesh) at a set time. It was to be a prayer, biblically pure in word and form, and appropriate for Jew or Gentile, that would allow all people to express the One Faith in the One God together, and at the same time. The inspirational prayer appeared in the next edition of the *United Israel Bulletin*.

One of the featured speakers at the meeting was Mr. Yakov Gladstone, who had spent much of his lifetime in aiding and guiding black Jews in both the U.S. and Israel. In 1984, he assisted the first organized group of Ethiopian *olim* to arrive in Israel through "Operation Moses." He personally was present at Ben-Gurion airport to welcome 15,000 of the arriving Ethiopian Jews. As a teacher, he spent time traveling throughout the country educating the Ethiopian youth as they integrated into a new culture. He also worked with Jewish organizations in New York to establish scholarships for Ethiopian and other economically deprived youth in Israel.

On June 23, 1992, Yitzhak Rabin was re-elected as the eleventh Prime Minister of Israel succeeding Yitzhak Shamir. Rabin was appointed the sixth Prime Minister in 1974, after the resignation of Golda Meir.

Rabbi Israel Mowshowitz, spiritual leader of a major Queens congregation and longtime supporter of United Israel, died on June 30, 1992. He was seventy-seven years old. The internationally known Rabbi became a spokesman for rabbis nationwide and was an advisor to New York Governor Mario Cuomo. Rabbi Mowshowitz enjoyed a long friendship with Governor Cuomo, a Roman Catholic, who often called him "my Rabbi." Rabbi Mowshowitz, was also a longtime friend of David Horowitz and played a vital role in the history of United Israel. At United Israel's 30th gala anniversary dinner, held in New York City on May 12, 1973, Rabbi Mowshowitz had delivered the invocation and offered these words of praise for the organization: "We gather here tonight to celebrate the 30th anniversary of United Israel World Union which has, through the years, been indeed a beacon of light to our people and the world—a mighty champion of the State of Israel and a disseminator of the spiritual and moral light of Torah to all men."

On December 14, 1992, David Horowitz again returned to Israel. This time however, he made an historic pilgrimage as the guest of Dr. James Tabor and special friends, Dennis and Kathy Jones, recent converts to Judaism. One of the explicit purposes of the journey was to visit the famous Cave of the Sanhedrin in Jerusalem, a place that held special significance for David. As he described in *Thirty-Three Candles*, it was at this cave that David Horowitz, as a young pioneer in British Mandate Palestine, had a mysterious and historic encounter with a truly prophetic figure, Moshe Guibbory, in December 1927. The encounter set in motion events that impacted David Horowitz's life for the next twenty years. The experience and subsequent insights led to the formation of United Israel World Union in 1944.

Accompanied by Jerusalem friend John Hulley, the little group gathered at the close of the day on Friday, the beginning of the Sabbath, to observe a short and simple ceremony at the cave. Candles were lit, and prayers were offered. It was Kislev 24.

Though other interesting things transpired on the trip, the group agreed that the visit to the sight of the Sanhedrin Cave was the most moving and significant. What no one realized at the time and did not find out until returning home to the U.S., was that the original encounter David Horowitz had with the prophetic Moshe at the Cave happened also on Friday evening, Kislev 24 in 1927—precisely sixty-five years ago to the day! (The 1993 winter edition of *United Israel Bulletin* later carried the full account of the historic Kislev 24 pilgrimage to Jerusalem.)

The 1992 winter edition of the *Bulletin* included two insightful and candid articles by Consultative Board member, Dr. James Tabor. In the first, entitled "Plain Talk About Christianity, Paganism and the Torah Faith," Professor Tabor speaks out plainly about the true Biblical Faith as revealed in the pages of the Torah and how classical Christianity developed from the late first century CE forward. In the second article, "An Open Letter from Professor James D. Tabor," he extends an urgent call for a return to Sinai and explains the background and development of the "Monthly Prayer for Redemption." The Bulletin carried the first public printing of the inspiring and biblically based prayer.

Chapter 47

An Historic Jubilee Celebration

Following my first meeting with David Horowitz in April 1992, we continued to communicate frequently. My business trips to New York almost always included time for a visit with David at his UN office. This incredible man, then the oldest and longest serving journalist at the UN, had been reporting from the world body since its inception. "I came here in 1947 to cover the UN debate on Palestine," David remarked, "and I never left. I witnessed the miracle of the birth of Israel with its repercussions to this present day."

Although the Madrid Peace Conference of 1991 had produced few results, bilateral talks had continued sporadically throughout 1992. Meanwhile, Israeli and PLO officials began holding secret meetings in Oslo, Norway. The Israelis were willing to meet directly with the PLO because Yassar Arafat, ironically, was prepared to be much more flexible than the non-PLO delegation. To ensure that the meetings remained secret, elaborate measures were taken so that the Israelis and Palestinians were never seen together. They arrived at different airports, stayed in different hotels, and were closely guarded by intelligence officers. The meetings were held at an isolated farmhouse, in safe houses, and other secure locations.

Whereas the Oslo talks were being conducted secretly, Israeli and Palestinian negotiators were still engaged in public talks that had originated in the Madrid Conference. Neither the members of the Palestinian delegation nor their PLO advisor, Nabil Shaath, knew about the back-channel meetings. But the secrets in Oslo were to be revealed to the world shortly.

Nineteen-ninety-three arrived and Bill Clinton was sworn in on January 20th as the 42nd President of the United States. Thirty-seven days later, a truck bomb was detonated below the North Tower of the World Trade Center in New York City. The powerful bomb was intended to send the North Tower crashing into the South Tower, bringing both towers down and killing tens of thousands of people. It failed, but still killed six people and injured more than a thousand. The mastermind of the attack was a Pakistani operative named Ramzi Yousef, who had been an associate of Osama bin Laden during the Afghanistan War. Sadly, it would not be the only time these New York City landmarks proved to be the target of terrorist attacks.

In April, United Israel World Union celebrated truly historic occasions. The dual celebrations marked fifty years of global activities on behalf of a unified Israel and the universal values of the Torah Faith, and the celebration of the 90th birthday of United Israel Founder and President David Horowitz.

United Israel's Jubilee celebration took place on April 11, 1993 at the renowned B'nai Zion American-Israel Friendship House in Manhattan. Over 130 guests joined David Horowitz and the Jubilee's Co-Chairmen, Hebert Solomon and Dr. James Tabor, for the gala affair. Well-known San Diego attorney, Herbert Joel Solomon, opened the celebration by welcoming the guests "to honor one of the great men of the 20th Century," and called it a mitzvah to have been given the opportunity to fulfill the commandment of "honoring thy father." Herbert Solomon was the son of United Israel President David Horowitz. Mr. Solomon then called on longtime United Israel friend, Rabbi Irving J. Block of the Brotherhood Synagogue, to give the invocation. Following the invocation, Rabbi Block introduced his associate, Cantor Eliezer Brooks, who mesmerized the audience with a beautiful and moving rendition of "Yerushalayim Shel Zahav." Co-Chairman Solomon then asked world renowned Cantor Joseph Malovany to offer a special song in honor of David Horowitz. Cantor Malovany, making reference to Horowitz as a two-time honoree of the "Defender of Israel" Award, sang an exquisite rendition in Hebrew of "O' Jerusalem."

Eight days later, Cantor Malovany was in Warsaw, Poland to give a special vocal presentation in commemoration of the 50th anniversary of the Warsaw Ghetto Uprising. Also in attendance were Israeli Premier Yitzak Rabin and Vice President Al Gore of the United States. Poland's President, Lech Walesa, delivered the commemorative address.

Following the introductions of several members of Horowitz's family and dignitaries in attendance, Co-Chairman Solomon proceeded to acknowledge the many warm greetings and congratulations from scores of friends and *Bulletin* readers from all parts of the nation and abroad. Among them were special tributes from leading Rabbis, Professor Yonah Alexander of George Washington University, Bar-Ilan University chancellor Emmanuel Rackman and Amitzia Guibbory. Included in the many acknowledgements was a personal note to Horowitz from Nobel Prize winner Elie Wiesel, who referred to him as "my wonderful friend."

Professor Dr. James Tabor began an impressive array of program speakers which included B'nai No'ach leader, J. David Davis, noted Nazi Hunter Charles Allen, Jr., Pastor Kenneth Rawson, veteran UN staff colleague Al Weinstein, writer and author, Dr. Manfred Lehmann, poet Wolf Pasmanik, Mason Louis Warter, journalist colleague John Cappelli, and Metropolitan Opera Orchestra violinist Shem Guibbory. It was an all-star cast of speakers.

At this point, Herbert Solomon introduced the esteemed honoree David Horowitz, the founder of United Israel World Union. Horowitz spoke eloquently and passionately about his early years as a pioneer in British Mandate Palestine, his spiritual quest with its sometimes strange and mysterious twists, and the movement he founded based upon the principles of Israel's ancient laws. Horowitz, at ninety years of age, whose achievements are enough to have consumed several lifetimes, was still articulating the prophetic ideal of Abrahamic Faith for all humanity.

As the Jubilee celebration drew to a close, Horowitz was presented with a unique gift by Mr. Dennis Jones—a beautifully framed photograph of the Cave of the Seventy Sanhedrin. Standing at the entrance of the historic cave were Professor James Tabor, Dennis and Kathy Jones, David Horowitz and John Hulley. The photograph was taken during David Horowitz's historic return to the cave on Kislev 24 during Hanukkah 1992.

I remember being struck by the overwhelming feeling of the history represented at the Jubilee affair. The personalities, their amazing lives and accomplishments, the diversity, yet all had converged to pay tribute to a truly remarkable man and the respected organization he had founded five decades ago. It was a rare moment in time that I was privileged to witness two historic milestone events: David Horowitz had reached the nonagenarian plateau, and United Israel World Union was entering its second Jubilee period.

On April 19th, a fifty-one-day standoff at the Branch Davidian compound near Waco, Texas ended with a fire that killed seventy-six people, including leader David Koresh. The Branch Davidians, a sect that separated in 1955 from the Seventh-day Adventist Church, was led by David Koresh and lived at Mount Carmel Center ranch in the community of Elk, Texas, just nine miles from Waco. The group was suspected of weapons violations causing a search and arrest warrant to be obtained by the ATF (Bureau of Alcohol, Tobacco, Firearms and Explosives), and involvement by the FBI.

Professor James Tabor and his colleague, Phillip Arnold, cooperated with the FBI during the Waco crisis in an effort to interpret the beliefs of the Branch Davidians during the negotiations by communicating with Koresh through taped recordings. In what became a vain effort, the two tried to educate the FBI on the apocalyptic aspects of the group and, at the same time, use the texts to persuade Koresh to bring the episode to a peaceful end. Although their discussions were yielding progress, the decision was made by the authorities to end the siege by force. Tabor and Dr. Eugene V. Gallagher later co-authored an insightful book entitled, *Why Waco? Cults and the Battle for Religious Freedom in America* (University of California Press, 1995), offering a thorough analysis of the tragic confrontation and raising provocative questions about government's role and the state of freedom of religion in America today.

The secret talks between Israeli and PLO officials in Oslo yielded a measure of success. In August 1993, the delegations had reached an agreement. In the "Letters of Mutual Recognition," the PLO acknowledged the State of Israel and pledged to reject violence, and Israel recognized the PLO as the official representative of the Palestinian people. The arrangement lasted for a five-year interim period during which a permanent agreement was negotiated.

On September 13, 1993, the Oslo Accords (referred to as Oslo I at this point), were signed by Shimon Peres and Mahmoud Abbas, and witnessed by Israeli Prime Minister Yitzhak Rabin, PLO Chairman Yasser Arafat, and U.S. President Bill Clinton at an official signing ceremony in Washington, DC. Israel's concession was that it legitimized the PLO on the basis of its words. It remained to be seen if its deeds would be consistent with them.

Chapter 48
A New Beginning

As United Israel World Union entered its second Jubilee period, the organizational structure began to experience change. Mr. Gregg Sitrin, who joined the United Israel Bulletin staff as associate editor in 1988 and was elected Secretary-Treasurer in 1989, provided much needed assistance to David Horowitz at his UN office. Dr. James Tabor, who had met Horowitz in 1990, was becoming increasingly involved in United Israel's efforts and agreed to serve as an officer, assisting David in producing the *Bulletin* and other related matters. I also agreed to serve on the United Israel Board.

In a message by Dr. Tabor which appeared in the Jubilee edition of the *Bulletin* in 1993, he addressed the need for reorganizational planning while reaffirming the commitment to the original statement of purpose and task in the Constitution and By-Laws of the organization.

On October 2-3, 1993, during the Sukkoth holidays, Dr. James Tabor and I visited the President of United Israel and his wife Nan at their northern New Jersey cottage and discussed future plans for the revitalization of the fifty-year movement. The little cottage located in the township of Blairstown in New Jersey was situated in a woodsy setting just off Mt. Vernon Road. There was a small pond nearby. The cottage retreat provided a respite from the busy activities of city life and the hot Manhattan summer heat. Their little dog always accompanied them.

During our historic visit, we spent time in David's vine-draped Sukkah in a mood of prayerful communion and a reading of selected passages from the Prophets relating to the occasion. In connection with the revitalization of the movement, Dr. Tabor and I agreed to join United Israel as officers, setting in motion intensified activities to begin in 1994. Professor Tabor also agreed to work with David as co-editor of the *Bulletin*. During the meeting an active program was outlined for the coming year.

David Horowitz had reached the age of ninety which imposes its natural limitations, but he maintained a passion and vigor that seemed to belie his age. In a grateful tone, however, he agreed that he "could use a little help."

The Oslo negotiations seemed to be changing the dynamics of Middle East diplomacy while creating the momentum for peace. Israel was negotiating directly with one of its bitterest enemies, the Soviet Union had collapsed, and the united Arab front against Israel was showing signs of breaking down. King Hussein of Jordan wasted little time in negotiating agreements and normalizing relations with Israel. Would real and lasting success toward peace finally be achieved, or was this just another mirage?

The winter 1993 edition of the *United Israel Bulletin* carried several newsworthy announcements and articles. One of them featured a report on the 8th Annual B'nai Noah Conference that took place in Athens, Tennessee on November 7-10, 1993. This unique annual gathering brought together both Jews and non-Jews who are oriented toward Torah faith based on the Seven Laws of Noah. Hundreds gathered to hear an impressive array of speakers, including Rabbi Israel Chait, Dean of the B'nai Torah Yeshiva in Far Rockaway, NY; Rabbi Solomon Zweiter, professor at Bar Ilan University in Israel; and Rabbi Chaim Richman of The Temple Institute in Jerusalem. Also speaking were United Israel's Dr. James Tabor; publisher and computer chronology researcher Mr. Gene Faulstich; and local B'nai Noach leaders J. David Davis and Jack Saunders.

The *Bulletin* also featured a story of the Jerusalem-based research on the Lost Tribes of Israel being compiled by researcher and author John Hulley. Dr. Tabor first met Hulley on a visit to Israel in 1990. His subsequent involvement with United Israel bears a look back at a most interesting career.

John Hulley graduated from Harvard College with high honors, majoring in Economics. He spent his professional career as an economist in the U.S. government and achieved special recognition for his services developing the Marshall Plan for European recovery. He later served as a senior economist at the World Bank headquarters in Washington, DC.

Hulley's papers appeared in many professional journals and his essay, "Dynamics of Life in the Universe," was selected as required reading at the War College of the U.S. Air Force where astronauts train. Additionally, he had two other papers published by The Congressional Committee on Science and Technology. Following a conversion to Judaism, Hulley relocated to Jerusalem where he spent time writing and lecturing on science and religion. For the past decade he was engaged in research, while writing a comprehensive, multi-volume work which sets forth, in the most rigorous historical and scientific manner, the migration and identification of the ten northern tribes of ancient Israel. Hulley's life, friendship, and important research continued to play an instrumental role in future activities of United Israel World Union.

On December 30, 1993, an agreement was signed between a small state and an even smaller one. This accord was unique, historic, and transcended geographic borders. The agreement established diplomatic relations between the Vatican and the State of Israel. The Hanukkah songs and the Israeli national anthem, "Hatikva," reverberated in sharp contrast to the words uttered by Pope Pius X in reply to the founder of the Zionist movement, Theodor Herzl, who in 1903 asked him to support the idea of creating a Jewish state. Pope Pius X responded: "The Jews did not recognize our God. Therefore, we cannot recognize any right on their part to the Holy Land." Ninety-four years later, on the evening of December 23, 1997, His Eminence Cardinal Edward Idris Cassidy participated in the ceremony of the lighting of the first candle of Hanukkah on behalf of His Holiness Pope John Paul II. Another candle was also lit. It was to mark the 50th anniversary of the State of Israel.

On February 25, 1994, following the difficult negotiations between the Israelis and the PLO, an Israeli extremist named Baruch Goldstein walked into the Tomb of the Patriarchs in Hebron and opened fire on the Muslim worshipers with an assault rifle, killing twenty-nine Palestinians before being overpowered and then beaten to death by survivors. It was by far the worst act of terrorism ever committed by an Israeli, and naturally inflamed the Arab world.

The massacre was widely denounced in Israel with Israeli Prime Minister Yitzhak Rabin condemning the attack and describing Goldstein as a "degenerate murderer" and an embarrassment to Judaism. Violence escalated however, as the Islamic radical organization Hamas retaliated with two suicide bus bombings against Israeli citizens.

At the 66th Academy Awards presentation held on March 21st in Los Angeles, Steven Spielberg's epic Holocaust drama *Schindler's List* won seven Oscars including Best Picture and Best Director. The Library of Congress later selected it for preservation in the National Film Registry in 2004, and in 2007 the American Film Institute ranked the film 8th on its list of the 100 best American films of all time. Often listed among the greatest films ever made, it didn't do badly at the box office either, earning $321.2 million worldwide on a $22 million budget.

United Israel World Union officially marked the beginning of a new era at its 51st Annual Meeting held at the Dumont Plaza Hotel in Manhattan on April 3, 1994. The watershed event brought the organizational changes needed to provide continued leadership and growth to the world movement. United Israel President David Horowitz called the meeting to order with the kindling of a special candle. It was a rare and unique candlestick that had been given to him as a parting gift by Moses Guibbory as Horowitz was about to embark on his voyage back to America aboard the S.S. Vulcania on May 15, 1934. Horowitz's remarkable encounter with the mysterious and prophetic figure is recounted in *Thirty-Three Candles* (World Union Press, 1949).

The business agenda of the meeting brought the election of new officers and board members. David Horowitz continued as President. Professor James D. Tabor was elected to the new position of Executive Vice President and I accepted the nomination to serve as Vice President replacing the late Eddie Abrahams who had served in that capacity for more than three decades. Newly-elected to the Board of Directors were J. David Davis, Dennis Jones, Rebecca Buntyn, LaTrenda Deem and Dr. Gene C. Lavers, a New York University professor. Other existing members were re-elected for another term.

Fifty years had passed since the prophetic vision of a United Israel was founded upon the principles of Israel's ancient laws. The movement, now a world structure lauded by leaders in many fields, closed the final years of the 20th Century with new leadership in place and poised to begin a new millennium. The organization was still led, however, as it always had been, by its founder, David Horowitz, who was quick to point out that the great lawgiver, Moses began his best work after the age of eighty.

Chapter 49
A Prophet with Honor

The summer 1994 edition of the *United Israel Bulletin* was released and was filled with important announcements and newsworthy articles. Coverage was given to the historic 51st Annual Meeting and the new leadership structure now in place. It included a full recap of the pivotal gathering and brief bios of the two new officers.

Newly elected Executive Vice President, Dr. James Tabor wrote a review of Rabbi Rafael Eisenberg's momentous new book, *Survival—Israel and Mankind*, (New York and Jerusalem: Feldheim Publishers, 1991). Rabbi Eisenberg was an author, a profound Torah scholar, and possessed a clear and perceptive understanding of history and the human condition. In Dr. Tabor's insightful review he mentioned two classic works by Rabbi Eisenberg: *East-West Conflict: Psychological Origin and Resolution*, published in 1967, and *A Matter of Return*, published in 1980 (both of which Tabor had reviewed in the previous issue of *United Israel Bulletin*). As Dr. Tabor pointed out, Rabbi Eisenberg died in Jerusalem in 1976 after a prolonged illness. His beloved wife, Ilse Eisenberg, with the editorial assistance of Abraham Sutton, completed *Survival—Israel and Mankind*.

In mid-August 1994, I received an unexpected package from Jerusalem. It was from the late Rabbi Eisenberg's widow, Ilse Eisenberg. In an enclosed letter, Mrs. Eisenberg congratulated me on joining the leadership of United Israel and also shared some unknown information about the Rabbi. An Eisenberg association with David Horowitz and the activities of United Israel dated back to 1967 when, as head of the United Nations Press Corps, Horowitz was instrumental in sending autographed copies of Rabbi Eisenberg's *The East-West Conflict* to multiple heads-of state. He received true affirmation from many of them affirming the valuable work and its message to all mankind. Mrs. Eisenberg spoke of her late husband passing away in 1976 leaving behind an unfinished manuscript constituting a sequel to *East-West Conflict* and of the challenge and reward of its ultimate publication. Still a reader of *United Israel Bulletins*, she offered praise for Dr. Tabor's earlier review of the book, calling it "so beautifully, wisely, and incisively reviewed." Enclosed with the letter from Mrs. Eisenberg was a copy of *Survival—Israel and Mankind* beautifully personalized with her best wishes to me for health, success and peace. She added a postscript: "Survival" was being translated into French with future language translations planned.

Methodical progress continued to be made between Israel and the PLO despite efforts by Hamas to derail the peace process. On May 4, 1994, the Gaza-Jericho Agreement (a follow-up treaty to the Oslo I Accord) was concluded. The Treaty provided for limited Palestinian self-rule in the West Bank and Gaza Strip within five years. Other provisions of the agreement included a timetable for the withdrawal of Israeli troops from those areas.

Following the Gaza-Jericho Agreement, the "Palestinian National Authority" was established to be the interim self-government body to govern the two areas. Yasser Arafat became the first president on July 5th with the formal inauguration of the PNA.

Other Middle East peace initiatives continued to show promise as Israel and Jordan signed the "Washington Declaration" on July 25th that formally ended the state of war that had existed between them since 1948. On August 8th, the Wadi Araba crossing was established, becoming the first border crossing between the two countries.

William E. Goodin, originally a member of the Worldwide Church of God and later one of the founders of the West Olive, Michigan congregation of United Israel, passed away on July 31, 1994.

In the August 14, 1994 edition of *The New York Times*, renowned reporter Francis X. Clines published an article about David Horowitz and his long career at the UN. Entitled "At Keyboard, A Prophet with Honor," Clines wrote of his interview with Horowitz about his seven decades of service in journalism. The article highlighted many of the key events in Horowitz's career from his arrival in 1947 to cover the Palestinian question, to his many journalism awards, and being elected President of the United Nations Correspondents Association. He described David as "still hacking away at his typewriter from a paper-stacked desk to cover the latest story in the Middle East epic of turmoil, despair, and uneasy hope, while offering his own keen and clear-eyed assessment of unfolding events." Clines concluded with the account of a dialogue exchange beginning in 1945 between David Horowitz and King Abdullah of Jordan (then called Trans-Jordan). Horowitz had appealed to the King to consider the Torah and the Holy Koran as the basis for adjudicating peace between the two contending political forces.

The correspondence between Horowitz and the grandfather of the present King Hussein of Jordan continued for nearly two years moving to its cordial conclusion. Fittingly, it was the grandson of King Abdullah who codified that sentiment in a peace agreement with his Israeli neighbors.

On October 26, 1994, Jordan became the second Arab country to sign a peace treaty with Israel. The Israelis had always believed it would be possible to reach an agreement with Jordan and viewed King Hussein as a reliable partner. The Treaty of Peace between the State of Israel and the Hashemite Kingdom of Jordan was signed in a ceremony held in the historic Biblical region of the Arava valley of Israel near the Jordanian border. President of Israel Ezer Weizman shook hands with King Hussein as U.S. President Bill Clinton and Secretary of State Warren Christopher looked on. Thousands of colorful balloons were released as the event ended. It isn't hard to imagine ninety-one-year-old journalist David Horowitz smiling as he filed the breaking story.

It was mid-October, and I was on my way to Israel accompanied by my son, Kent, who was making his first trip to the Holy Land. We were joining with Dr. James Tabor and United Israel board member, J. David Davis, both having left on September 13th, arriving in time to observe Yom Kippur with Jerusalem researcher John Hulley. The purpose of the trip was multifaceted. Professor Tabor was there to consult with Hebrew Bible scholars regarding a new translation of the Bible that he had been preparing for the past two years and to follow up on several projected archaeological projects of interest. We had the opportunity to spend important time in the Galilee region, especially at the holy city of Tz'fat (Safed), investigating some of the ancient tomb sites reported by Isaac ben Luria (The Ari) and his disciples. Rabbi Chaim Richman of the Temple Institute in Jerusalem accompanied us on the Safed excursion. Another highlight of the trip was a visit to the site of Cave number one near Qumran, where Bedouins discovered the first batches of Dead Sea Scrolls in 1947. The authentic site of the cave had remained virtually unknown, even to most tour guides in Israel. The winter 1994-95 issue of *United Israel Bulletin* carried a full report of the historic trip.

On December 10, 1994, the Norwegian Nobel Committee awarded the Nobel Peace Prize to Yasir Arafat, Shimon Peres and Yitzhak Rabin for their efforts to create peace in the Middle East.

On Christmas Day, December 25, 1994, David Horowitz's beloved wife Nan passed away at the age of eighty-four. First meeting at a New Year's Eve party in Greenwich Village in 1949, David and Nan were married for forty-three years.

By the end of the year, Jordan had opened an embassy in Tel Aviv, and Israel had established one in Amman. Several other Arab states began to pursue business and diplomatic contacts with Israel. At year's end more than 150 nations had diplomatic relations with Israel—more than double the number only a decade earlier. As a new year dawned, these positive developments caused many in the international community to feel optimistic about peace progress in the Middle East.

Then the unthinkable happened.

Chapter 50
Of Hope and Sorrow

Nineteen-ninety-five began with raised hopes for a final resolution of the century-old conflict between Palestinians and Israelis. With Oslo I and the Gaza-Jericho agreements in place, Israel and the PLO continued their negotiations. A peace treaty had been signed between Israel and Jordan, but roadblocks remained for broader success. Israeli-Lebanese talks continued to be held hostage by Syria. Any hope for progress toward a peace treaty with the existing Lebanese government could not be accomplished before first reaching an agreement with Syria, but Assad never permitted any substantive discussions. Continued terrorist attacks by Iranian-backed Hizbollah militants and Hamas extremists also sought to derail the peace progress.

The operational change within the United Israel World Union organization was flowing seamlessly. David Horowitz, slowed some-what by age, continued his tireless routine of coverage of UN activities from his pressroom office with the drive and persistence of a man in his sixties. He also continued to guide the efforts of the United Israel organization he founded in 1944, albeit, with fresh assistance from a recently elected new leadership group.

It was announced in the spring that Rabbi Chaim Richman of Jerusalem formed a unique new organization called "Light to the Nations." Rabbi Richman, the Director of Public Affairs at the Temple Institute in Jerusalem, is a friend and active supporter of the B'nai Noah movement and has spoken at various B'nai Noah conferences in the United States. We had met with Rabbi Richman during our visit to Israel in October 1994. "Light to the Nations" would operate as a Jerusalem-based organization dedicated to bringing the light of Torah to all who sincerely wish to learn. It will offer true-Torah Biblical study, commentary, newsletters, lectures and seminars, both in Israel and the United States.

The 52nd Annual Meeting of United Israel was held in New York City at the Shelbourne Hotel before a large and enthusiastic crowd on the afternoon of April 30, 1995. Earlier in the day a devoted group of United Israel associates and lifetime friends of Horowitz gathered at the hotel to remember and pay tribute to Nan Reilly Horowitz, devoted wife of David, who had passed away on December 25, 1994, quite literally, in his arms in their Manhattan apartment.

At the afternoon annual meeting, an announcement that efforts to restore and reopen the Broadway office of United Israel, which for years had been used mostly for archives and storage, would take place. Professor James Tabor reported on his recent trip to Europe and his visits to Berlin, Malmo, Sweden, and the Czech Republic. I also reported on a recent meeting with Esther Jungreis, founder and director of "Hineni," and her most positive attitude toward the B'nai Noah movement. Prominent San Diego attorney and son of David Horowitz, Herbert Joel Solomon, was unanimously elected as a new member of the Board of Directors.

The spring 1995 issue of *United Israel Bulletin* covered the huge success of the Ninth Annual B'nai Noah Conference held in Athens, Tennessee, in November of 1994. The unique gathering was made up of Gentiles drawn to Torah faith, and orthodox Rabbis and Torah scholars for a weekend of fellowship and study. J. David Davis, a member of the United Israel Board and leader of the Emmanuel Congregation in Athens, hosted the conference. Two officers and three board members of United Israel attended the affair.

In June, Rabbi Irving J. Block, long-time faithful friend of United Israel and a member of its Consultive Board, retired from the renowned Brotherhood Synagogue in New York, which he had founded many years ago. In his parting sermon, Rabbi Block presented a masterful record of lifelong service. He chanted the invocation at United Israel's 50th Anniversary Jubilee fete at New York's B'nai Zion Hall on April 11, 1993.

In the September 15, 1995 issue of the *New York Jewish Week*, David Horowitz was the subject of a cover story entitled, "Dispatches from First Avenue," by writer Stewart Ain. His interview covered some of the highlights of Horowitz's almost fifty years of covering UN affairs. "I'm the oldest and longest active correspondent at the UN," remarked Horowitz, with obvious pride. "I'm ninety-two. I don't believe it myself. I started in 1947 when the UN was in Lake Success. It moved here in 1951. I watched them put up this building. It was a slum area."

Reflecting on his career at the UN, Horowitz said Abba Eban was Israel's best spokesperson there and that Benjamin Netanyahu ran a close second "in oratory and alertness." He said it was Netanyahu who blew the whistle on former UN Secretary General Kurt Waldheim's Nazi past. "The revelation came as a surprise," Horowitz said, "because I knew Waldheim well and found that he had always tried to ingratiate himself with the Jewish people." Recalling a lighter, memorable moment when an ambassador from the United States said in one of his speeches that he wished the Jews and Arabs would just behave like good Christians, Horowitz said, "everybody laughed."

The quest for peace continued as Israel and the Palestinians signed a new agreement at the White House on September 28th that came to be known as Oslo II. The key and complex interim agreement expanded the area of Palestinian self-rule beyond Gaza and Jericho and allowed them greater control over their affairs.

On October 27, 1995, The United Nations Correspondents Association (UNCA) celebrated "Fifty Years of Reporting the World from New York." The gala dinner and dance was held at the UN's prestigious Delegates Dining Room. The 50th Anniversary Award went to Ted Turner of CNN for the contribution made by his network to covering the UN and its operations. Well-known newsman Bernard Shaw accepted the award on behalf of Mr. Turner. A special award was presented to journalist David Horowitz for his lifetime of activity and contributions to the association, where he served as president in 1981. UN Secretary-General Boutros-Boutros Ghali presented the special medal to Mr. Horowitz.

The dangers of the Middle East were not on the minds of the thousands of Israelis who gathered in downtown Tel Aviv on November

4, 1995 to attend a rally in support of the Oslo Accords. The rally was called to show support for the government's peace policies and warmth for Prime Minister Yitzhak Rabin. At the end of the rally, Rabin joined Shimon Peres and one of Israel's leading pop singers on stage. He was showered with applause. Then, uncharacteristically, the normally reserved Prime Minister joined in a song of peace with the assembly. After the rally, Rabin walked down the city hall steps towards the open door of his car when a man approached him from behind and fired three shots, striking him in the back. Rabin was rushed to nearby Ichilov Hospital where he died on the operating table. In Rabin's pocket was a bloodstained sheet of paper with the lyrics to the well-known Israeli song "Shir LaShalom" (A Song for Peace), which was sung at the rally.

The nation was shocked, but what made it even more horrifying was that the assassin was a Jew, who believed the prime minister's policies had endangered the country. The assassin was Yigal Amir, a former Hesder student and far-right law student at Bar-Ilan University. Yigal Amir was captured immediately, tried, and convicted of the murder. He was sentenced to life in prison. Like former Egyptian President Anwar Sadat in 1981, another Nobel Peace Prize recipient had died at the hands of an extremist force.

Sixty heads of state, including President Clinton, British Prime Minister John Major, German Chancellor Helmut Kohl, and French President Jacques Chiraq, attended Rabin's funeral. Seven Arab countries also sent representatives. Egyptian President Hosni Mubarak (who had never been to Israel) and King Hussein of Jordan offered eulogies.

The murder of Prime Minister Rabin was one of the most traumatic events in Israeli history. Now it was time to muster the courage and the collective will to move on.

Chapter 51
Bibi's Big Promotion

Following the assassination of Prime Minister Yitzhak Rabin on November 4, 1995, Shimon Peres became acting Prime Minister of Israel and Minister of Defense, continuing to serve in this capacity for seven months, until the May 1996 elections.

With the arrival of the new leap year of 1996, Palestinians went to the polls on January 20th and re-elected Yasir Arafat as President of the Palestinian Authority. The next major step in the peace process was to be Israel's withdrawal of troops from most of the city of Hebron, but the actions of the Palestinians made it impossible for Peres to carry it out. Hamas and other Palestinian rejectionists groups did not accept the Oslo Accords and launched suicide bomb attacks on Israelis. There was also opposition within Israel from settler-led groups. Oslo remained only partially implemented.

The Brotherhood Synagogue was the site for the 53rd Annual Meeting of United Israel on April 21, 1996. The synagogue, located in the Gramercy Park section of Manhattan is a 19th century landmark building. The meeting was well-attended, and it was my distinct privilege to serve as the meeting's chairman for the forum. The program included a succession of speakers with Dr. James Tabor delivering the keynote speech. One organizational change took place. President Horowitz nominated Rebecca Buntyn, a present board member, to become United Israel's Administrative Assistant, a new organizational office. Mrs. Buntyn was unanimously elected to the new post.

Throughout early 1996, Iranian-backed Hezbollah escalated their attacks on Israel. Katyusha rockets were routinely fired on the Israeli communities adjacent to the Lebanese-Israeli border eventually culminating in one rocket salvo that resulted in thirty-eight Israeli casualties. In response, IDF forces were given the green light to strike back. On April 11ᵗʰ, "Operation Grapes of Wrath" was launched against targets in Lebanon. In a sixteen-day campaign, Israel conducted more than 1,100 air raids and extensive shelling, targeting infrastructure and terror hubs in southern Lebanon. The conflict was de-escalated on April 27ᵗʰ by a ceasefire agreement banning attacks on civilians.

Jerusalem-based researcher and United Israel friend, John Hulley released his first book titled: "Comets, Jews and Christians," (Jerusalem, Israel: Keterpress Enterprises, 1996). The extraordinary book is a study of the cultural and religious background of winners of Nobel prizes in science and how this unique symbiotic relationship offers hope in confronting one of the greatest threats to our survival.

Two significant compositions appeared in the spring issue of the *United Israel Bulletin*. Dr. James Tabor's article, "Four Major Themes," offered well-researched evidence related to the Lost Tribes of Israel from biblical and historical sources. The prophetic reunion of Judah and Israel is an indispensable component of the redemptive plan. David Horowitz wrote the exposition of a three-part series that I introduced in the spring issue entitled, "Are the terms Jew, Hebrew or Israelite synonymous?" The series explains the basic meaning of each term and follows the progression of meaning throughout the biblical account. The exposition was an updated version of a work Horowitz had previously published in 1978.

General elections were held in Israel on May 29, 1996. In a surprising development, Likud's candidate Benjamin Netanyahu became the youngest person ever elected to the position of Prime Minister when he upset the pre-election favorite Shimon Peres. The razor-thin margin of less than 1% victory occurred after initial exit polls had predicted a Peres win. Netanyahu also became the first Prime Minister born in the land after Israel became a sovereign nation again. Throughout his tenure as Israel's Ambassador to the United Nations, "Bibi" as his friends knew him, distinguished himself as a dynamic spokesman for the Jewish State on all vital matters pertaining to Israel's welfare and security. Handsome and articulate, a few of Bibi's UN colleagues had foreseen in him a future prime minister. One of those colleagues was David Horowitz.

Horowitz held the fondest of memories of Bibi and shared his personal thoughts on those UN years. Though he felt Netanyahu served at the UN with great dignity, respect and admiration, Horowitz described the most important quality shown by Bibi as "his spiritual qualities, his Jewishness, his attachment to Hebraic tradition." It never failed, Horowitz said, "whenever the UN Judaica Book Club held a Purim or Hanukkah reception, Bibi made it his business to attend and participate in the kindling of the candles. We all rejoiced as we brought the spirit of the Torah and the Biblical truths into the United Nations."

Nineteen-ninety-six was a presidential election year in the United States. On November 5th, Democratic incumbent President Bill Clinton won re-election, defeating the former Republican Senator from Kansas, Bob Dole, and Independent Presidential candidate Ross Perot of Texas. President Clinton became the first Democrat to win two consecutive presidential elections since Franklin D. Roosevelt in 1936, 1940, and 1944.

Just three months earlier, in August 1996, the founder of al-Qaeda, Osama bin Laden issued a call for jihad against the United States, on the grounds that it was trespassing on the sacred soil of Islam. It was for al-Qaeda, a declaration of war on the U.S.

On December 13, 1996, the UN Security Council recommended Ghanaian diplomat Kofi Annan to replace outgoing Secretary-General Boutros Boutros-Ghali of Egypt. Confirmed four days later by the vote of the General Assembly, Kofi Annan began his first term as Secretary-General on January 1, 1997.

New Year events were underway with Bill Clinton being sworn in for a second term as President of the United States and Madeleine Albright becoming the first female U.S. Secretary of State. In Israel, Yasser Arafat returned to Hebron after more than thirty years to join the celebration of the handover of the last Israeli-controlled West Bank city.

The April 1997 edition of the *International Diplomatic Observer*, a publication dedicated to serving the world diplomatic community, with offices in New York, Geneva, Madrid and Tokyo, carried the story of a special award given at a recent Earth Society event. At the ringing of a peace bell to begin the spring ceremony, David Horowitz was recognized with a special award for his contributions to world-wide environmental affairs and a life committed to reporting on international affairs. Horowitz was recognized as a former President of the United Nations Correspondent Association, and the most senior as well as one of the highest-ranking journalists at the UN. It was pointed out that Mr. Horowitz had known every Secretary-General as well as almost every head of state from every country connected to the UN over the last half-century.

In accepting his award on Earth Day, Horowitz pointed out to the gathering "that the slabs of stone used in the courtyard where the peace bell was located, were a gift from a former Prime Minister of Israel, and the arrangement of the stones were meant to signify the three areas of the UN: the General Assembly, the Security Council, and the Secretariat." That was news to many who attended that day. Mr. Michael H. Geoghegan, Chairman of the UN Earth Society, presented the special award to Mr. Horowitz.

In late spring, Horowitz received a surprise letter from Offenbach, Germany. It came from an old acquaintance of over forty years ago. His name was Hans David Binzer and his reasons for writing to David after such a long time had an inspirational impact on the old veteran journalist. Binzer wanted Horowitz to know his story. He was a convert to Judaism. He revealed how his conversion took place in September 1956 in Berlin after a long, friendly and helpful correspondence with Horowitz and with Joseph Schur in Tel Aviv. Schur was a friend and active supporter of United Israel World Union.

Binzer recounted the events of the many years that had passed since then. In 1960, he married a Jewish girl, a survivor of the Terezin Ghetto, and they had three children. His eldest daughter married a Jewish man from Poland, his younger daughter married an Israeli and was living in Haifa, and his son (not yet married) had taken over Han's import-export business in Germany. They were blessed with five grandchildren. His business activities had taken Hans to many countries of the world, but he considered the highlight of his travels to be his many visits to the Holy Land of Israel.

Hans Binzer closed his letter by expressing his appreciation: "I am now sixty-six years of age and together with my dear wife, we keep a happy and kosher life here in Offenbach, Germany. We have a Jewish population of about 800 and in two weeks, a new Jewish Community Center will be inaugurated." He concluded by saying: "My dear David, I want to thank you for all your efforts for us *gerim*, for leading us into the flock of the House of Israel."

Of the myriads of correspondence David Horowitz had received over his half-century of communicating with the world, the heartfelt letter from Hans Binzer remained among those he most treasured.

Chapter 52
A Meeting with the Prime Minister

When Benjamin Netanyahu was elected as the new Prime Minister of Israel in May of 1996, David Horowitz was elated. Their relationship dated back to 1984 when Netanyahu served as the Israeli Ambassador to the UN. Horowitz always felt that "Bibi," as he called him, possessed special qualities and abilities that destined him for greatness. He predicted as much when he published an article about Netanyahu in the mid-eighties titled "His Leadership Awaited."

Born in Tel Aviv, Benjamin Netanyahu was the first Israeli prime minister born in Israel after the establishment of the state and the significance didn't escape David Horowitz. He felt at long last a "new Israelite had been raised up to lead the re-born nation."

The historic Brotherhood Synagogue in Manhattan was again the site for the 54th Annual Meeting of United Israel World Union on April 13, 1997. I served as chairman for the meeting and long-time United Israel friend, Rabbi Hailu Moshe Paris, gave the invocation. Dr. James Tabor and B'nai Noach leader, J. David Davis, provided one of the meeting highlights when they presented a narrated slide show of a "Masada-like" mountain location in Los Lunas, New Mexico that contains a rock facing engraved with the Ten Commandments in ancient Hebrew. The Los Lunas Decalogue Stone is a large boulder on the side of Hidden Mountain, about thirty-five miles south of Albuquerque. The inscription is interpreted to be an abridged version of the Ten Commandments in a form of Paleo-Hebrew. Dr. Tabor visited the site in September 1996 with a group of associates for an initial survey of the evidence. He also interviewed Professor Frank Hibben, local historian and archaeologist from the University of New

Mexico. Professor Hibben, who first saw the text in 1933, was convinced the inscription is ancient and thus authentic.

The Decalogue Stone remains controversial. However, the historical and archaeological evidence was well-documented by epigrapher, Barry Fell in his impressive major study, "America B.C." (New York: Pocket Books, 1989). Interestingly, the Los Lunas Decalogue Stone is not the only American landmark of its kind with disputed provenances. Other disputed American Hebrew inscriptions include the Smithsonian Institution's Bat Creek inscription, and the Newark Ohio Decalogue Stone, Keystone, and Johnson-Bradner Stone.

A new friend of United Israel, Paul Elliott-Smith, who during World War II served in North Africa as an operative of U.S. Army Intelligence, delivered a riveting account of his experiences, including an account of his friendship with the late British-Israeli Colonel Moshe Pearlman. Colonel Pearlman, a journalist and immigrant from Britain, was the first IDF Operations Directorate spokesperson that was appointed in 1948 with the establishment of the State of Israel.

In business related decisions, President David Horowitz made a special presentation of the deed to the Blairstown, New Jersey property that he graciously transferred to the United Israel organization. Horowitz and his late wife Nan had owned the property for many years. Rebecca Buntyn, United Israel's Administrative Assistant, accepted the deed with gratitude on behalf of all constituents of United Israel, thanking Mr. Horowitz for his generosity. President Horowitz also nominated Dr. Steven Deem to become a member of United Israel's board of directors. Following an officer and board vote, Dr. Deem was unanimously elected. The annual meeting was followed by a reception hosted by Paul Elliott-Smith in his Manhattan apartment home.

Former President of Israel, Chaim Herzog died on April 17, 1997. Born in Belfast and raised in Dublin, Major-General Herzog was the son of Ireland's Chief Rabbi Yitzhak HaLevi Herzog. He served as the sixth President of Israel between 1983 and 1993. A lesser-known fact is that Herzog was the brother-in-law of Abba Eban, considered to have been Israel's greatest spokesman to the UN. Chaim Herzog was buried on Mount Herzl in Jerusalem.

Despite the January withdrawal of Israeli forces from Hebron and the turnover of civilian authority in much of the area to the Palestinian Authority, suicide bombings continued against Israeli civilians. Hamas claimed responsibility for most of the bombings, but clearly Netanyahu blamed Arafat for not doing enough to rein in the terrorist attacks.

Although he had stated differences with the Oslo Accords, Prime Minister Netanyahu continued their implementation, but his premiership saw a marked slow-down in the peace process. The political rift within Netanyahu's coalition didn't help matters. He was opposed by the political left-wing in Israel and lost support from the right because of his concessions to the Palestinians, particularly in Hebron. Eventually, the lack of progress of the peace process led to another round of negotiations.

The 1997 issues of the *United Israel Bulletin* were packed with news and insightful articles covering an array of subjects. Rebecca Buntyn, who recounted her recent visit to England and Wales in search of her past, wrote one such article. In her report, "Tribal Roots Point to Hebrew Origins," Rebecca returned to the lands of her forefathers to trace her genealogy. Her search eventually led to the little township of Corris, Wales and the valley of so many of her ancestors. The cemetery was situated on the grounds of the Carmel Corris, Talyllin, Wesleyan Methodist Church erected in 1810. The Welch inscriptions on the gravestones were startlingly close to Hebrew script. David Horowitz often said that the Welsh and Hebrew languages were strikingly similar. Further research revealed that the Celtic British Isles had a long history of Sabbath-keepers, believing that the day begins at sundown. Many Celtic believers were Arians (anti-Trinitarians) and were known to be Quartodecimans (observers of the Christian Passover on the 14th day of the first month in Spring). They eschewed unclean meats. The weeks of historic searching left Rebecca with a myriad of information to assimilate both intellectually and emotionally; however, it had imparted a strong sense of pride in her Welsh-Celtic-Hebrew influenced heritage.

New friend and United Israel member Ross Nichols contributed an insightful article entitled, "The Pen of the Scribes," a commentary on the transmission of the Biblical texts from antiquity to our present day.

In the winter issue of the *Bulletin*, the copy of a note from Eleanor Roosevelt to David Horowitz in 1949 was re-published, along with a photo of the two of them attending a UN Press Corp meeting. Mrs. Roosevelt was a regular reader of the *United Israel Bulletin*. Revisiting the Horowitz-Roosevelt connection was just another example of the far-reaching influence David Horowitz had with so many dignitaries. I was about to witness firsthand this special connection Horowitz held with a world leader.

During a business trip to New York in the summer of 1997, I visited David at the UN. We were having lunch together in the UN Secretariat Building cafeteria when I mentioned to him that I would be in Israel in October as a part of the Alabama Governor's trade mission team to develop commercial linkages with Israeli counterparts. Our delegation would be meeting with an impressive array of top Israeli Government officials. When he heard this, he excitedly asked, "Are you meeting with Bibi?" I replied, "Yes. We'll be meeting with the Prime Minister." David, with no hesitation, immediately said "You must take a message to Bibi for me. I have some things to say to him."

Chosen to be a part of the trade mission delegation, my wife Rebecca and I joined Governor and Mrs. Fob James, Alabama State Representatives and other business team members for the historic visit. Invited by the Israeli government as its official guest, our objective was to open the door for more economic development between Israel and the State of Alabama. A former director of Israel's government press office, Yoram Ettinger served as Alabama's trade representative in Israel. We arrived in Israel in time to participate in the Simchat Torah celebration at the Western Wall prior to spending five days in Jerusalem and four days in Tel Aviv.

During our nine-day visit, our delegation met at various times with top Israeli officials including Speaker of the Knesset, Dan Tichon, Minister of Finance Ya'acov Neeman, Mayor Ehud Olmert of Jerusalem, Natan Sharansky, Ariel Sharon, President Ezer Weizman, and of course, Prime Minister Benjamin Netanyahu.

Our final meeting was a private affair with the Prime Minister at the Knesset Building in Jerusalem. Members of the Israeli Press were present. After the introductions and formal exchange of customary gifts, the group reported on the week's progress and plans to move forward on several initiatives. During the meeting my wife Rebecca said, "Mr. Prime Minister, I have been asked to deliver a message to you personally from an old acquaintance of yours during your years in New York," as she handed the one-page letter from David Horowitz to him. Looking a bit surprised, Netanyahu carefully opened the letter and paused to peruse the message while everyone waited. Suddenly, he smiled and began to explain to the group who David Horowitz was while recalling a few of the memories of the long-past days when he served as the Israeli Ambassador to the UN. Appearing moved by the message he thanked us and commented that he would answer Horowitz personally.

When I later reported the story to Horowitz, he was thrilled. I imagined for a moment how U.S. Department of Justice official Martin Smith must have felt in 1948 after delivering another personal message from David Horowitz to Harry Truman just before the presidential election.

Chapter 53
Jubilee! Israel at 50

In early October 1997, David Horowitz received a prominent visitor at his World Union Press office at the United Nations. Kare Kristiansen, one of Norway's most distinguished diplomats was in the country to promote "Embassy 3000," the campaign sponsored by the Israeli-based Root and Branch Association to encourage all nations to recognize united Jerusalem as the eternal capital of Israel and to move their embassies in Israel to Jerusalem. Lowell Gallin, President of Root and Branch Association and author Susan Roth accompanied Dr. Kristiansen.

The Honorable Kare Kristiansen had agreed to serve as the Embassy 3000 International Chairman. Mr. Kristiansen—who famously resigned from the Nobel Peace Prize Committee when it awarded a peace prize to PLO Chairman Yasser Arafat—was the past President of the Norwegian Parliament, former Norwegian Minister of Oil and Energy, and former Chairman of Norway's Christian Democratic Party. An account of Mr. Kristiansen's historic visit to the UN appeared in the December 19, 1997 issue of the Jewish Press.

Following his New York and Washington visits to promote the Embassy 3000 campaign, Mr. Kristiansen attended another meeting, this time in Israel and it had a direct connection to our trade mission trip. As an International Council Member of Root and Branch Association, I worked with its president Lowell Gallin in a collective effort to arrange a meeting between Mr. Kare Kristiansen and Alabama Governor Fob James while in Israel on the trade initiative. I spoke directly with Governor James, who agreed to a meeting, while Lowell made the necessary arrangements for Mr. Kristiansen to fly in from Oslo to meet with us.

Our meeting took place in a Tel Aviv hotel room and also included Alabama House Representative Jim Carns and his wife Judy, Susan Roth, Ira Silberman, Samson Krupnick, Lowell Gallin, Governor and Mrs. James, the Honorable Kare Kristiansen, Rebecca, and me. The special meeting provided the impetus that led to the State of Alabama's endorsement of Embassy 3000, calling for a united Jerusalem as the eternal capital of the State of Israel and for all foreign embassies to be located there. Governor Fob James signed the State of Alabama House Resolution HJR 36 introduced by Representative Jim Carns of Birmingham, on February 3, 1998. An account of the historic meeting and its results appeared in the February 20, 1998 issue of the *Jerusalem Post* titled: "Next Year in Jerusalem."

The spring of 1998 marked several milestone events. The State of Israel would be observing the Jubilee Anniversary of its 50th year as a re-born State while United Israel celebrated its 55th year as an organization. On April 4, 1998, at Il Monello Restaurant in Manhattan, a group of family and friends gathered to celebrate the extraordinary life of David Horowitz. It was his 95th birthday. Herbert and Elene Solomon, son and daughter-in-law of the honoree, hosted the soiree to honor their remarkable Patriarch. Letters of tribute from around the world, including Holland, England, France, and Germany were read and acknowledged. There was also a hand-written note that arrived the day before the celebration. It was from Israeli Prime Minister Benjamin Netanyahu congratulating David on reaching his 95th birthday. The splendid finale included a beautiful birthday cake, a lively rendition of Happy Birthday, hugs all around and a "L'Chaim" toast to the honored guest.

The Brotherhood Synagogue was the site for the 55th Annual Meeting of United Israel World Union on April 5, 1998. The large gathering included many family members and special guests that had attended David's birthday celebration the previous day. Mr. Horowitz introduced his family members including his grandniece, Francesca Bori from Los Angeles. Speakers included Ms. Susan Roth, author of the Kabbalistic book, *Moses in the Twentieth Century*; longtime friend Tikvah Feinstein, who had just published her book, *Taproot*; and special guest, Bishop T. L. Hill, who gave a moving account of his spiritual odyssey. Reports were also given by Dr. James Tabor, B'nai Noach leader

J. David Davis, and Rabbi Irving J. Block. In the business session, Ms. Susan Roth was unanimously elected a member of the United Israel board of directors.

In May, the State of Israel looked both up and inward on its 50th anniversary Independence Day as it celebrated across a divided Jewish state. A team of Air Force fighter pilots scrawled a big blue and white "50" in the sky over Jerusalem as crowds below cheered. Prime Minister Benjamin Netanyahu played host to U.S. Vice President Al Gore and 190 guests from Israel's impoverished towns at a gala featuring the country's top entertainers. The Prime Minister's words offered a chilling reminder of the re-born State's struggles in the face of incredible odds and future challenges it faced. "Fifty years ago, it was a question whether the Jewish people would exist at all," Netanyahu said. "And yet you see we gathered the final life force within us and from an unprotected people, we now have a state of our own in our ancient homeland." The Prime Minister reiterated Israel's determination to keep control of all Jerusalem but focused on the need to make peace. "For thirty years we fought. For twenty years we've been trying to attain peace. For thirty years we've been searching for how not to die. For twenty years, we're looking at how to live," he said during the gala celebration.

A poll by the Israeli newspaper *Ha'aretz* found one subject on which the large majority of Israelis agree: eighty-two percent believe Israel will be around to celebrate its centennial.

On June 23, 1998, former New York City Council President and prominent attorney Paul O'Dwyer died after a long illness. The Irish-born immigrant was a champion of liberal causes and strong advocate for human rights. He fought for the creation of Israel, organized black voters in the South, and argued for Puerto Rican rights. He was also a long-time friend of David Horowitz and was the lawyer who successfully defended Horowitz against the libel suit brought against him by Hungarian Nazi war criminal Ferenc Koreh in 1977. Paul O'Dwyer was ninety.

In September, President Clinton met with Israeli Prime Minister Benjamin Netanyahu and PLO leader Yasser Arafat at the White House in a new effort to stimulate progress in the negotiations. This led to the "Wye River Memorandum," an agreement negotiated between

Israel and the Palestinian Authority at a summit in Wye River, Maryland, held on October 15-23. Israel agreed to withdraw from an additional thirteen percent of the West Bank over a three-month period and to release 750 Palestinian prisoners. The Palestinians said they would arrest Palestinian terrorists, formally revoke the Palestinian covenant's controversial articles, and take measures to prevent anti-Israel incitement.

In December, Israel carried out the first of the three withdrawals (amounting to about nine percent of the West Bank) and released the required number of prisoners. The Palestinians, however, were failing to follow through by refusing to arrest terrorists, prevent incitement or confiscate weapons. Palestinians continued to riot throughout the territories.

Israelis were not happy. Once again, Israel had given up territory without seeing a peaceful response. Members of Netanyahu's governing coalition were becoming incensed. The opposition who supported the Wye Agreement was also dissatisfied by Netanyahu's inability to keep the peace process moving toward a final resolution. It became a perfect storm. The result was the collapse of Netanyahu's government on December 21, 1998, and the decision to hold new elections in May 1999.

On December 3rd, the United Nations Correspondents Association celebrated its 50th anniversary, thanking all the journalists who contributed to UNCA's half century of history. Special recognition was given to the pioneers and veterans who were still working after more than two decades. Thirteen names were called. One of those people stood out from the remaining twelve: David Horowitz, the founding member of UNCA and a witness to all *fifty* years.

Before the year ended, I received a personal letter from Bjornemyr, a little Norwegian village located on the west coast of the municipality of Nesodden. It was from the Honorable Cabinet Minister Kare Kristiansen. In his letter, Mr. Kristiansen offered his sincere thanks for my support of the Embassy 3000 Campaign on behalf of Israel and my efforts in helping to bring about the successful State of Alabama's official endorsement. He closed by saying that he hoped to one day have the privilege of visiting our great state. I wish he could have, but Kare Kristiansen, Norway's great statesman and world citizen passed away on December 3, 2005 without fulfilling his wish.

Chapter 54
Brotherhood of Man

In its Proclamation on Aging, the United Nations General Assembly decided to declare 1999 as the International Year of Older Persons. Meant to draw attention to the recognition of humanity's demographic coming of age, the year was celebrated with numerous events scheduled within the UN and in member countries to mark the event. Had the UN decided it needed a poster-person to publicize such a declaration, it certainly had to look no further than to one of its own. Senior citizen journalist David Horowitz, who turned ninety-six in April, surely could have been considered the leading candidate.

On February 7, 1999, King Hussein of Jordan died. Within a few hours, Crown Prince Abdullah II recited the same oath his father took nearly five decades earlier, becoming the new King of Jordan. King Hussein's rule had extended through the Cold War and four decades of Arab-Israeli conflict. In 1994, he became the second Arab head of state to make peace with Israel after Egyptian President Anwar Sadat in 1978.

The state funeral took place in Amman on February 8th with the largest gathering of royalty and world leaders since the 1995 funeral of Israeli Prime Minister Yitzhak Rabin. President Bill Clinton and former presidents George H. W. Bush, Jimmy Carter and Gerald Ford represented the United States. Prime Minister Benjamin Netanyahu led the Israeli delegation. Among the number of tributes paid to the late king was this moving message from Israel's Prime Minister Netanyahu: "With great sadness we bid farewell to you, king and friend, the peace between our peoples will be a testament to your abiding belief in a lasting peace between the sons of Abraham. Rest in peace, your majesty." His Majesty King Hussein, the father of modern Jordan, will always be remembered as a leader who guided his country through strife and turmoil to become an oasis of peace, stability, and moderation in the Middle East.

The historic Brotherhood Synagogue in Manhattan was once again the site for United Israel World Union's 56th Annual Meeting held on April 11, 1999. Cantor Eliezer Brooks gave the invocation and inspired the attendees with his chanting of traditional songs. Cantor Brooks, who pursued his cantorial studies at Yeshiva University, was well known for his musical concerts at synagogues and centers of Jewish life in the greater New York area.

United Israel welcomed two special guests for the meeting, both long-time former United Nations personalities: Marcia Cooper Pinchas, who worked in the Security Council, and Maria Garcia, a South American marrano, whose family had returned to Judaism. A young Maria Garcia met veteran journalist David Horowitz years earlier when she gained an entry-level position at the UN. It was Horowitz who provided guidance and counsel as she navigated her way through those early UN days. In a moving tribute, she spoke of his influence in her life. "Actually, my faith in HaShem (God) began at your office in the United Nations. I gained an unavoidable feeling of bonding with my Jewish roots. I now observe the Sabbath and keep the dietary laws. I'll always be grateful for your guidance." She then offered her appreciation for his mentorship. "You tutored me, made sure I got names and figures accurately for my articles and reports. You guided me in how to respond in situations of political difficulty and how to be fearless in my approach. I learned many lessons from you. I will always be immensely grateful for your friendship." Maria Garcia is now Director of the South American Institute of Language and Culture, an organization that teaches all levels of Spanish, Portuguese, French and English languages and offers translation services.

Following the customary reports and a keynote message from Executive Vice President, Dr. James Tabor, the business session produced two new additions. Mrs. Betty Givin was unanimously elected as a new member of the board of directors, and Ms. Sarah King was unanimously elected to the post of recording secretary for the organization. David Horowitz made special mention of a newly released book written by Rabbi Irving J. Block entitled, *A Rabbi and His Dream: Building the Brotherhood Synagogue* (New York: KTAV Publishing 1999). In the spirited autobiography, retired Rabbi Block recounts his often-stormy forty-two years in the rabbinate and his founding of the Brotherhood Synagogue in Greenwich Village in 1954.

In this very synagogue in the Gramercy Park borough of Manhattan, where so many United Israel meetings have taken place, Rabbi Block worked to make religious brotherhood a living reality. Rabbi Block was a longtime friend of David Horowitz and a member of United Israel's Consultative Board, and it was through that association that many of us were privileged to know him. Yet, we knew so little about the life and vision of this remarkable man.

Irving J. Block was born in Bridgeport, Connecticut and served in the U.S. Army in World War II. With an accounting degree from the University of Connecticut, he began studies at the Hebrew University in Jerusalem. During his studies in Israel, he joined the Hagganah Defense League and participated in Israel's war for independence, for which he was recognized with the Israeli Victory Medal. Ordained as a Rabbi in 1953 by the Hebrew Union College-Jewish Institute of Religion, he subsequently received the degree of Master of Hebrew Letters, and in 1978, an Honorary Doctor of Divinity.

In 1954 he founded the Brotherhood Synagogue and for the next twenty years shared quarters with the Village Presbyterian Church, led by the Reverend Dr. Jesse W. Stitt. The two congregations entered into a covenant of brotherhood, not only sharing space, but also programing together in the arts and social action. Both Rabbi and Pastor carried their message of ecumenical harmony all over the United States as well as to Germany and Israel. A break came in 1974 after Pastor Stitt left and Brotherhood's ever-growing congregation was fortunate to acquire and restore a historic Quaker Meeting House, originally built in 1859, located in beautiful, serene Gramercy Park. Rabbi Irving J. Block, who often reminded us that "the idea of brotherhood is as ancient an idea as the Bible," retired from the rabbinate in 1994.

On April 12, 1999, retired astronaut John Glenn, the first American to orbit the earth, was the guest speaker for the International Longevity

Center as a part of the UN's program on aging. He addressed a large assembly in the Dag Hammarskjold Auditorium at the UN Head-quarters. When Glenn was told about David Horowitz and his long career at the UN, he responded with a personal note to Horowitz expressing his best regards and Happy Birthday wishes, calling him "a great example of good aging in action."

David Horowitz was indeed an example of good aging, even with its natural process. He now walked with a cane and worked from his Manhattan apartment on most days while making the trek to his UN office on others. He had a trusty aide in Baggett Mathews and the wonderful assistance of Gregg Sitrin, Maria Garcia, Naomi Farrell, and others to help carry on the UN duties. He continued to write his columns, handle his correspondence and contribute to the *Bulletin*. "Staying active" was his motto.

Movement on the peace process had halted during the election campaign in Israel. Early general elections were held on May 17th following a vote of no confidence in the government. The incumbent Likud Prime Minister Benjamin Netanyahu ran for re-election. Opposition Labor Party candidate Ehud Barak, promising renewed negotiations with the Palestinians and a withdrawal from Lebanon by July 2000, won the election in a landslide victory. In a penetrating assessment of Netanyahu's defeat, journalist Horowitz offered a response in his syndicated column "At the UN" on June 11, 1999. In the article, "How did Bibi miss the Boat," Horowitz stated that Netanyahu never lived up to his original election campaign pledges, and made unnecessary concessions in Hebron, the West Bank, and the Wye Plantation Agreement. Revealing a more personal side of a previous relationship, Horowitz continued:

When I realized the new path he (Netanyahu) had chosen, which was altogether unbiblical, I wrote him a series of letters from the UN reminding him of the underground days and the sacrifices young Israelis made for the Medinah. In one of the letters I sent him an Israeli post office montage showing postage-size photos of the Israeli hero, Dov Gruner and several of his co-fighters whom the ruthless British hanged in the Acco prison.

"They gave their lives for the State," I told him. "Let's honor them by remaining firm to their convictions not to sacrifice land for peace." Horowitz then candidly stated: "This was not the Bibi I so admired at the UN during his tour of duty there, where he excelled in his defense of Israel and justice. His colleague, Jeanne Kirkpatrick, and he became a good UN team on behalf of Israel."

Returning to the election results, David remarked, "I am not at all gloomy about Israel. This only means that one good man has been replaced by another." Then he added: "Let's not give up on Bibi. He's a good man whose best days may lie ahead."

That would seem to be so. As of this time, Benjamin Netanyahu has been elected Prime Minister of Israel four times, matching David Ben-Gurion's record. If his current government lasts a full term, upon its completion he will become the longest-serving Prime Minister in the history of Israel.

Part Six

Chapter 55

A New Millennium

They called it the great Y2K scare. Everyone was anticipating the arrival of the new millennium. January 1, 2000 was the day that our entire lives were going to be changed. For months before the stroke of midnight, analysts speculated that entire computer networks would crash, causing widespread dysfunction for a global population that had become irreversibly dependent on computers to hold, disseminate, and analyze its most vital pieces of information. Because computer memory space was pricey, programmers could save memory by using two digits for the date instead of four. Therefore, when the year changed to 2000, it was feared that entire computer systems would fail to function. The new millennium could bring the apocalypse. Yet, when the clocks and calendars did actually change to the year 2000, computers barely had any problems. After a season of Y2K anxiety and millenarian doomsayers, the new year arrived with nothing more than the expected hangover.

In a now forgotten event, Israel and Syria actually engaged in peace talks early in the new millennium. From January 3-10, Israel and Syria held peace talks in Shepherdstown, West Virginia. Israeli Prime Minister Ehud Barak led the Israeli delegation and Foreign Minister Farouk al-Sharaa led the Syrian delegation. The Peace Conference finally came to a dead end and was later followed by failed negotiation attempts to renew it.

From March 12-26, Pope John Paul II visited Israel, thus becoming just the second Pope to visit the Jewish state. During his stay, the Pope visited Yad Vashem (the Israeli national Holocaust memorial) and the

Western Wall, placing a note inside it in which he prayed for forgiveness for the actions of the church against Jews in the past.

On April 16, 2000, United Israel World Union held its 57th Annual Meeting at historic B'nai Zion in Manhattan. It was at this same renowned location in 1993 that United Israel held its Jubilee, celebrating fifty years of global activities on behalf of a united Israel and the universal values of the Torah faith. It was again my privilege to serve as chairman of the event. First time attendee Ms. Jeanne Rees, who studied voice for years with renowned Faye Foster in New York, sang "Jerusalem of Gold" and a selection from the Shabbat liturgy, "M'dor Dor." Professional cellist Miss Francesca Bori, grandniece of David Horowitz, presented two selections on the cello; a first and second suite from Johann Sebastian Bach and "Song of the Birds" by Pablo Casals. Other first-time attendees were recognized, including David and Kay Levitan, Brian Jones and Beth Holley, Ross and Bridget Nichols, and Faith Harrison. It was announced that Director of the South American Institute of Culture and Education, Ms. Maria Garcia, had recently begun work on a Spanish translation of David Horowitz's autobiography *Thirty-three Candles*.

In a meeting highlight, board member Susan Roth presented David Horowitz with a magnificent collector's edition of *The Golden Book of Psalms*. The beautifully illustrated edition by world-renowned Israeli artist Shuki Freiman was one of only 320 signed and numbered copies of the work of art. As the owner and director of the publishing house, S.J.R. Associates, Ms. Roth was instrumental in the development and creation of the exquisite publication. She had been present at the book's launch at the Jerusalem Hilton in January and personally presented the first numbered copy of the limited edition to Israeli Ashkenazic Chief Rabbi Yisrael Meir Lau.

Mr. Joseph Peeples, President of The Jerusalem Historical Society was a guest speaker at the meeting. Mr. Peeples, a long-time friend of David Horowitz, had worked with him when he was a United Nations press employee in the 1950s. He spoke glowingly of his long association with David. Dr. James Tabor delivered the keynote address titled: "The Unique Biblical Vision of United Israel—A Millennial Perspective." The moving message also included a personal tribute to David.

Rabbi Hallu Moshe Paris spoke briefly and closed the meeting with a prayer and blessing in Hebrew, then translated it into English. The successful first meeting of United Israel in the new millennium had been a grand affair.

On May 25th, Israel withdrew IDF forces from the "security zone" in southern Lebanon, in compliance with U.N. Resolution 425, after twenty-two years in which the area was occupied by Israeli forces. The UN certified full Israeli withdrawal.

News broke on June 10th that Syrian President Hafez al-Assad was dead. He died of a heart attack while on the telephone with Lebanese Prime Minister Selim Hoss. Hafez al-Assad was the 18th President of Syria and the longest serving ruler in the Middle East spending twenty-nine years in office. He was sixty-nine years of age. His son, Bashar al-Assad, succeeded him as president.

In July, United States President Bill Clinton convened a summit meeting at Camp David between new Israeli Prime Minister Ehud Barak and Palestinian Authority chairman Yasser Arafat. The lengthy summit took place from July 11-25 and was an effort to end the Israeli-Palestinian conflict. The summit failed with the latter two blaming each other for the failure of the talks. There were four principal obstacles to agreement: territory, Palestinian refugees right of return, Jerusalem, and the Temple Mount.

On September 28, 2000, Israeli opposition leader Ariel Sharon, together with a Likud party delegation, visited the Temple Mount. The stated purpose for Sharon's visit of the compound was to assert the right of all Israelis to visit the Temple Mount. Seen by Palestinians as highly provocative, violence broke out as angry demonstrators began throwing stones at police. It soon erupted into rioting. The incident triggered the outbreak of the Second Intifada (uprising), also known as the Al-Aqsa Intifada, a period of intensified Israeli-Palestinian violence. Sharon's visit was only the spark that set off the uprising, not its root cause. Seven years of the Oslo peace negotiations had failed to deliver peace or a Palestinian State, and frustrations were further intensified by the collapse of the Camp David Summit in July. Unlike the first intifada, Palestinian tactics centered on suicide bombings, rocket attacks, and sniper fire, which Israel met with even deadlier force. The long, deadly

Palestinian uprising continued for years, finally ending in 2005, but not before about 1,000 Israelis and 3,200 Palestinians were killed.

On October 12, 2000, the USS *Cole* was the target of an attack while it was being refueled in Yemen's Aden Harbor. The guided missile destroyer was struck when two suicide bombers detonated explosives carried in a small boat near the warship. The explosion killed seventeen sailors and injured thirty-nine others. The terrorist organization al-Qaeda claimed responsibility for the attack. Osama bin Laden praised the operation, though his precise role in it remains unclear.

On November 7th, Republican candidate George W. Bush, the incumbent governor of Texas and son of former president George H. W. Bush, narrowly defeated the Democratic candidate Al Gore, the incumbent vice president and former Tennessee senator, as well as various third-party candidates including Ralph Nader. This was the closest presidential election in U.S. history, with a .009% margin (537 votes) separating the two candidates in the decisive state, Florida. The narrow margin triggered a recount and ensuing litigation, ultimately reaching the Florida Supreme Court and the United States Supreme Court. The high court's contentious 5-4 decision in *Bush v. Gore*, was announced on December 12, 2000, effectively awarding Florida's votes to Bush and granting him the victory.

On December 10th, Israeli Prime Minister Ehud Barak surprised the nation when he announced he was resigning and would push for re-election as prime minister in sixty days to seek a fresh mandate to tackle what he called the country's emergency situation. Under Israeli law, if the prime minister resigns, special elections for prime minister must be held within sixty days. In such a situation however, only standing Knesset members can seek the post. The surprise act of brinksmanship from Ehud Barak now led to a new election for Prime Minister in February of the New Year, an election that held its own surprise.

As the year 2000 wound down, there was yet another award in store for journalist David Horowitz. On December 12th, he was given a Life Achievement in Journalism Award by the United Nations Correspondents Association and made an Honorary Member for life. It was a most fitting way of recognizing the career of the Dean of United Nations Correspondents.

Chapter 56

Day of Terror

2001: A Space Odyssey was a 1968 epic science-fiction film produced and directed by Stanley Kubrick 33 years ago. Time had finally caught up with the futuristic fictional period. Two-thousand-one was here and we were witnessing the beginning of the 21st century and the first year of the 3rd millennium.

On January 20th, George W. Bush was sworn in as the 43rd President of the United States. He was the second president in our history to have been a son of a former president, the first having been John Quincy Adams.

Elections for prime minister were held in Israel on February 6, 2001 following the resignation of the incumbent, Ehud Barak in December of 2000. Labor's Barak stood for re-election against Likud's Ariel Sharon. Disillusioned with Barak's inability to conclude a peace agreement or stem the violence of the intifada, Israelis voted Sharon into office in a landslide victory. He became the 11th Prime Minister of the State of Israel.

As was the case with the man he replaced, Ariel Sharon was a decorated Israeli war hero. He was a commander in the Israeli army from its creation in 1948. He participated prominently in the 1948 War of Independence as well as in the 1956 Suez Crisis, the Six-Day War of 1967, and the Yom-Kippur War of 1973. As Minister of Defense, he directed the 1982 Lebanon War. Sharon was considered the greatest field commander in Israel's history, and one of the country's greatest military strategists and tacticians.

April marked two milestone events as United Israel founder David Horowitz celebrated his 98th birthday on April 9th and United Israel held its 58th Annual Meeting on April 15th in Manhattan.

The spring issue of the *United Israel Bulletin* carried several articles of well-timed interest. Professor James Tabor's article, "Arm of Yah" offered a biblical concept of Jehovah as a "wayfaring man," one designated as the "arm" or "arms" of Jehovah, a common theme in scripture. In an article entitled, "At the United Nations," President David Horowitz wrote an intriguing commentary on how the founding fathers patterned our new nation after the Republic of Moses. The article was written to commemorate the recent World Conference of Religious Leaders assembled in New York. His article paid special tribute to the late Oscar S. Strauss' book, *The Origins of Republican forms of Government*. Mr. Strauss (1850-1926) had served as an American diplomat in Turkey under Presidents Grover Cleveland and William McKinley.

United Israel Bulletin Managing Editor Gregg Sitrin wrote a personal account of how he met David Horowitz and became involved in the United Israel organization. While working with famous Nazi-hunter, Dr. Charles Kramer in 1984, he picked up a copy of the *United Israel Bulletin* at Kramer's office. Intrigued with the content, Sitrin contacted the editor, David Horowitz and was added to the mailing list. When the Palestinian intifada broke out in 1987, Sitrin's interest was rekindled in getting involved with a Jewish organization that truly supported the Jewish state. Again, he contacted David Horowitz, who invited him to his UN office for a visit. From there, Gregg Sitrin became an important member and associate of United Israel and the dependable aide to whom David would refer to as "my right-hand man."

In the summer of 2001, the militant Sunni Islamist organization al-Qaeda, founded by Osama bin Laden, released recruiting videotape that was widely circulated throughout the Middle East. This fueled speculation that al-Qaeda might be on the verge of striking again after the USS *Cole* bombing in October of 2000. Yet, al-Qaeda had acted in so many different places, using so many different techniques, and in connection with so many different Arab and Muslim causes that it was difficult to predict how they would strike next.

On September 11, 2001, we had our painful answer.

At 8:45 a.m. on a clear Tuesday morning, an American Airlines Boeing 767 loaded with 20,000 gallons of jet fuel crashed into the north tower of the World Trade Center in New York City. The impact left a gaping, burning hole near the 80th floor of the 110-story skyscraper, instantly killing hundreds of people and trapping hundreds more in higher floors. Eighteen minutes later, a second Boeing 767, United Airlines flight 175, appeared out of the sky, turned sharply toward the World Trade Center and sliced into the south tower near the 60th floor.

As millions watched the events unfolding in New York, American Airlines Flight 77 circled over downtown Washington, D.C., and slammed into the west side of the Pentagon military headquarters at 9:45 a.m. Meanwhile, a fourth California-bound plane, United Flight 93, was hijacked about forty minutes after leaving Newark International Airport in New Jersey. The flight crashed into a field near Shanksville, Pennsylvania at 10:03 a.m. after several brave passengers fought the hijackers.

America was under attack.

The terrorist attacks of September 11, 2001, were a profoundly shocking event to the U.S. government and public. The attacks killed 2,996 people, injured over 6,000 others, and caused at least $10 billion in property and infrastructure damage and $3 trillion in total costs. Not since the British had burned down the White House in 1814, almost two centuries earlier, had America's enemies succeeded in attacking the continental United States.

Civilian aircraft traffic in the U.S. did not resume until September 13th and the New York Stock Exchange remained closed for trading until September 17th, the longest closure since the Great Depression. On September 20th, in an address to a joint session of Congress and the American people, U.S. President George W. Bush declared a "War on Terror," not simply going after the immediate sponsors of the attacks, but also holding accountable those nations that harbored terrorist groups. This position became known as the "Bush Doctrine."

Two new actions were taken in response to the September 11th attacks. On October 8th, President Bush announced the establishment of the Office of Homeland Security followed by the signing of the Patriot Act into law on October 26th.

On October 12, 2001, the Norwegian Nobel Committee awarded the Nobel Peace Prize for 2001, in two equal portions, to the United Nations and to its Secretary-General, Kofi Annan, for their work "for a better-organized and more peaceful world." Annan was awarded the peace prize for having revitalized the UN and having given priority to human rights. Kofi Annan of Ghana, was the seventh Secretary-General of the UN, serving from 1997 to 2006, and was the first to emerge from the ranks of United Nations staff.

David Horowitz had been a part of the long history of the United Nations beginning in 1947 when the UN was still in its temporary home in Lake Success, New York. He had reported on almost every aspect of the UN, particularly the Middle East, and on human rights issues. He was asked on several occasions about his more than fifty years at the world organization and his view of the UN in this dawn of the new millennium. He provided a unique personal assessment of the world body.

"The ideal of the United Nations is the future of the world," offered Horowitz, it is not an accidental development, it is a providential development. It exists to promote international co-operation. The assembly of nations is still in its infancy. What is a mere fifty years in the course of millenniums of history involving continuous wars with the fall and rise of empires?... One must bear in mind that this world organization, born out of the Holocaust of World War II, to repeat, is in its infancy. Prior to the advent of the UN, each nation went its own way. There was no common understanding among them on the basic needs of humanity: on matters of human rights versus exploitation, on health, children, food, technology, women's rights, labor, etc. Today, at least, a beginning has been made."

From his long-held vantage point, Horowitz still viewed Israel's role at the UN through the lens of his Torah faith and working observations. "Israel is home after a 2,000-year bitter and tortuous exile and viewed by the media as the miracle of the age," summarized Horowitz.

"But it's only part of the prophetic story. Israel has taken her place at the table of nations, but still remains the most neglected member state. World peace and economic stability are dependent on Israel's peace and re-gathering. When the nations come to understand Israel's relevance and significance within the international arena, hopefully things will happen for the world organization. After all, it was Israel, a nation in antiquity, that gave the world the first International Charter of human rights and judicial laws of justice in the form of the Torah."

It was a "back to the future" expression of hope for all nations from a UN veteran journalist as his long career drew to a close.

The September 11th attack on the United States galvanized American and international resolve as never before to fight terror. The president warned the Taliban rulers in Afghanistan, where al-Qaeda was based, to hand over Osama bin Laden or risk a massive assault. The Taliban refused to comply. In November and December 2001, the Taliban and al-Qaeda were ousted from their major strongholds in Afghanistan. A pro-U.S. Afghan government, led by Hamid Karzai, was established in Kabul. The Bush administration failed to capture or kill Osama bin Laden, who appeared to have slipped over the border from Afghanistan into western Pakistan.

The stage was set for some remarkable transformations in America's entire foreign policy posture. The war on terror was just beginning.

Chapter 57

Witness to a Century

By early 2002, the Bush administration was clearly broadening the scope of its "war on terror" to take on foes without demonstrable ties to the attacks of September 11th. The first sign of this shift came in President Bush's January 2002 State of the Union address, in which the president declared that America was menaced by an "axis of evil" consisting of Iraq, Iran, and North Korea.

On January 3rd, the Israeli Navy seized a cargo ship trafficking fifty tons of weapons to the Palestinian National Authority. They were intended to support the amplified uprising against Israel. The Palestinian intifada against Israel had continued in intensity with a number of suicide attacks and bombings. By March, the rate of attacks had increased to its highest level. In addition to numerous shooting and grenade attacks, the month of March saw fifteen suicide bombings carried out in Israel, an average of one bombing every two days.

The wave of suicide bombings culminated with the Passover massacre in Netanya on March 27th, in which thirty people were killed at the Park Hotel while celebrating Passover. In total, 130 Israelis, mostly civilians, were killed in Palestinian attacks during March 2002, a month that came to be known in Israel as "Black March."

As spring turned into summer, veteran journalist David Horowitz was no longer making his occasional visits to his UN office. Confined to his Manhattan apartment, his days were largely spent answering correspondence, writing, and following current events on television and in The New York Times. Volunteer staff members Gregg Sitrin and Naomi Farrell provided assistance at the World Union Press office at the UN.

On Sunday, October 27, 2002, Gregg Sitrin called to inform us that David Horowitz had died. He passed away peacefully in his Upper East Side Manhattan apartment sometime between the close of the Sabbath and Sunday morning. He was ninety-nine-years-old. Gregg had called David's son, Herbert Solomon, in San Diego to inform the family and also our United Israel Executive Vice-President Dr. James Tabor.

The sudden news came as a shock, even considering David's advanced age. For years, my wife Rebecca and I had called David on Friday evenings to wish him a joyful Shabbat Shalom. In our last conversation, David was in good spirits and talkative. In fact, he had a joyful and very alert visit with his good friends Maria Garcia and Sonia Nusenbaum on the Sabbath afternoon before he passed away.

Dr. Tabor later pointed out that the Torah and Haphtarah reading this week, which began on Saturday at sundown, is Genesis 23-25 (Chai' Sarah) and I Kings 1, dealing with the deaths of Sarah, Abraham, and King David. It seemed that throughout David's life key events in which he participated were marked by significant Torah/Haphtarah readings, culminating now with this account on the very week he left us.

Friends and family members gathered at Riverside Memorial Chapel on the Upper West Side of Manhattan on Tuesday, October 29th, for a service to honor the life of the beloved patriarch. Despite a profound feeling of loss, it was a lovely celebration of life and the cherished memories we all held. David Horowitz's grandson, professor Bruce Solomon of Indiana University, sang part of the liturgy. Dr. James Tabor delivered the eulogy. A simple pine box holding David's body was draped with the Israeli flag. A single candle burned from a tall candlestick at the head of the casket. It was a profoundly moving experience.

From the chapel, we all drove to Sharon Gardens, the Jewish section of multi-ethnic Kensico Cemetery in Valhalla, New York, for a brief graveside service. A Rabbi officiated and several of us offered our personal remarks. It was a Jewish burial with the simple pine box containing the linen cloth-shrouded body, a back-to-basics simplicity that honors life's final act. The ashes of David's late wife Nan were also placed in the grave with David, as he had requested. We took turns shoveling soil on the casket.

The October day was beautiful as a crisp breeze blew through the falling, multi-colored leaves of the season. Journalist Vanni Cappelli once asked David Horowitz about his birthday and he replied, "I was born in the springtime when everything comes alive." Somehow it seemed fitting that he would pass from us as we entered creation's season of rest.

As we were coming to grips with the loss of David, it seemed we were experiencing a strange chain-reaction of concurrent events. Four days after David's death, Rabbi Irving J. Block, founder of the Brotherhood Synagogue in Manhattan and one of the most esteemed religious leaders in the city, died following a long bout with the complications of Parkinson's disease. He was seventy-nine years old. Rabbi Block was a longtime friend of David Horowitz and ardent supporter of United Israel World Union. The Brotherhood Synagogue hosted several of United Israel's annual meetings over the years.

On November 17, Abba Eban, eloquent defender and voice of Israel during the perilous first thirty years of its independence, died in a hospital near Tel Aviv. He was eighty-seven years old. Eban served as Israel's representative at the United Nations during the independence struggle of 1948, its ambassador to both Washington and the UN during the Middle East war of 1956, and its foreign minister during the 1967 and 1973 Middle East wars. David Horowitz and Abba Eban were good friends when both served together at the UN. David covered many of Eban's UN activities while reporting for the World Union Press. He considered Abba Eban to be Israel's greatest diplomat and spokesperson. In a little-known fact, it was Eban who helped arrange a critical meeting between the Zionist patriarch Chaim Weizmann and President Harry S. Truman in the weeks before Mr. Truman decided that the United States would recognize Israeli independence in 1948.

No issues of *United Israel Bulletin* were published in 2002. The *Bulletin* remained suspended and did not resume publication until the summer of 2004.

United Israel World Union now entered a new era. Plans were set in place to hold the 60th Anniversary Annual Meeting on April 13, 2003, at historic B'nai Zion in Manhattan. It was the first without its founder and beloved leader. It also became the last United Israel annual meeting to be held in New York. The 60th Anniversary Meeting of United Israel was a landmark affair. There was the restructuring of organizational leadership, including the election of a new president, key officers, and board members, and a possible re-location of the editorial and business offices. Bulletin publication plans and the use of growing social media were among the many activities addressed. New president, Dr. James Tabor also announced that following the meeting, attendees were invited to the Kensico Cemetery in Valhalla for the official unveiling of the tombstone of David Horowitz at his gravesite. A short graveside memorial was conducted.

David Horowitz was gone, and it was hard to imagine a world without him in it. Born in 1903, he was witness to a century, the tenth and final century of the 2nd millennium. A chain of events that heralded significant changes in world history that defined the era dominated the 20th century. World War I and World War II, nuclear power and space exploration, nationalism, and decolonization were just a few of the history-altering events.

World War II left about sixty-million people dead. Out of the carnage, the United Nations emerged as the successor to the League of Nations. It was established as an international forum in which the world's nations could discuss issues diplomatically, and to promote international co-operation. It was this world organization that David Horowitz entered at its inception and was now leaving with an unparalleled legacy as the Dean of United Nations Correspondents. His sixty-year presence cast a long shadow.

Chapter 58
A Colleague's Tribute

Following the death of David Horowitz, I had the privilege to meet with one of his longtime colleagues at the UN. His name was Serge Beaulieu, and I met with him in his 3rd floor United Nations Bureau office on the morning of October 30, 2002. Serge was UN Bureau Chief for CNS News and Haiti's Majorite National Broadcaster on Radio Liberte. He had known David Horowitz for many years dating back to the late 1950s. When I asked him about his relationship with David, he spoke openly about David's UN career and his impact on others, including his own life and career.

He recalled how David befriended him when he first arrived at the UN and influenced his decision to become a UN correspondent. He also spoke of David's unflinching devotion to the new Jewish state and its early struggles at the UN to gain statehood. Of course, I heard the stories, some humorous, some personal, and others about the world organization that only brothers-in-trade could know. It became apparent that here was a man whose life and career was deeply affected by another in his profession. Touched by the life of his friend and colleague, Serge Beaulieu wrote a moving tribute only two days after Horowitz's death. It was released to his media sources and to all members of the Foreign Press Association. Upon leaving his office, he gave me a copy of his article.

In honoring the life and legacy of David Horowitz, we are pleased to share the following special message written by CNS News UN Bureau Chief Serge Beaulieu:

United Nations, October 29, 2002 (CNS News)

David Horowitz: 1903-2002
The Man of Thirty-Three Candles

It is hard to walk the corridors of the United Nations and not see the silhouette of David Horowitz, dean of the U.N. press corps. In the third-floor press section, behind a mountain of papers, one had to go very close to discover the man we described as the institutional memory of the United Nations.

I met David under unusual circumstances in the late 1950s when I had been assigned to Israel. I was lost in the vast corridor complex of the United Nations, looking for the field service where I was supposed to get my travel documents. I had no idea where I was or what direction to go. With my heavily accented English, I asked a man with a friendly face if he knew the office of Mr. De Lauro. It was a time when everybody knew and fraternized with everybody else at the UN. It was the time of the: "we the people of the UN" organization.

"Of course," the man said, leading me to the correct bank of elevators. "By the way, my name is David Horowitz. What's yours and where are you from?" When he learned that I was on my way to Israel, he stopped the elevator at the next floor and said that if I wasn't in a rush I should come to his office so we could chat. I followed him and found myself somewhere in the UN sitting behind a pile of papers, listening to a man I barely knew who was showing me photos of different scenes in Israel and talking with passion about the birth and history of the Jewish State. His discourse was so intense, more than an hour passed. He caught my interest when he spoke of the importance of Haiti's vote in the creation of the state of Israel, and I was very happy with my first encounter with David Horowitz. He certainly made me feel important.

I was already a successful broadcaster in my own country, but David insisted that I should become like him—

a UN correspondent. At the time, I had no idea of what a UN correspondent did. But the suggestion took hold in my mind, and I thought about what I might do when my current assignment was over. I had a week's stay in New York before flying to Jerusalem. We were lodged at the Tudor Hotel across from the UN on 42nd Street. The cafeteria of the UN, which was located on the 4th floor at that time, and David Horowitz's office, became the places for a daily rendezvous where I was taught about the duties and responsibilities of a UN correspondent. That was when I decided I wanted to be one, too.

From my post in Jerusalem, I maintained contact with David Horowitz. Upon my return to New York, I was introduced to Joe Nichols, the UN press accreditation officer for radio and television, who formally issued me a UN press credential pass. It was the time of decolonization, when the UN was looking for its real vocation. It appeared to me that David's mission, in addition to his devotion to the Israeli state, was also to help Third World people feel at home in UN headquarters. The Western elitist press corps was present, but not omnipresent, at the UN The Third World was active and represented in full force.

It was also the time of the U.S. Civil Rights Movement, where Jews and Blacks appeared to have embraced each other for a common cause. While Jack Greenburg and Thurgood Marshall collaborated on legal questions, Malvin Goode from ABC, Gerald Fraser at *The New York Times*, and Jean Perry at the *Daily News* made their entrances as members of the Western elitist press corps.

While the highly educated black writer, Margaret Cartwright, was active in the UN press corps, H. Berry from the Indonesian News Agency, Sam Queko from the Ghana News Agency, and Oswald Sykes from the *Amsterdam News*, and others also represented a powerful force. For whatever reason, we all placed our confidence in David Horowitz and elected him president of our Foreign Press Association. Under

Horowitz's presidency, the Foreign Press Association became a travel center; we went all over the United States and Canada. At the inauguration of the Montreal Expo, the entire foreign press flew to Montreal, where I was the French interpreter for David Horowitz in his encounter with Montreal's Mayor Jean Drapeau.

On one of our trips around the United States, I recall visiting a restricted General Electric plant in Valley Forge, Pennsylvania. It was the time of the Cold War. During a briefing on "Life Under Water" by one of the GE scientists, he negligently left in plain view next to him a letter from an upper level U.S. intelligence source putting him on alert that among us there was a suspicious Polish correspondent. The elderly scientist did not realize that David and I could see the document. With a gentle smile, David discreetly pointed to direct the scientist's attention to the paper, saving the man from embarrassment. Later on, David and I had a private chuckle, since part of our delegation included Russian, Hungarian, and other members of the Communist press.

Although David was a fanatic when the Jewish State was discussed, he was consistently promoting reconciliation between Christians and Jews. He always found a Biblical passage to explain his points. No one felt uncomfortable with his position, and he never asked anyone to defend his point of view, just to listen. He was not arrogant, although his knowledge and memory about the UN were without precedent. As the UN grew in size, so did the legendary pile of papers on David Horowitz's desk. He continued to work, and even though he was quite ill the last year of his life, on occasion he came to the UN in a wheelchair with a nurse attendant and sat behind his papers, pounding out his words on his ancient typewriter.

"Truth is stranger than fiction," David said. He devoted his life to his causes, seemingly ignoring the material world. He was a quiet-spoken man who never raised his voice and could often be seen eating a simple meal behind his cluttered desk on the third floor. His legacy is his correspondence with the world's highest dignitaries and the collection of photos of legendary heads of state and UN secretary-generals that decorated his office.

Lately, the UN seems to have no place for piles of papers, but we hope that the memories of David Horowitz will not disappear in this process. Colleagues at the UN will remember him fondly. Sadly, the developing world has lost a friend that some never even knew.

Serge Beaulieu died two years later on December 12, 2004 at the age of sixty-six. As Bureau Chief of CNS News, he provided analysis about Africa, Latin America, the Caribbean and the United Nations. He hosted a daily talk show broadcast on Radio Liberte in Haiti. Acknowledged as having one of the most brilliant minds of his generation, Serge Beaulieu dedicated his life to making both his homeland of Haiti and the world at large a better place. He had achieved a highly successful career as a United Nations correspondent, with a little help from a friend along the way.

Chapter 59

Forty Years in Room 373 at the UN with David Horowitz

By John Cappelli
Chapter excerpt from Memorie d'un cronista d'assalto
("Memories of a Crusading Journalist")
Milan: l'Ornitorinco Editori, 2016
Translation by Vanni Cappelli

At the UN I worked for forty years from 1960 in Room 373, sharing it with David Horowitz, which was the sole element of continuity in that long period of time. David was old enough to be my father; he passed away at the age of 99 and a half years in October of 2002. It was a great pity that he didn't last a bit more: everyone at the UN was ready, from Secretary General Kofi Annan down, to celebrate the only 100th birthday the world organization had ever known.

As it turned out, the only commemoration was a toast raised with Italian wine in our room on that day, April 9, 2003, by David's assistant Greg Sitrin and my son Vanni, who looked on David as his grandfather.

David was always in the office before me; he came on foot from his apartment at Second Avenue and 70th Street, never missing a day of work except in his last three years, when he had to often visit the doctor. On his desk he always had a candle lit, in total violation of the house rules, but no one was going to challenge the dean of the UN press corps, who had covered everything from the founding San Francisco conference in 1945, on a relatively minor point. He blew the candle out only when both of us were away from the room at the same time.

David, the son of a celebrated Orthodox cantor, and a pure Zionist, never belonged to a synagogue. After the untimely death of his first wife, their only son perished in the Holocaust; his second wife, Anna, who everyone called Nan, was Irish. He was Swedish, born in Malmo in 1903, and on account of this Dag Hammarskjold came frequently to Room 373. My desk was right by the door, and so I was the de facto official greeter of all the numerous visitors who came to see David.

U Thant was another frequent visitor, as he was the only secretary general who had ever been a journalist, and so had a special rapport with the press.

David wrote a weekly column, "Behind the Scenes at the UN," under the aegis of his own news service, World Union Press; it ran in dozens of newspapers across the United States and in Israel, and was read by people such as Golda Meir, Benjamin Netanyahu, and Elie Wiesel.

David was a passionate lover of opera, and in his final years had the particular distinction of being the last person alive who could say that he personally knew Enrico Caruso. It was no accident that the first thing I saw upon entering Room 373 was a photo of Caruso standing with a group of Metropolitan Opera company employees that included David, which dated from his years there as an office boy. The teenager of course wore his magnificent smile, the David smile we all came to love. Of Caruso he would always speak warmly not only of his gregarious character but of how fantastic he had been in his final role, Eleazer in Halevy's La Juive, and how carefully the great tenor had prepared for it, seeking out advice from many authoritative Jews.

In my early days at the UN I served my trial period as a new arrival, sitting and writing my pieces in the open bull pen on the third floor, right outside the office of the spokesman of the secretary general, before being assigned a permanent desk. The door of Room 373 opened right onto this area, and that is how I met David. In no time, he set himself to cutting through the red tape of the UN bureaucracy, and soon brought me into his office.

I had the honor, on the first Hannukah of our colleagueship, of lighting the first candle on his menorah.

In return for all his generosity to me, I would translate the letters sent to him from Israel by the inhabitants of the Italian village of San Nicandro, who had converted to Judaism en masse and then emigrated to the new Jewish state. David knew perfectly well that my newspaper, *Paese Sera* of Rome, was a journal of the left, and that I was an atheist; yet in our forty years together, we never had an argument about God, the Arab-Israeli conflict, or any other issue.

David was an intimate friend of Menachem Begin, and a frequent visitor to Israel in the years of fire, both before and after the foundation of the state. He didn't fight in the Irgun, but Nan Horowitz did, and he would recount this to me with pride.

He had on his desk a keepsake which he treasured, a letter from King Abdullah I of Jordan, which formed a part of his path breaking correspondence with that monarch, and used to tell me, "Here you can read the first dialogue of our time aimed at bringing peace between Jews and Muslims."

In November 1975, Resolution 3379 of the General Assembly, which condemned Zionism as racism, threatened the peaceful environment that we had created in Room 373. For me, it was a watershed. A wording as blatant and one-sided as that contained in this resolution had never been seen at the UN; for me, it was pure racism. The question arose as to what line *Paese Sera* would take on it, especially since most journals of the left had applauded it. Going through the text line by line over the telephone with my editor in Rome, I made my opinion of the resolution clear, and then finished my plea with a passionate challenge: "If *Paese Sera* does not denounce this resolution, how can I ever come here and sit next to David Horowitz again?!" I won my case, and had the great satisfaction of showing David the editorial in which we condemned it.

Epilogue

In the two years following the death of founder David Horowitz, United Israel World Union underwent significant changes.

New organizational leadership was implemented. Dr. James D. Tabor was elected the new President replacing David Horowitz. I was elected the new Executive Vice President replacing James. Other elected officers were Dennis Jones as Vice President, Timothy Thompson as Treasurer, and Rebecca Buntyn as Secretary.

The organization still had a fourteen-member board of directors. It would later be purposely reduced through attrition.

Ms. Naomi Farrell, longtime associate of David Horowitz, assumed correspondence duties at the United Nations, writing under the auspices of World Union Press, the oldest accredited news agency at the UN. David Horowitz founded the World Union Press in 1945 as the press arm of United Israel World Union. Ms. Farrell, a former vice president of the UN Society of Writers, had served as a reporter for the Globe and Mail of Canada, the Jerusalem Post, and Al Ahram.

As a part of the transitional period, the editorial offices of United Israel were relocated to Charlotte, North Carolina. A David Horowitz Memorial Library was established in his honor. The library houses a vast collection of historical materials including documents, photos, and artifacts related to the history of United Israel and David's career at the United Nations.

The United Israel Bulletin publication was resumed with a special 61st Anniversary issue released in the summer of 2004. The attractively redesigned version was being published regularly, with a spring, summer, and winter issue. A completely redesigned web site was becoming increasingly more important for worldwide communication.

United Israel World Union held its 61st Annual Meeting and Conference on April 9-11, 2004, at the Courtyard Marriott Conference Center in Charlotte, North Carolina. It was the first ever meeting of the organization in its new headquarters. The theme for the conference was: "United Israel: Past, Present, and Future."

A new chapter in the history of United Israel World Union was underway.

Sixty years earlier, United Israel and the United Nations both emerged from a dark and frightening period of history. The foundational precepts of international peace and security, justice, human rights, responsible social and economic development, and responsible steward-ship of our planet and its environment, stand as core principles of both organizations. They are reflected in the Preamble and Charter of the UN. They are also integral to United Israel as basic tenants drawn directly from the pages of the Torah and the Prophets.

David Horowitz founded one organization and was a charter member of the other. He spent over a half-century promoting the higher purpose of each organization. He was a man of great faith, committed to the vision of the Hebrew Prophets and the ideals of the Kingdom of God: namely that justice, righteousness, and the knowledge of God might fill the earth.

David was also a visionary. He watched a century of world history unfold, a major portion spent at what he referred to as the "Parliament of Man," a world body brought together in an effort to avoid the tragic failures of the past and pursue the elusive ideals of righteousness. He viewed unfolding world events through the lens of biblical prophetic revelation with a keen perception. He played a crucial role in the miracle of a re-born Israel after a 2,000-year exile, always stressing the point that Israel had a major role to play on the world scene.

One of the stated purposes of United Israel was to disseminate research and information relative to the biblical concept of the unification of all Israel. A central theme of the Hebrew Prophets is the reunification of Judah, the Jewish people, with the dispersed descendants of Ephraim/Israel. This re-gathering is to take place at a time when many around the world will awaken to a consciousness of their forgotten heritage and seek to unite with Judah to fulfill the universal aspects of the divine plan. "Then, and only then," stated David Horowitz, "could mankind hope to turn their swords into plowshares and enter the vision of A House of Prayer for All Peoples."

A few years ago, I discovered a copy of an old publication while searching through endless boxes of archived material. It was a June 1936 issue of the late D. Paul Ziegler's *Torch of Israel*. The issue carried a picture of General Allenby on its cover. In it was an article by Ms. Tacy Weinreber, who lived in the early part of the twentieth century and was a student of the Bible and prophecy. Ms. Weinreber was one of the first Americans to foresee an "Atlantic Union of Nations" on the basis of her knowledge of Biblical prophecy.

In her article, titled: "One Continent: One Flag," Ms. Weinreber made this prediction, among others:

> Any alliance formed between Israel and Judah, as outlined in Ezekiel 37:16, must consist of the protestant people. Once we grasp this fact, we may pass on to the next feature.
>
> First…we believe that somewhere in New York City, all unknown to himself, God has a prepared Jew, who is destined to act as intermediary in this affair. Then what shall happen? In the 22nd verse of this same chapter Ezekiel 37, we read: "And I will make them one nation in the land upon the mountains of Israel…"

Tacy Weinreber's prophecy of June 1936 appeared nearly a decade before United Israel World Union or the United Nations came into existence.

I've thought so many times about David Horowitz: of the privilege I had of knowing him and the cherished memories of spending time with him in long conversations. He was a wise man. He enriched my life in ways I'm still discovering. His faith was his anchor. I'll never forget the times he would look me in the eye, poking the air with his finger, and saying, with that sparkle in his eyes; "Ralph, it will surely happen!"

Today, United Israel World Union has completed seventy-five years of global activities on behalf of a unified Israel and the universal values of the Torah faith. With an incredible legacy to uphold, there's still work to be done. The day may yet come when the lofty ideals of the United Nations and United Israel are realized. It's the cry of a weary world threatened still by ancient hatreds and new plagues, but still seeking redemption and restoration.

All people during their season of reflection and hope wish for Peace on Earth and Goodwill toward Men. The long arc of history may yet bend toward justice. Maybe, just maybe it will surely happen.

Select Bibliography

Writing a work of history requires hours of investigation to flesh out an episode or a subject and bring it to life in the pages of a book. Subject interviews, archival searches, institutional databases, websites and the works of other authors are a few of the resources used. David Horowitz's private archive is currently housed at the United Israel World Union editorial office and the David Horowitz Memorial Library in Charlotte, North Carolina. All letters and documents cited derive from this source and were actively used in the chapters.

Primary MS Sources

Newspapers, Periodicals, Electronic Sources:
B'nai B'rith Messenger
The Boston Globe
The Chicago Tribune
The Congressional Record
Epiphany Bible Students Association
The Foreign Press Association
The Foreign Press News
International Diplomatic Observer
The Jerusalem Post
Jewish Press
The Jewish Standard
The Jewish Week
Las Vegas Israelite
The New York Times
South American Institute of Language and Culture

United Israel Bulletin, 1945-2004
United Israel World Union Archives
United Nations Archives (WUP)
The UN Correspondent
Wikipedia Encyclopedia
World Union Press UN Bureau

Books

Abraham, I. (1969). *Origin and History of the Calcutta Jews*. Calcutta: Asian Printers

Gordis, D. (2014) *Menachem Begin: The Battle for Israel's Soul*. New York: Knopf Doubleday

Horowitz, D. (1949). *Thirty-Three Candles*. New York: World Union Press

Horowitz, D. (1990). *Pastor Charles Taze Russell*. New York: Shengold Publishers

Newman, R. (1981). *Concise History of Israel*. Quincy, MA: The Abraham Press

Rosenne, S. (1978). *Israel and the United Nations*. New York: American Jewish Year Book

Sadat, A. (1978). *In Search of Identity: An Autobiography*. New York: HarperCollins

Yaqub, S. (2003). The United States and the Middle East: 1914 to 9/11. Chantilly, VA: The Teaching Company

About the Author

Ralph Buntyn is the Executive Vice President and Associate Editor of United Israel World Union. A historian and researcher, his many articles and essays have appeared in various media outlets including *The Jerusalem Post, United Israel Bulletin* and *The Southern Shofar.*

After a distinguished career with a Fortune 500 company, he retired as a Senior Vice-President of Marketing in 2003. As a member of the state business delegation he was responsible for developing joint economic trade opportunities between the State of Alabama and the State of Israel. He was instrumental in efforts leading to the passage of Alabama House of Representatives Resolution HJR 36 supporting the Embassy 3000 Campaign to encourage the nations of the world to recognize united Jerusalem as the eternal capital of the State of Israel and to move their embassies in Israel to Jerusalem.

He is a past member of the International Council for Jerusalem-based Root & Branch Association, where he served as International Co-Chairman on Torah, Economics and Business.

Ralph's activities include home-scale permaculture and sustainable living, historical research, traveling and writing. He and his wife Rebecca live in Asheville, North Carolina.